Fantastic Four

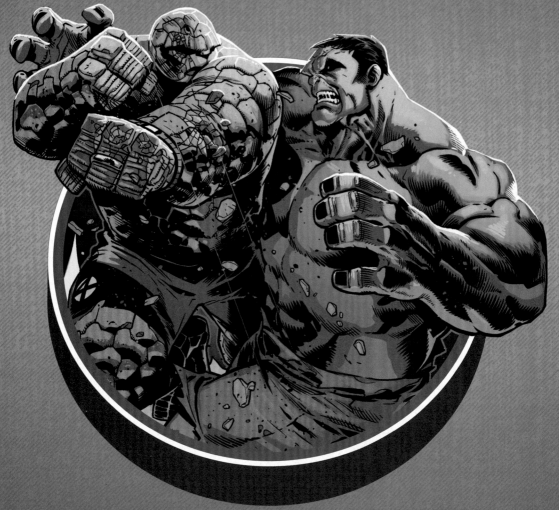

Thing Vs. Immortal Hulk

COLLECTION EDITOR **Jennifer Grünwald**
ASSISTANT MANAGING EDITOR **Maia Loy**
ASSISTANT MANAGING EDITOR **Lisa Montalbano**
EDITOR, SPECIAL PROJECTS **Mark D. Beazley**

VP PRODUCTION & SPECIAL PROJECTS **Jeff Youngquist**
BOOK DESIGNER **Adam Del Re**
SVP PRINT, SALES & MARKETING **David Gabriel**
EDITOR IN CHIEF **C.B. Cebulski**

FANTASTIC FOUR VOL. 4: THING VS. IMMORTAL HULK. Contains material originally published in magazine form as FANTASTIC FOUR (2018) #12-13, FANTASTIC FOUR: 4 YANCY STREET (2019) #1 and FANTASTIC FOUR: NEGATIVE ZONE (2019) #1. First printing 2020. ISBN 978-1-302-91725-8. Published by MARVEL WORLDWIDE, INC., a subsidiary of MARVEL ENTERTAINMENT, LLC. OFFICE OF PUBLICATION: 1290 Avenue of the Americas, New York, NY 10104. © 2020 MARVEL No similarity between any of the names, characters, persons, and/or institutions in this magazine with those of any living or dead person or institution is intended, and any such similarity which may exist is purely coincidental. **Printed in Canada.** KEVIN FEIGE, Chief Creative Officer; DAN BUCKLEY, President, Marvel Entertainment; JOHN NEE, Publisher; JOE QUESADA, EVP & Creative Director; TOM BREVOORT, SVP of Publishing; DAVID BOGART, Associate Publisher & SVP of Talent Affairs; Publishing & Partnership; DAVID GABRIEL, VP of Print & Digital Publishing; JEFF YOUNGQUIST, VP of Production & Special Projects; DAN CARR, Executive Director of Publishing Technology; ALEX MORALES, Director of Publishing Operations; DAN EDINGTON, Managing Editor; SUSAN CRESPI, Production Manager; STAN LEE, Chairman Emeritus. For information regarding advertising in Marvel Comics or on Marvel.com, please contact Vit DeBellis, Custom Solutions & Integrated Advertising Manager, at vdebellis@marvel.com. For Marvel subscription inquiries, please call 888-511-5480. **Manufactured between 1/17/2020 and 2/18/2020 by SOLISCO PRINTERS, SCOTT, QC, CANADA.**

10 9 8 7 6 5 4 3 2 1

A brilliant scientist — his best friend — the woman he loved — and her
fiery-tempered kid brother! Together, they braved the unknown terrors of outer space
and were changed by cosmic rays into something more than merely human! They became the…

FANTASTIC FOUR

Thing Vs. Immortal Hulk

FANTASTIC FOUR #12-13

Dan Slott
WRITER

Sean Izaakse
ARTIST

Marcio Menyz
COLOR ARTIST

VC's Joe Caramagna
LETTERER

Esad Ribić
COVER ART

FANTASTIC FOUR: 4 YANCY STREET

Gerry Duggan
WRITER

Greg Smallwood, Mark Bagley & **Scott Hanna, Luciano Vecchio,** AND **Pere Pérez**
ARTISTS

Greg Smallwood & **Erick Arciniega**
COLOR ARTISTS

VC's Joe Caramagna
LETTERER

Greg Smallwood
COVER ART

FANTASTIC FOUR: NEGATIVE ZONE

"ETHICAL DILEMMAS IN MODERN SCIENCE"

Mike Carey
WRITER

Stefano Caselli
ARTIST

Erick Arciniega
COLOR ARTIST

"WHAT ARE THE FANTASTIX FOR?"

Ryan North
WRITER

Steve Uy
ARTIST

VC's Cory Petit
LETTERER

Kim Jacinto & **Rain Beredo**
COVER ART

Shannon Andrews Ballesteros
ASSISTANT EDITOR

Alanna Smith
ASSOCIATE EDITOR

Tom Brevoort
EDITOR

The Fantastic Four created by Stan Lee & Jack Kirby

The Fantastic Four foiled Doctor Doom's plan to steal Galactus' power, defended Yancy Street from the Dark Elf King Malekith's army and are finally coming together as a team. With all the craziness around them, Ben and his new bride, Alicia, haven't been able to go on a honeymoon — until now! They've earned a relaxing break...right?

"The Honeymoon Crasher"

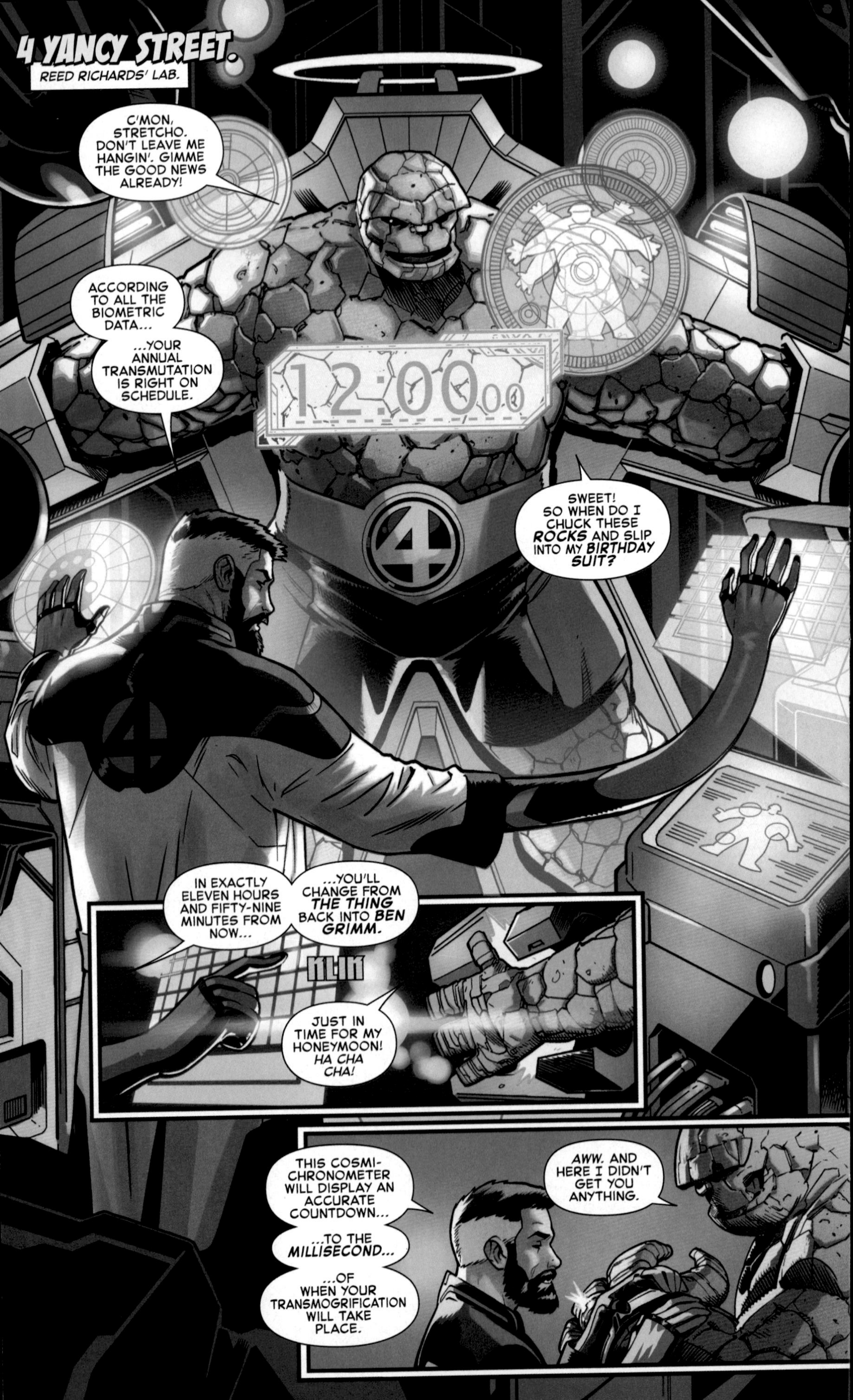
4 YANCY STREET.
REED RICHARDS' LAB.
C'MON, STRETCHO. DON'T LEAVE ME HANGIN'. GIMME THE GOOD NEWS ALREADY!
ACCORDING TO ALL THE BIOMETRIC DATA...
...YOUR ANNUAL TRANSMUTATION IS RIGHT ON SCHEDULE.
12:00 00
SWEET! SO WHEN DO I CHUCK THESE ROCKS AND SLIP INTO MY BIRTHDAY SUIT?
IN EXACTLY ELEVEN HOURS AND FIFTY-NINE MINUTES FROM NOW...
...YOU'LL CHANGE FROM THE THING BACK INTO BEN GRIMM.
KLIK
JUST IN TIME FOR MY HONEYMOON! HA CHA CHA!
THIS COSMI-CHRONOMETER WILL DISPLAY AN ACCURATE COUNTDOWN...
...TO THE MILLISECOND...
...OF WHEN YOUR TRANSMOGRIFICATION WILL TAKE PLACE.
AWW. AND HERE I DIDN'T GET YOU ANYTHING.

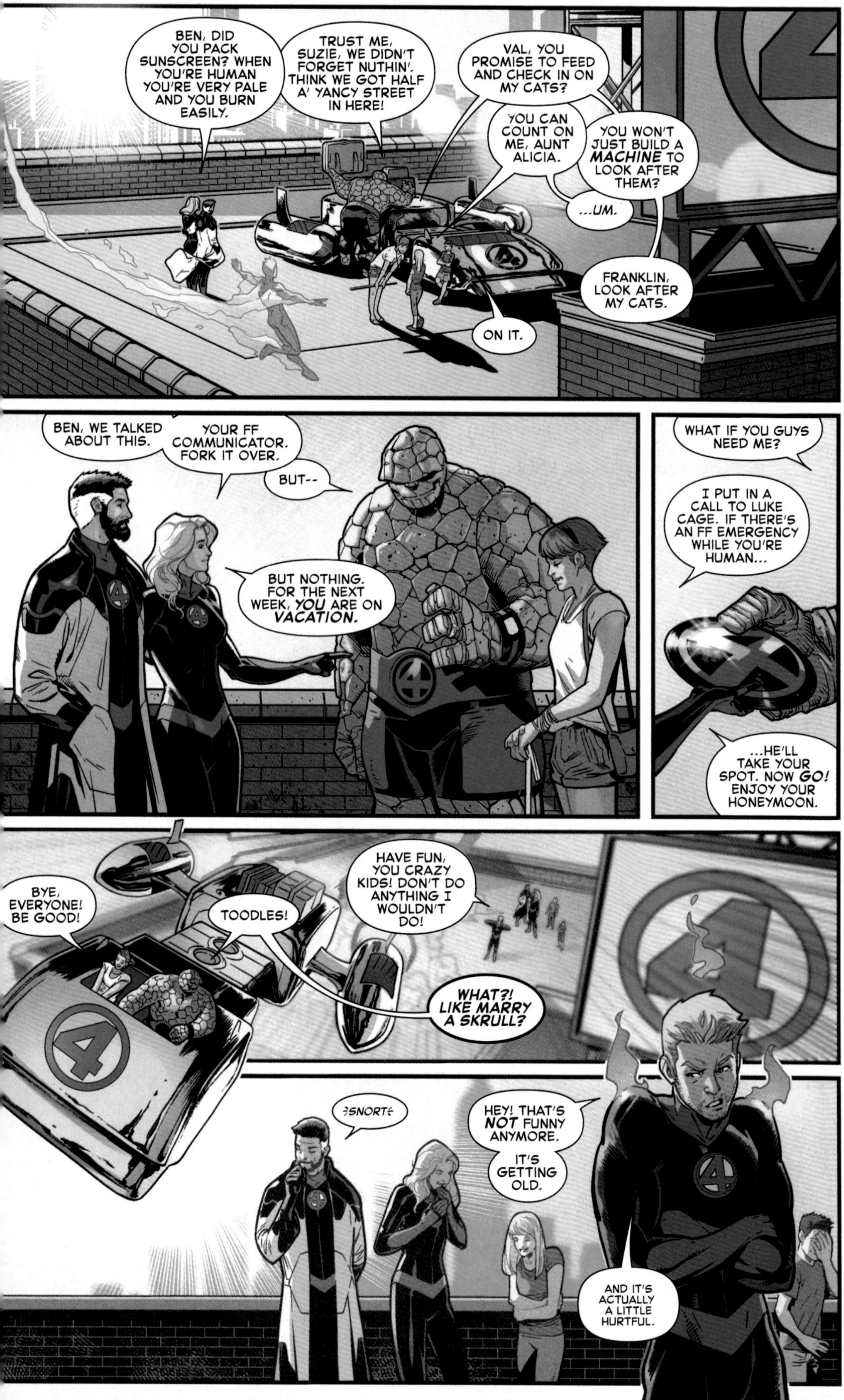

BEN, DID YOU PACK SUNSCREEN? WHEN YOU'RE HUMAN YOU'RE VERY PALE AND YOU BURN EASILY.
TRUST ME, SUZIE, WE DIDN'T FORGET NUTHIN'. THINK WE GOT HALF A' YANCY STREET IN HERE!
VAL, YOU PROMISE TO FEED AND CHECK IN ON MY CATS?
YOU CAN COUNT ON ME, AUNT ALICIA.
YOU WON'T JUST BUILD A MACHINE TO LOOK AFTER THEM?
...UM.
FRANKLIN, LOOK AFTER MY CATS.
ON IT.
BEN, WE TALKED ABOUT THIS.
YOUR FF COMMUNICATOR. FORK IT OVER.
BUT--
BUT NOTHING. FOR THE NEXT WEEK, YOU ARE ON VACATION.
WHAT IF YOU GUYS NEED ME?
I PUT IN A CALL TO LUKE CAGE. IF THERE'S AN FF EMERGENCY WHILE YOU'RE HUMAN...
...HE'LL TAKE YOUR SPOT. NOW GO! ENJOY YOUR HONEYMOON.
BYE, EVERYONE! BE GOOD!
TOODLES!
HAVE FUN, YOU CRAZY KIDS! DON'T DO ANYTHING I WOULDN'T DO!
WHAT?! LIKE MARRY A SKRULL?
SNORT
HEY! THAT'S NOT FUNNY ANYMORE.
IT'S GETTING OLD.
AND IT'S ACTUALLY A LITTLE HURTFUL.

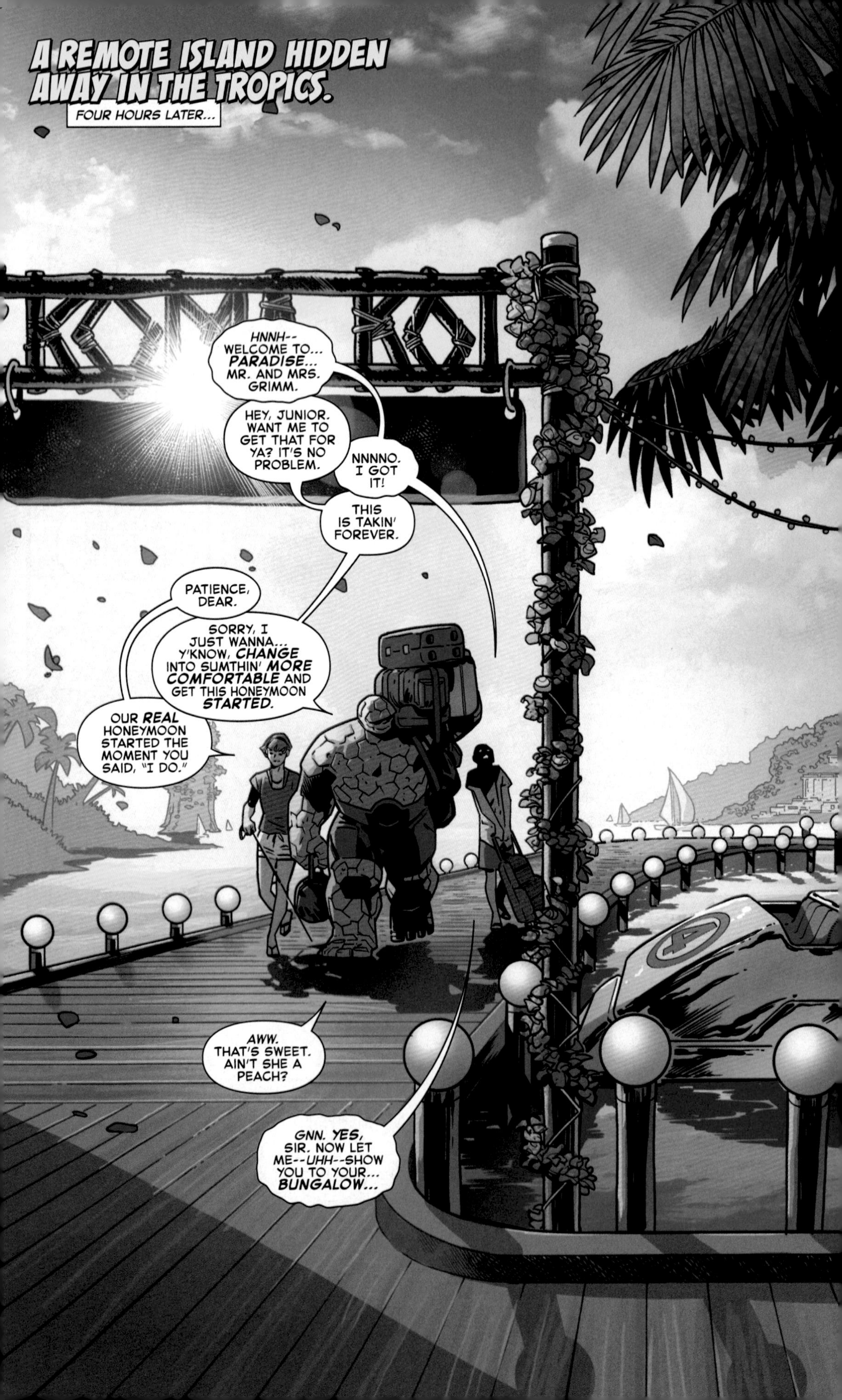
A REMOTE ISLAND HIDDEN AWAY IN THE TROPICS.
FOUR HOURS LATER...
HNNH-- WELCOME TO... PARADISE... MR. AND MRS. GRIMM.
HEY, JUNIOR. WANT ME TO GET THAT FOR YA? IT'S NO PROBLEM.
NNNNO. I GOT IT!
THIS IS TAKIN' FOREVER.
PATIENCE, DEAR.
SORRY, I JUST WANNA... Y'KNOW, CHANGE INTO SUMTHIN' MORE COMFORTABLE AND GET THIS HONEYMOON STARTED.
OUR REAL HONEYMOON STARTED THE MOMENT YOU SAID, "I DO."
AWW. THAT'S SWEET. AIN'T SHE A PEACH?
GNN. YES, SIR. NOW LET ME--UHH--SHOW YOU TO YOUR... BUNGALOW...

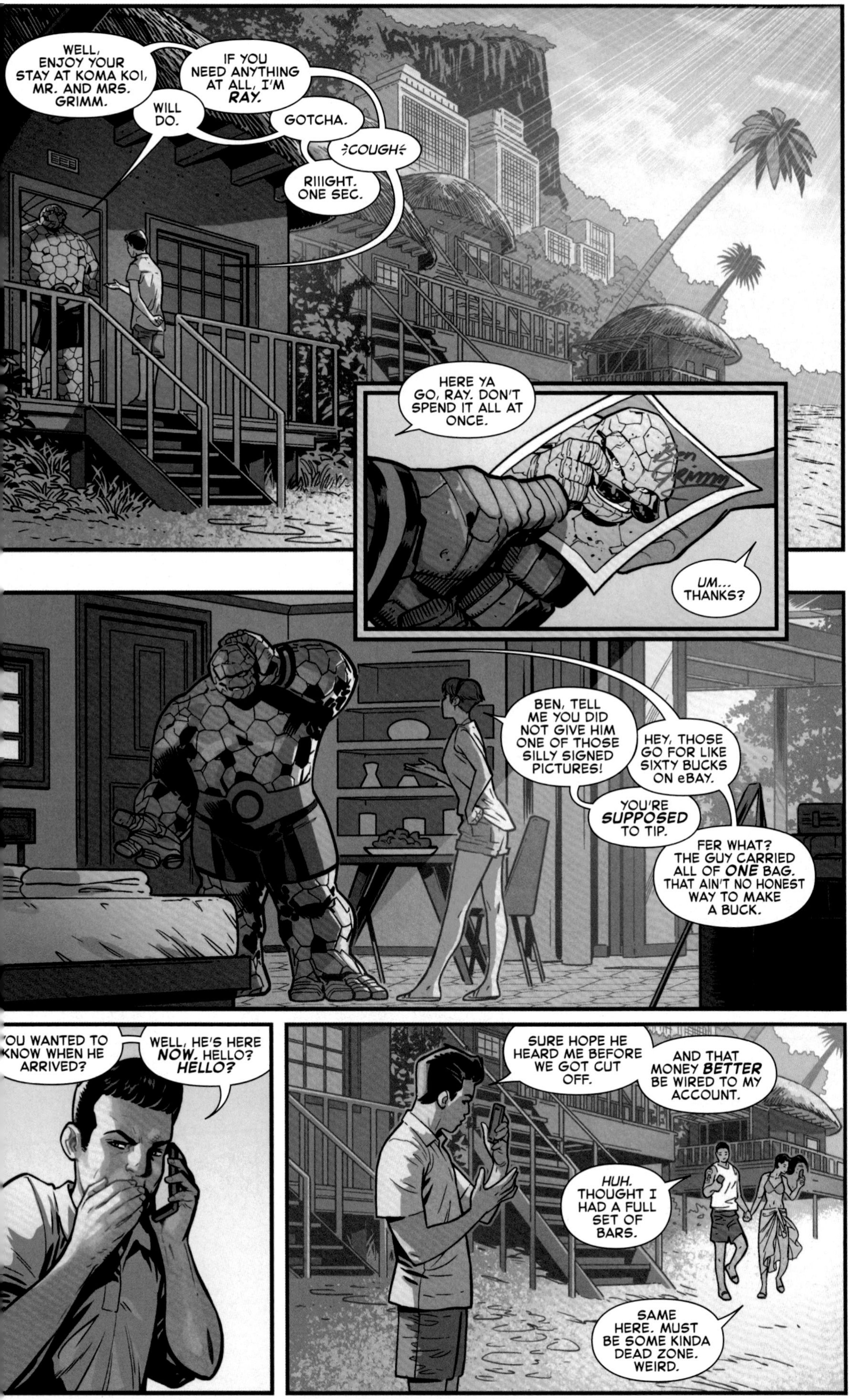
WELL, ENJOY YOUR STAY AT KOMA KOI, MR. AND MRS. GRIMM.
IF YOU NEED ANYTHING AT ALL, I'M RAY.
WILL DO.
GOTCHA.
COUGH
RIIIGHT. ONE SEC.
HERE YA GO, RAY. DON'T SPEND IT ALL AT ONCE.
UM... THANKS?
BEN, TELL ME YOU DID NOT GIVE HIM ONE OF THOSE SILLY SIGNED PICTURES!
HEY, THOSE GO FOR LIKE SIXTY BUCKS ON eBAY.
YOU'RE SUPPOSED TO TIP.
FER WHAT? THE GUY CARRIED ALL OF ONE BAG. THAT AIN'T NO HONEST WAY TO MAKE A BUCK.
OU WANTED TO KNOW WHEN HE ARRIVED?
WELL, HE'S HERE NOW. HELLO? HELLO?
SURE HOPE HE HEARD ME BEFORE WE GOT CUT OFF.
AND THAT MONEY BETTER BE WIRED TO MY ACCOUNT.
HUH. THOUGHT I HAD A FULL SET OF BARS.
SAME HERE. MUST BE SOME KINDA DEAD ZONE. WEIRD.

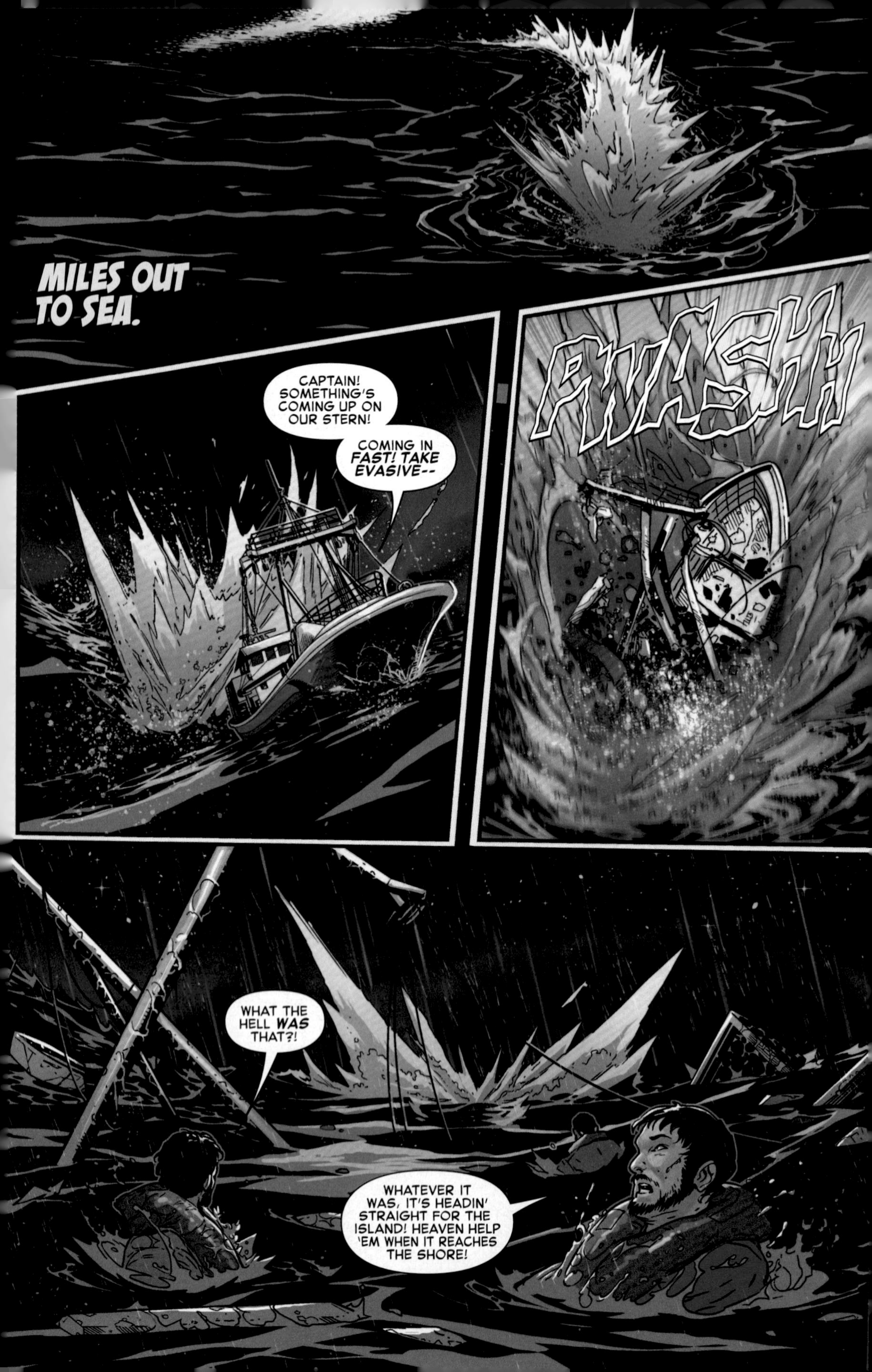

MILES OUT TO SEA.
CAPTAIN! SOMETHING'S COMING UP ON OUR STERN!
COMING IN FAST! TAKE EVASIVE--
FWASHH
WHAT THE HELL WAS THAT?!
WHATEVER IT WAS, IT'S HEADIN' STRAIGHT FOR THE ISLAND! HEAVEN HELP 'EM WHEN IT REACHES THE SHORE!

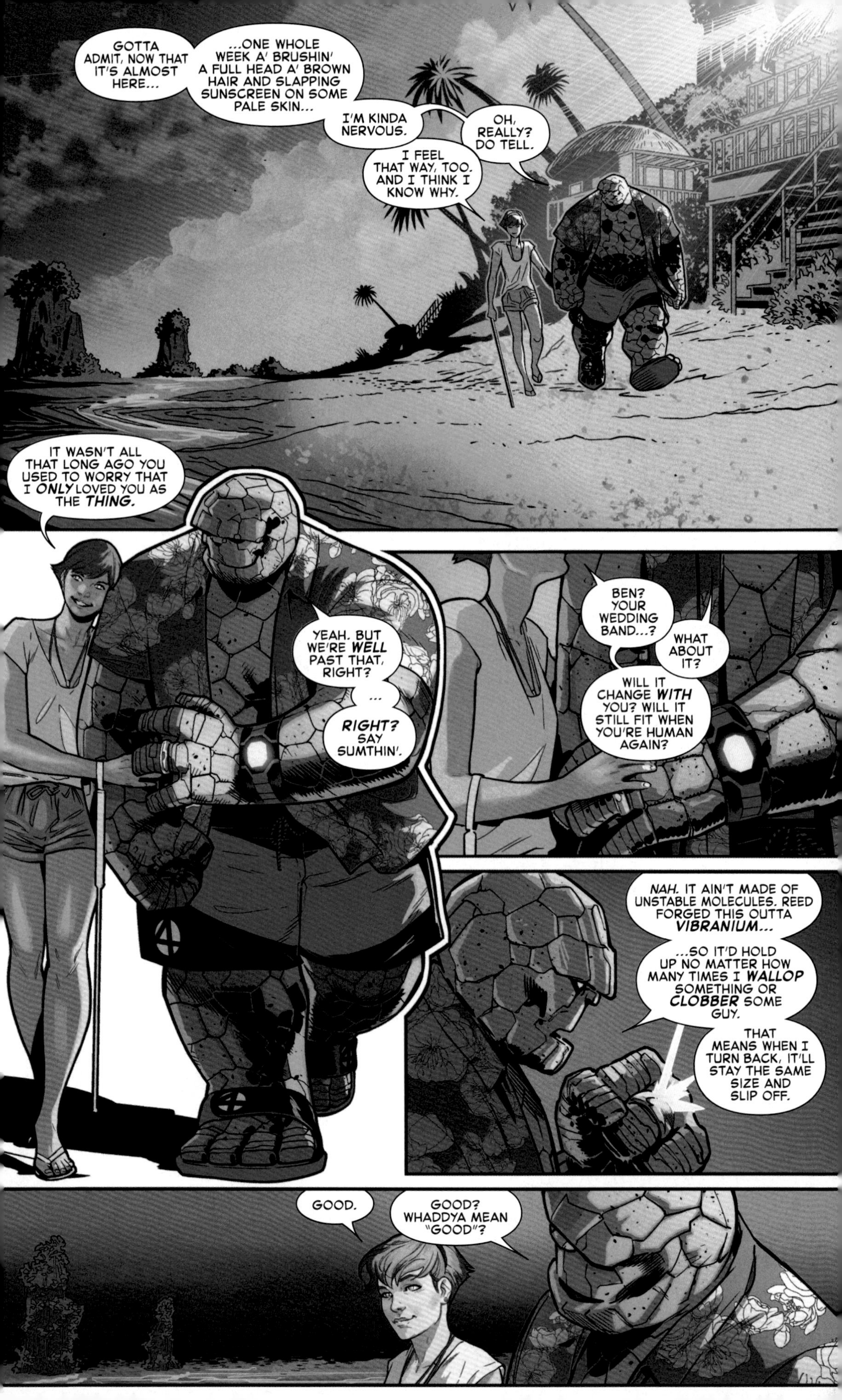
GOTTA ADMIT, NOW THAT IT'S ALMOST HERE...
...ONE WHOLE WEEK A' BRUSHIN' A FULL HEAD A' BROWN HAIR AND SLAPPING SUNSCREEN ON SOME PALE SKIN...
I'M KINDA NERVOUS.
OH, REALLY? DO TELL.
I FEEL THAT WAY, TOO. AND I THINK I KNOW WHY.
IT WASN'T ALL THAT LONG AGO YOU USED TO WORRY THAT I ONLY LOVED YOU AS THE THING.
YEAH. BUT WE'RE WELL PAST THAT, RIGHT?
...
RIGHT? SAY SUMTHIN'.
BEN? YOUR WEDDING BAND...?
WHAT ABOUT IT?
WILL IT CHANGE WITH YOU? WILL IT STILL FIT WHEN YOU'RE HUMAN AGAIN?
NAH. IT AIN'T MADE OF UNSTABLE MOLECULES. REED FORGED THIS OUTTA VIBRANIUM...
...SO IT'D HOLD UP NO MATTER HOW MANY TIMES I WALLOP SOMETHING OR CLOBBER SOME GUY.
THAT MEANS WHEN I TURN BACK, IT'LL STAY THE SAME SIZE AND SLIP OFF.
GOOD.
GOOD? WHADDYA MEAN "GOOD"?

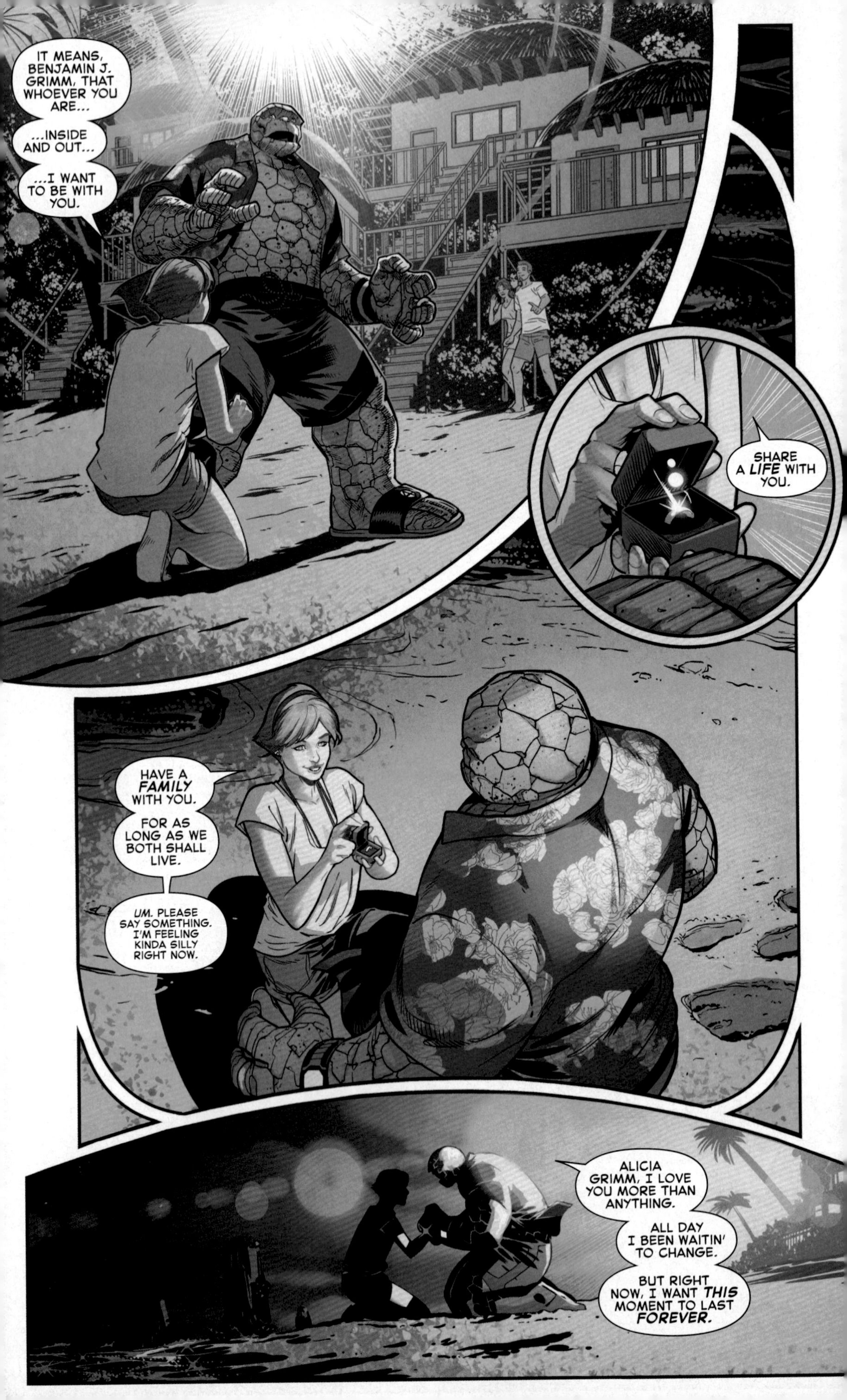
IT MEANS, BENJAMIN J. GRIMM, THAT WHOEVER YOU ARE...
...INSIDE AND OUT...
...I WANT TO BE WITH YOU.
SHARE A *LIFE* WITH YOU.
HAVE A *FAMILY* WITH YOU.
FOR AS LONG AS WE BOTH SHALL LIVE.
UM. PLEASE SAY SOMETHING. I'M FEELING KINDA SILLY RIGHT NOW.
ALICIA GRIMM, I LOVE YOU MORE THAN ANYTHING.
ALL DAY I BEEN WAITIN' TO CHANGE.
BUT RIGHT NOW, I WANT *THIS* MOMENT TO LAST *FOREVER.*

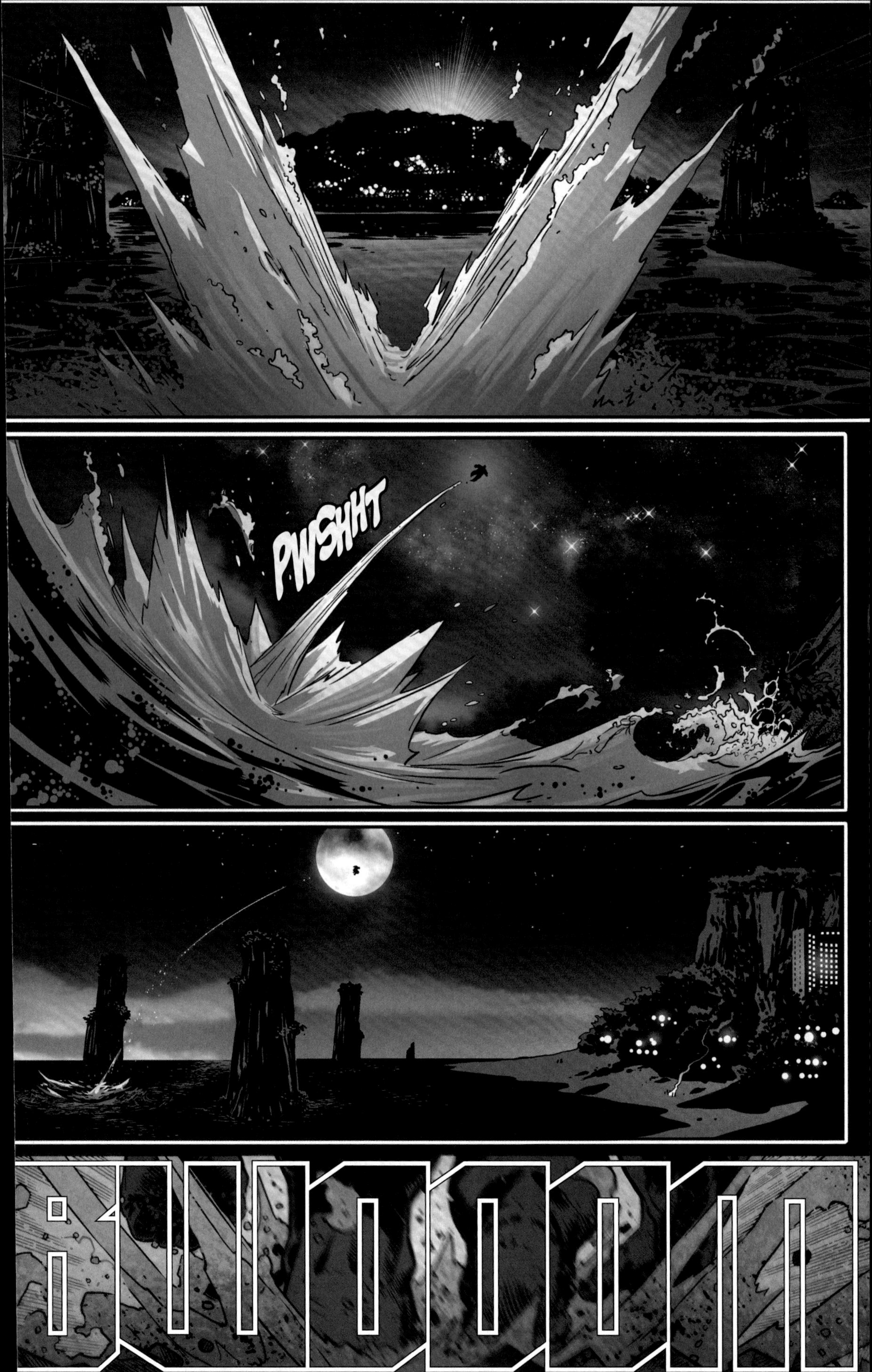
PWSHHT
BWOOOM

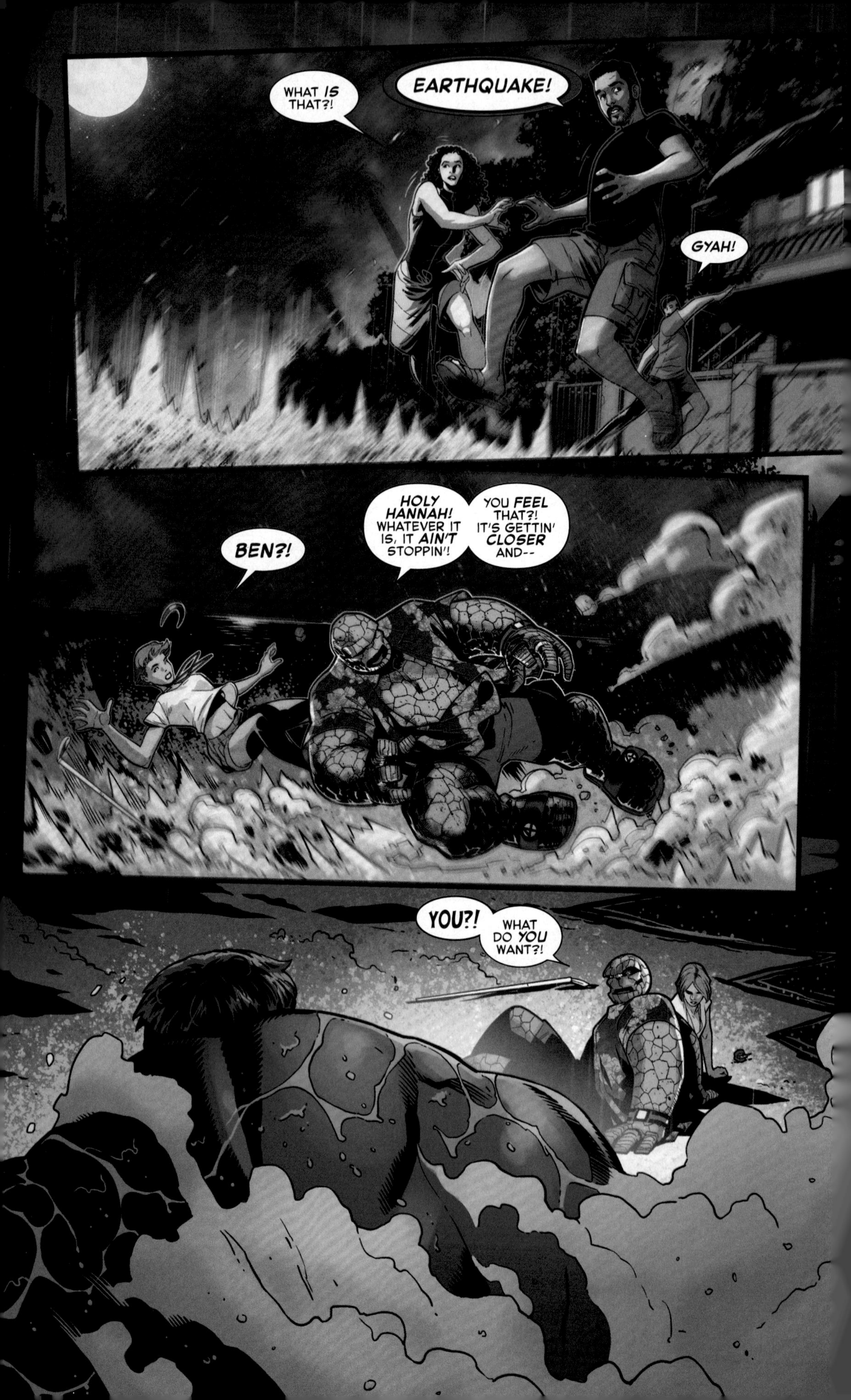

WHAT IS THAT?!
EARTHQUAKE!
GYAH!
BEN?!
HOLY HANNAH! WHATEVER IT IS, IT AIN'T STOPPIN'!
YOU FEEL THAT?! IT'S GETTIN' CLOSER AND--
YOU?!
WHAT DO YOU WANT?!

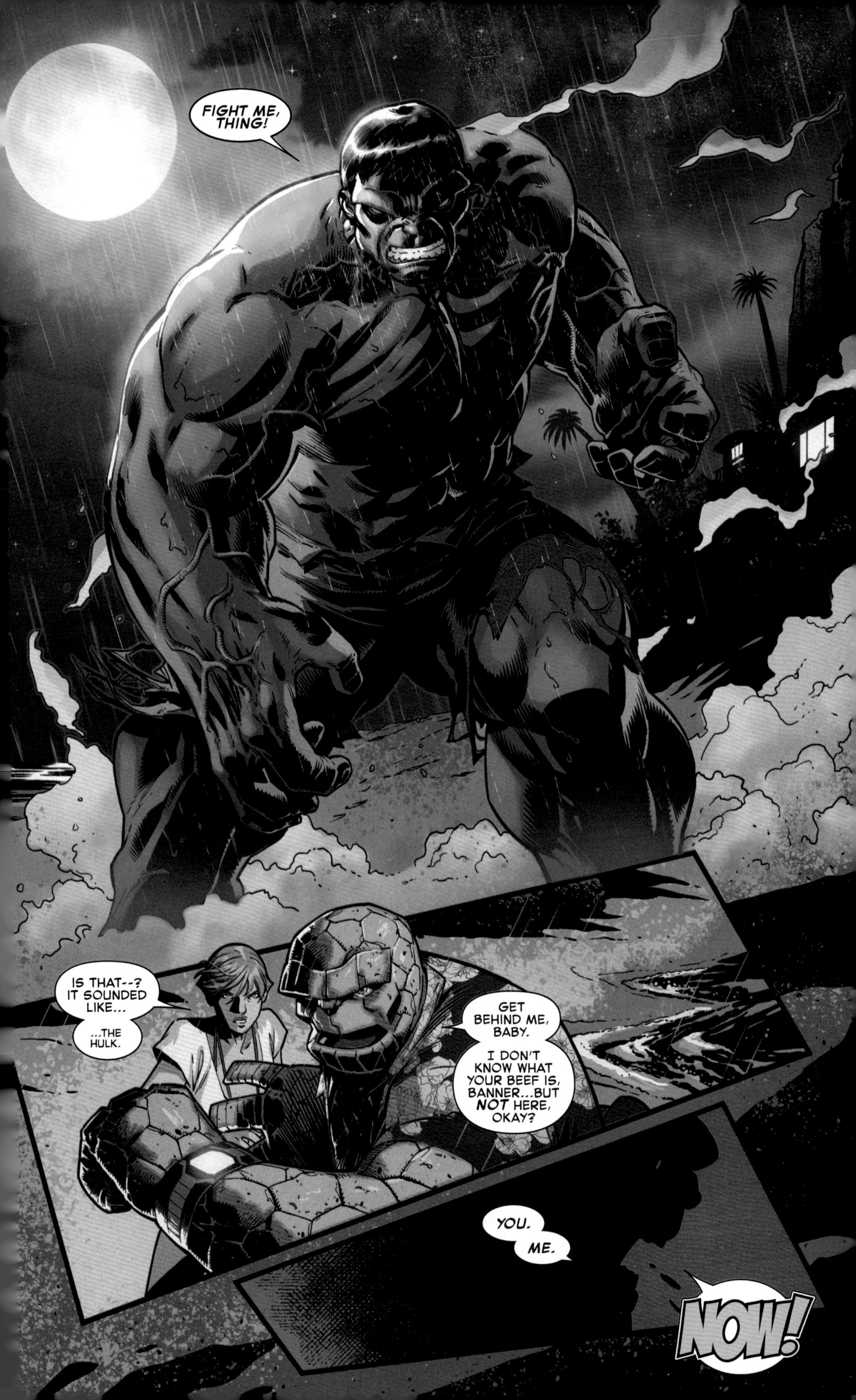
FIGHT ME, THING!
IS THAT--? IT SOUNDED LIKE...
...THE HULK.
GET BEHIND ME, BABY.
I DON'T KNOW WHAT YOUR BEEF IS, BANNER...BUT NOT HERE, OKAY?
YOU.
ME.
NOW!

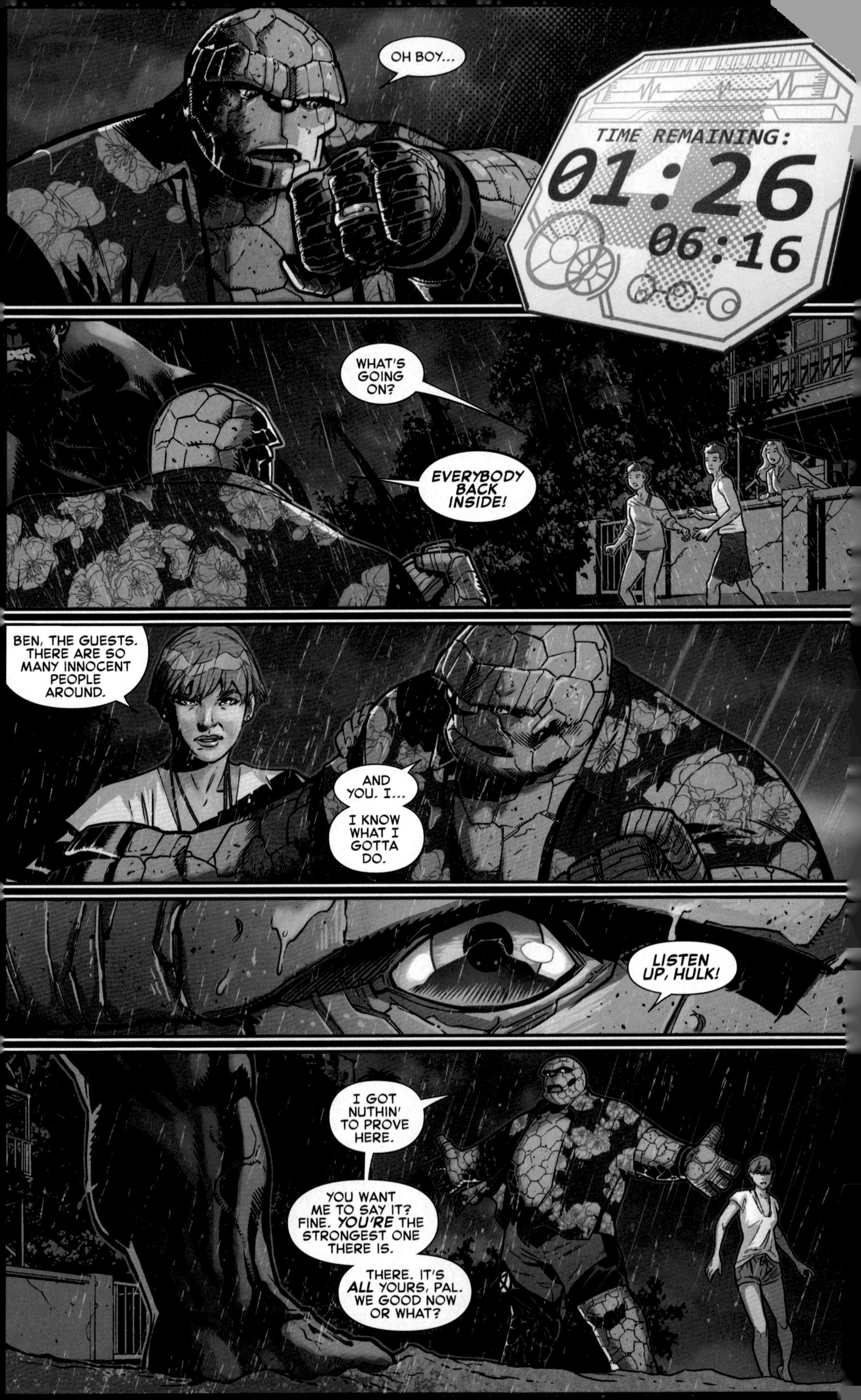
OH BOY...
TIME REMAINING:
01:26
06:16
WHAT'S GOING ON?
EVERYBODY BACK INSIDE!
BEN, THE GUESTS. THERE ARE SO MANY INNOCENT PEOPLE AROUND.
AND YOU. I...
I KNOW WHAT I GOTTA DO.
LISTEN UP, HULK!
I GOT NUTHIN' TO PROVE HERE.
YOU WANT ME TO SAY IT? FINE. YOU'RE THE STRONGEST ONE THERE IS.
THERE. IT'S ALL YOURS, PAL. WE GOOD NOW OR WHAT?

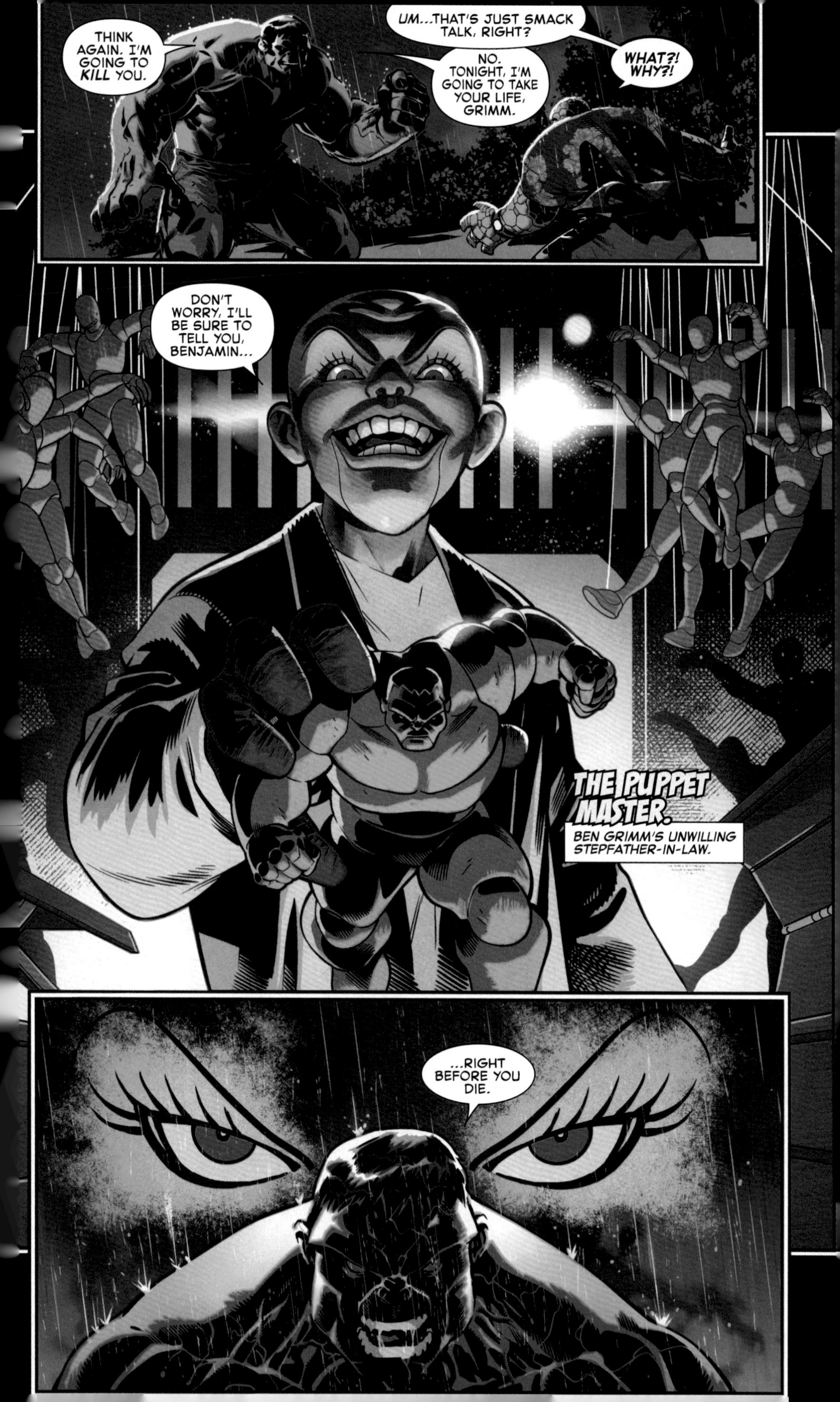

THINK AGAIN. I'M GOING TO *KILL* YOU.
UM...THAT'S JUST SMACK TALK, RIGHT?
NO. TONIGHT, I'M GOING TO TAKE YOUR LIFE, GRIMM.
WHAT?! WHY?!
DON'T WORRY, I'LL BE SURE TO TELL YOU, BENJAMIN...
THE PUPPET MASTER.
BEN GRIMM'S UNWILLING STEPFATHER-IN-LAW.
...RIGHT BEFORE YOU DIE.

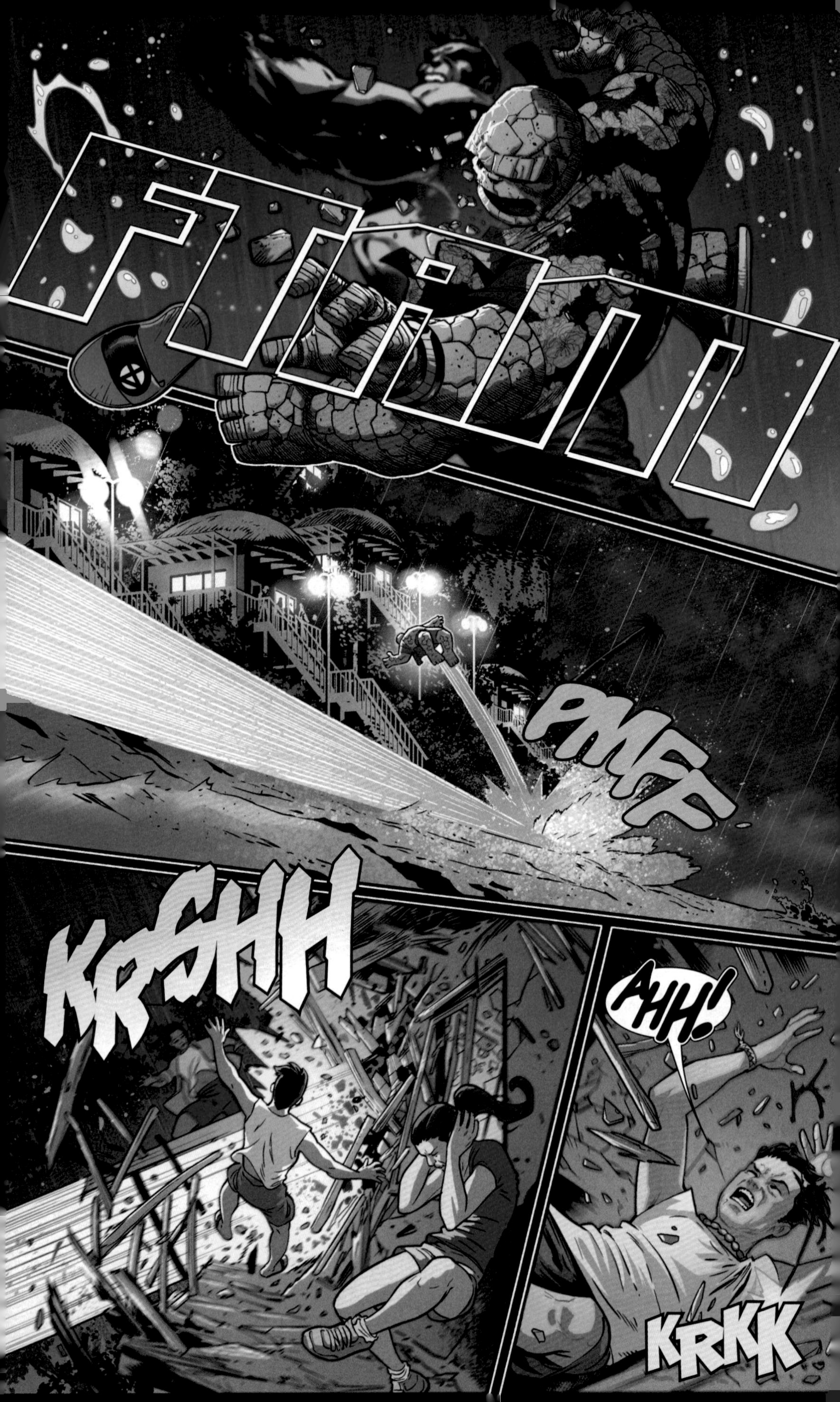

PMFF
KRSHH
AHH!
KRKK

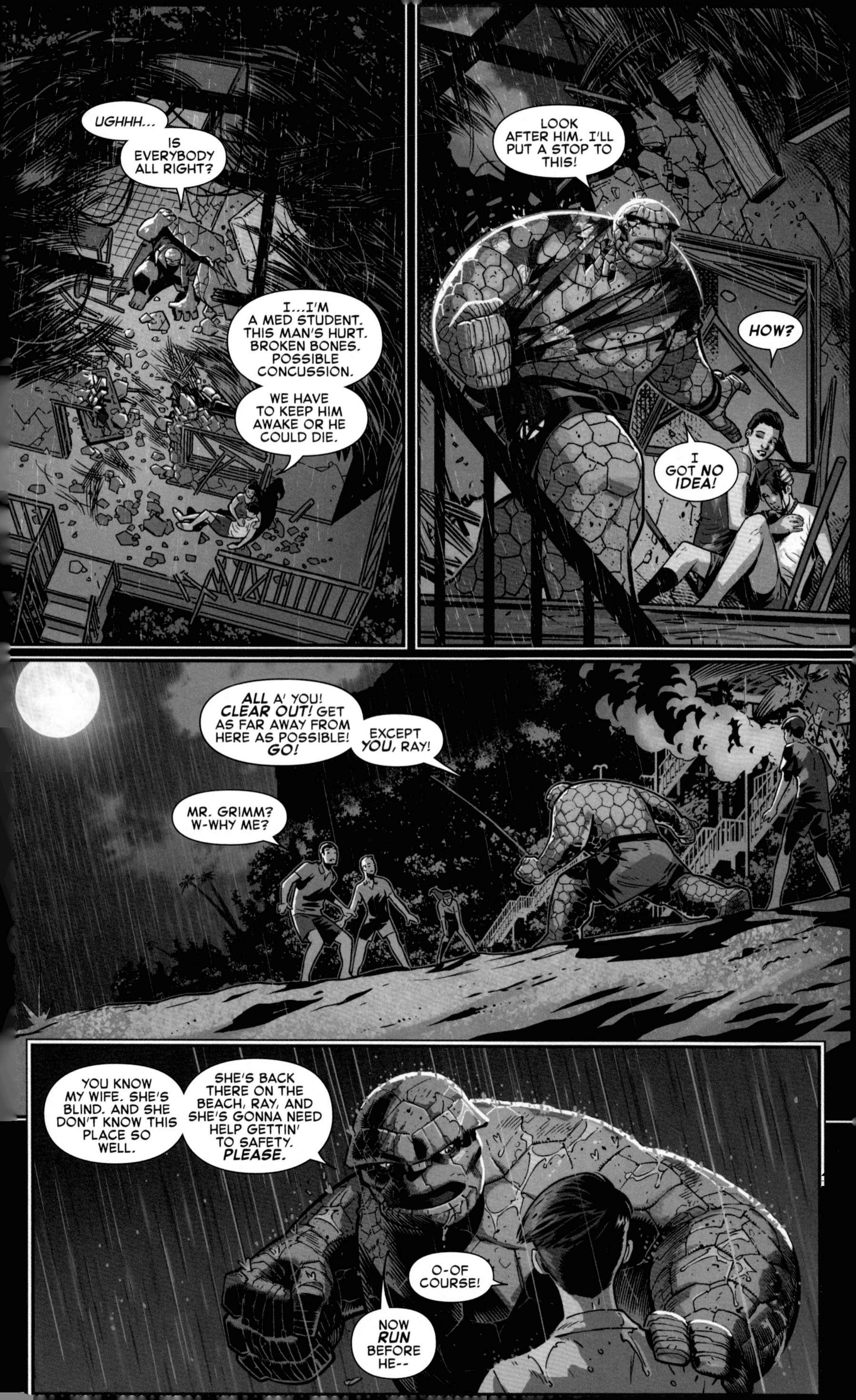
UGHHH...
IS EVERYBODY ALL RIGHT?
I...I'M A MED STUDENT. THIS MAN'S HURT. BROKEN BONES. POSSIBLE CONCUSSION.
WE HAVE TO KEEP HIM AWAKE OR HE COULD DIE.
LOOK AFTER HIM. I'LL PUT A STOP TO THIS!
HOW?
I GOT NO IDEA!
ALL A' YOU! CLEAR OUT! GET AS FAR AWAY FROM HERE AS POSSIBLE! GO!
EXCEPT YOU, RAY!
MR. GRIMM? W-WHY ME?
YOU KNOW MY WIFE. SHE'S BLIND. AND SHE DON'T KNOW THIS PLACE SO WELL.
SHE'S BACK THERE ON THE BEACH, RAY, AND SHE'S GONNA NEED HELP GETTIN' TO SAFETY. PLEASE.
O-OF COURSE!
NOW RUN BEFORE HE--

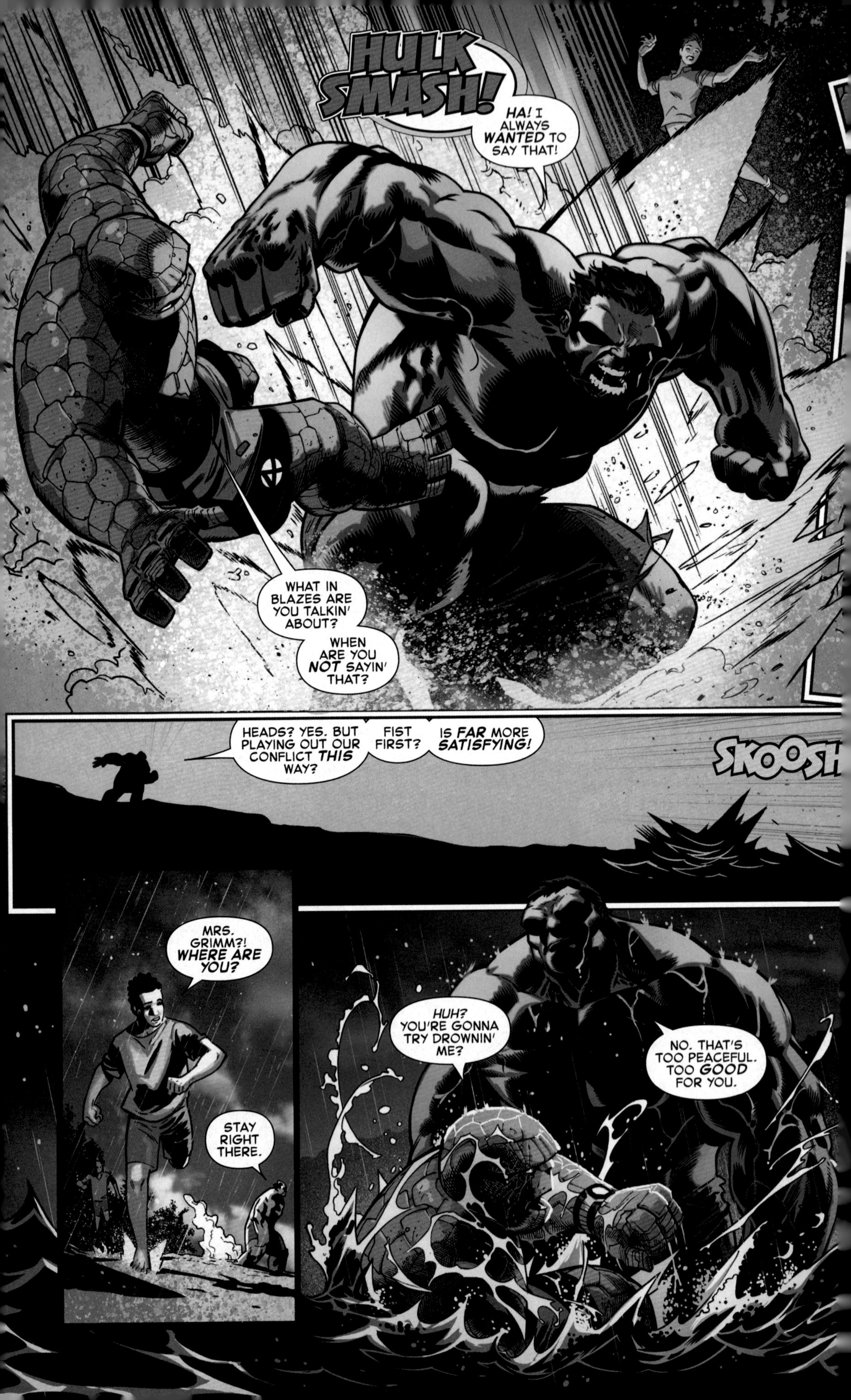
HULK SMASH!
HA! I ALWAYS WANTED TO SAY THAT!
WHAT IN BLAZES ARE YOU TALKIN' ABOUT?
WHEN ARE YOU NOT SAYIN' THAT?
HEADS? YES. BUT PLAYING OUT OUR CONFLICT THIS WAY?
FIST FIRST?
IS FAR MORE SATISFYING!
SKOOSH
MRS. GRIMM?! WHERE ARE YOU?
STAY RIGHT THERE.
HUH? YOU'RE GONNA TRY DROWNIN' ME?
NO. THAT'S TOO PEACEFUL. TOO GOOD FOR YOU.

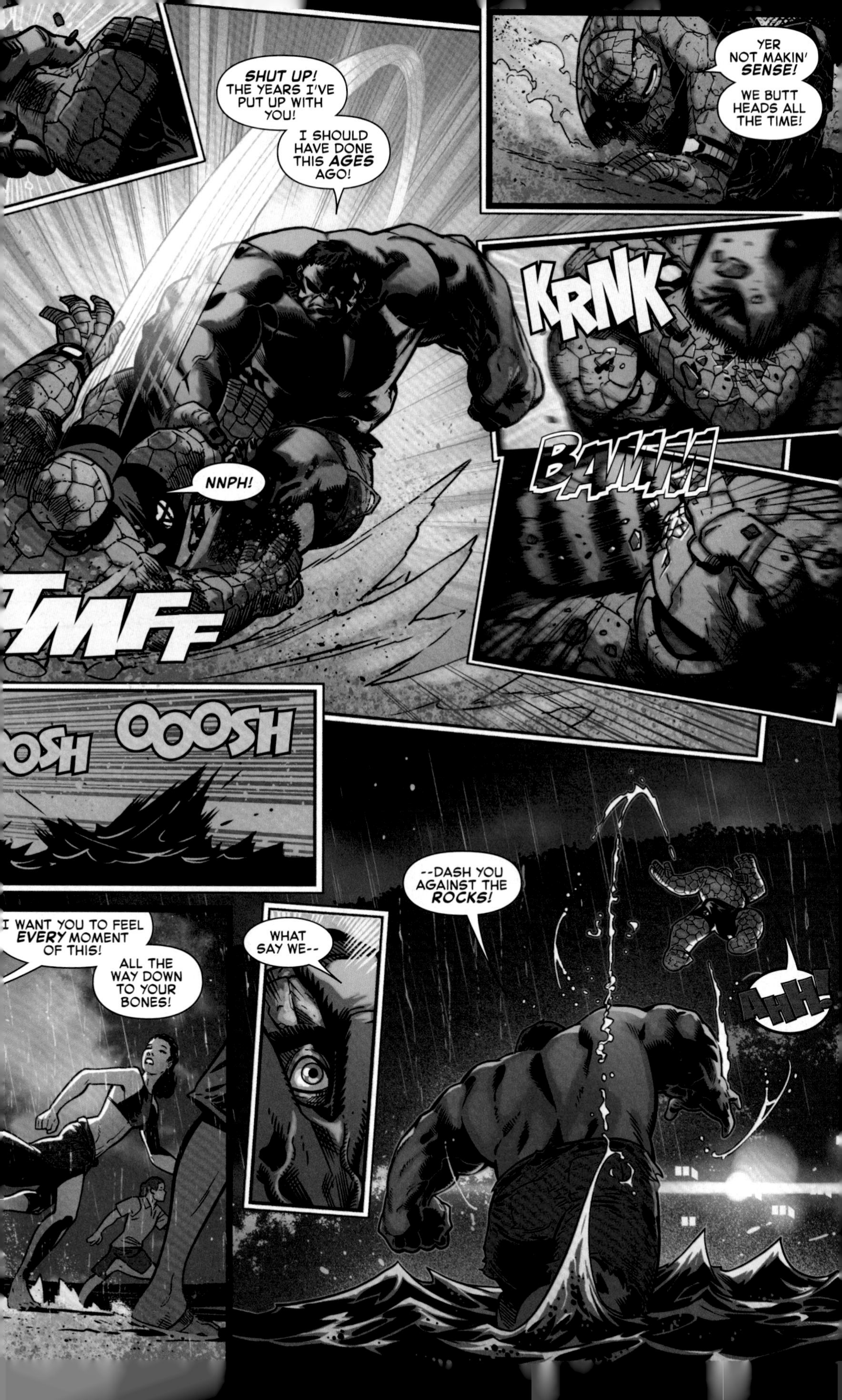

SHUT UP! THE YEARS I'VE PUT UP WITH YOU!
I SHOULD HAVE DONE THIS AGES AGO!
YER NOT MAKIN' SENSE!
WE BUTT HEADS ALL THE TIME!
KRNK
NNPH!
BAMM
TMFF
OSH
OOOSH
I WANT YOU TO FEEL EVERY MOMENT OF THIS!
ALL THE WAY DOWN TO YOUR BONES!
WHAT SAY WE--
--DASH YOU AGAINST THE ROCKS!
AHH!

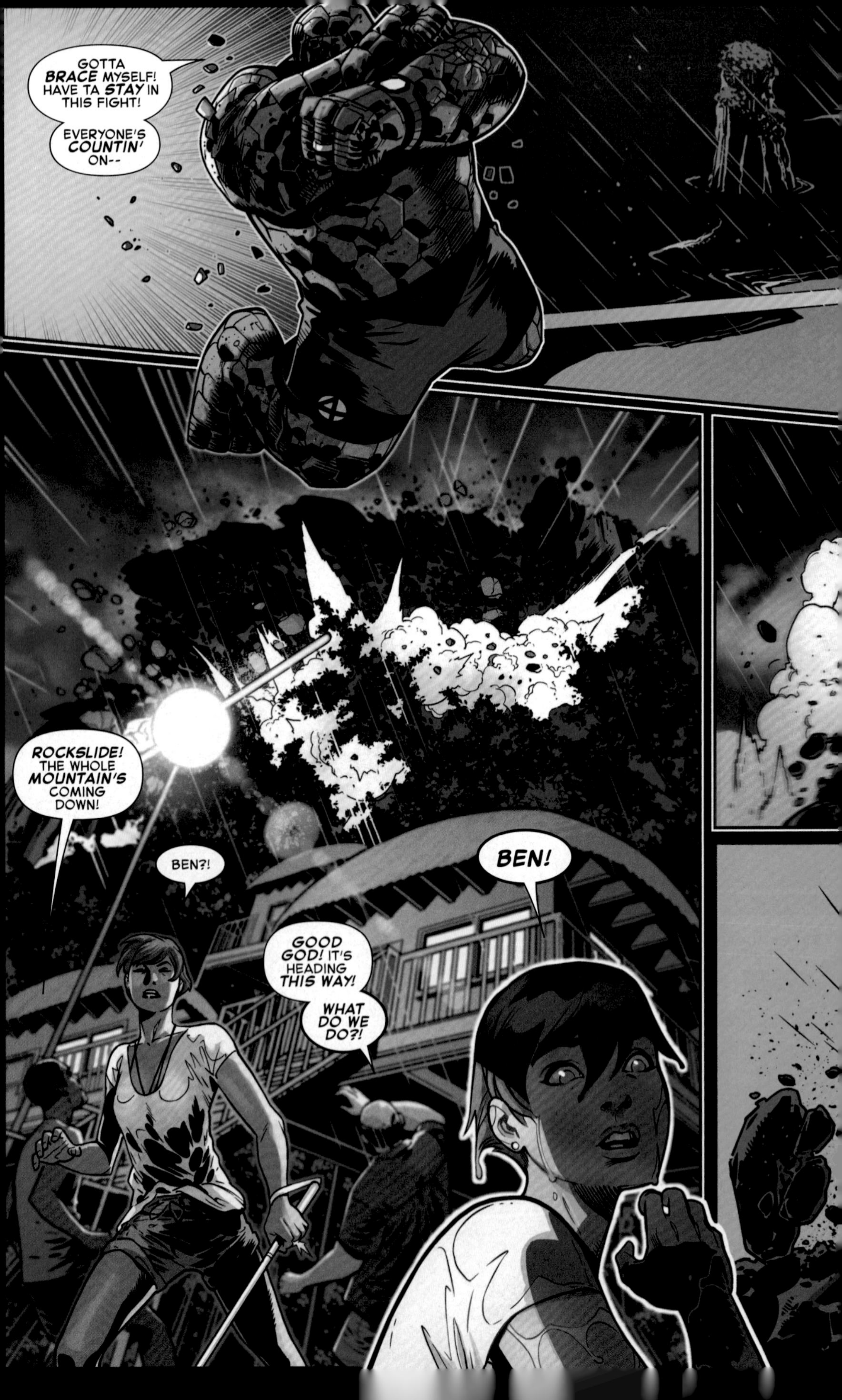
GOTTA BRACE MYSELF! HAVE TA STAY IN THIS FIGHT!
EVERYONE'S COUNTIN' ON--
ROCKSLIDE! THE WHOLE MOUNTAIN'S COMING DOWN!
BEN?!
BEN!
GOOD GOD! IT'S HEADING THIS WAY!
WHAT DO WE DO?!

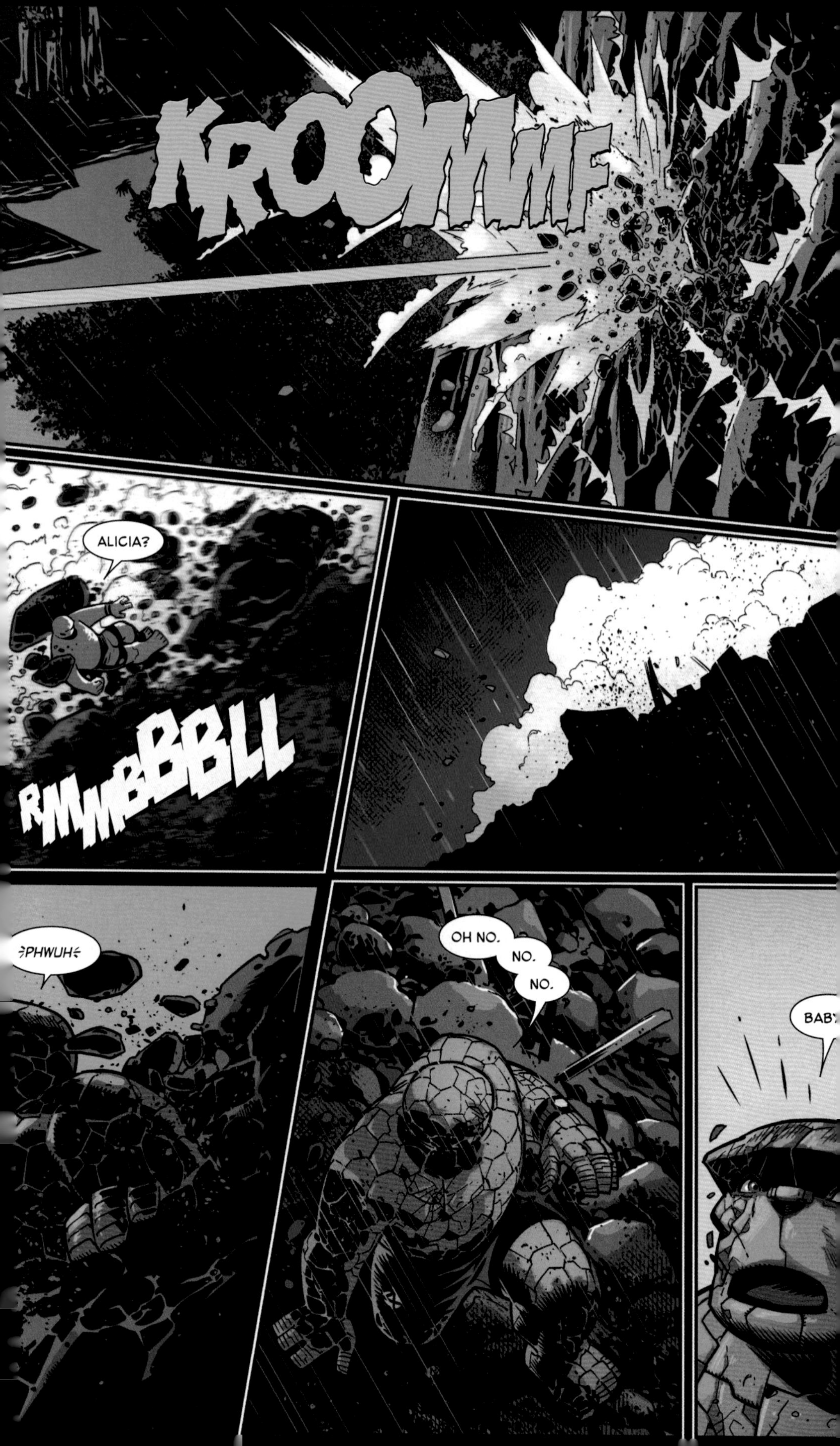
KROOMMF
ALICIA?
RMMBBBLL
PHWUH
OH NO.
NO.
NO.

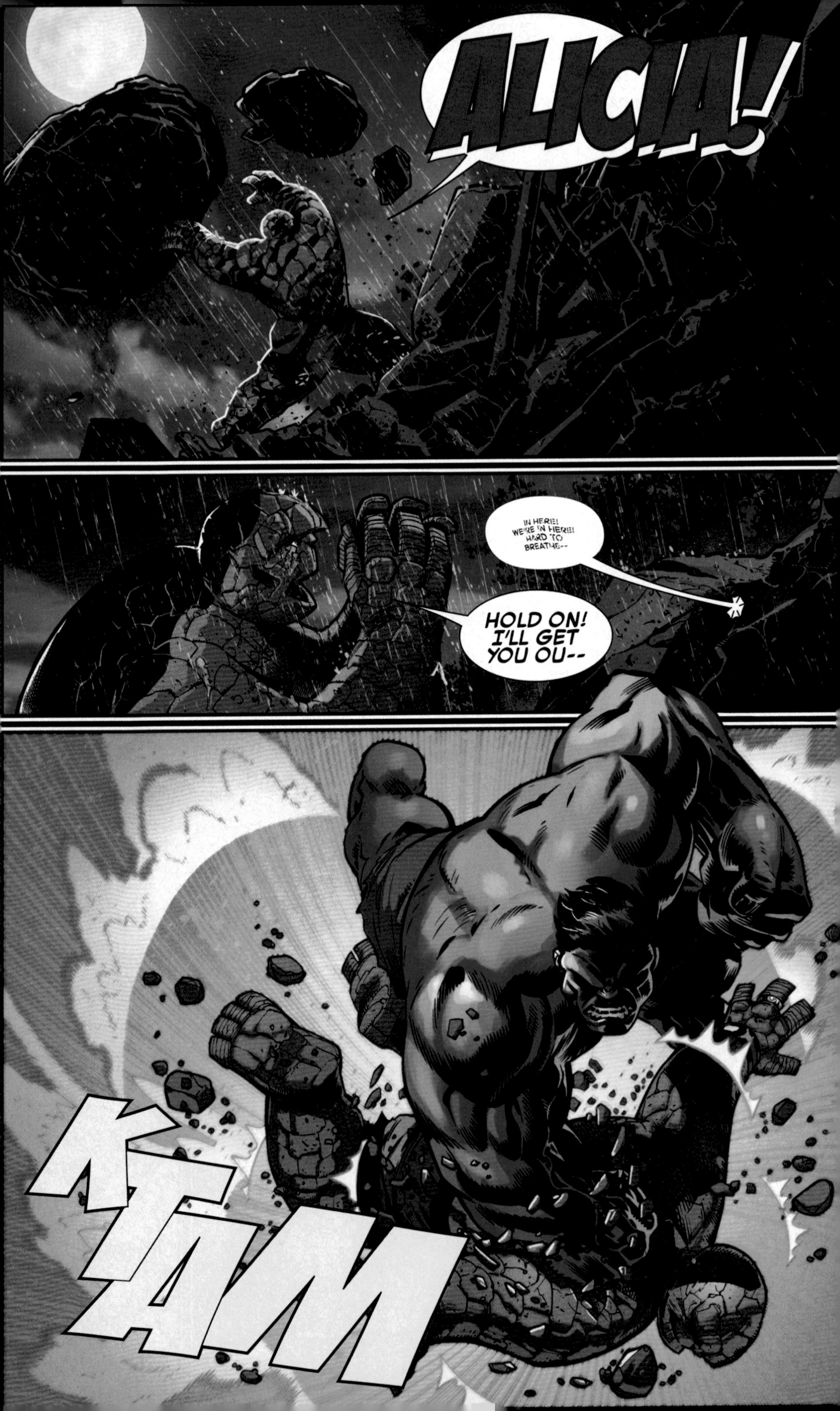
ALICIA!
IN HERE! WE'RE IN HERE! HARD TO BREATHE--
HOLD ON! I'LL GET YOU OU--
KTAM

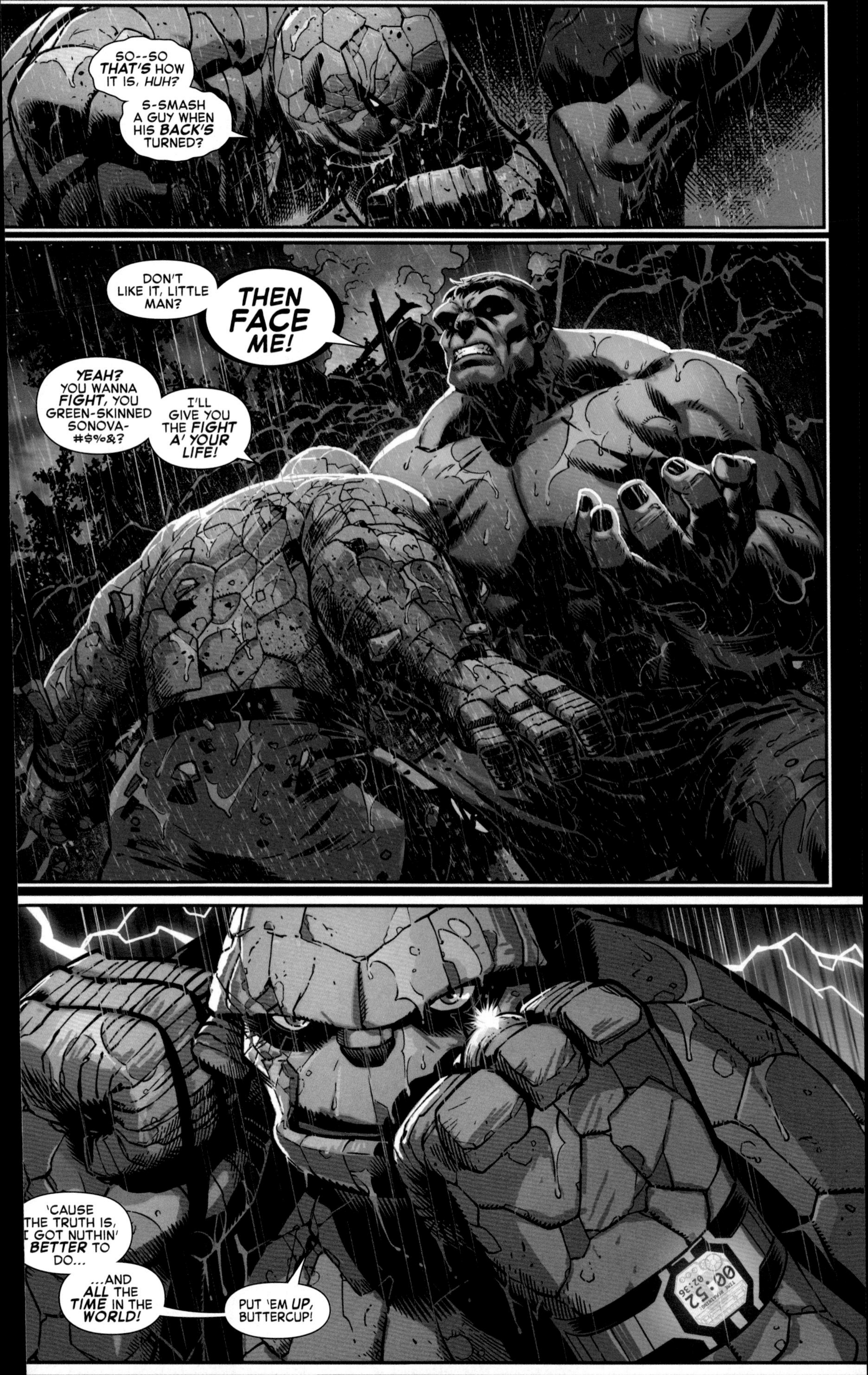
SO--SO THAT'S HOW IT IS, HUH?
S-SMASH A GUY WHEN HIS BACK'S TURNED?
DON'T LIKE IT, LITTLE MAN?
THEN FACE ME!
YEAH? YOU WANNA FIGHT, YOU GREEN-SKINNED SONOVA-#$%&?
I'LL GIVE YOU THE FIGHT A' YOUR LIFE!
'CAUSE THE TRUTH IS, I GOT NUTHIN' BETTER TO DO...
...AND ALL THE TIME IN THE WORLD!
PUT 'EM UP, BUTTERCUP!

"The Fight of Your Life"

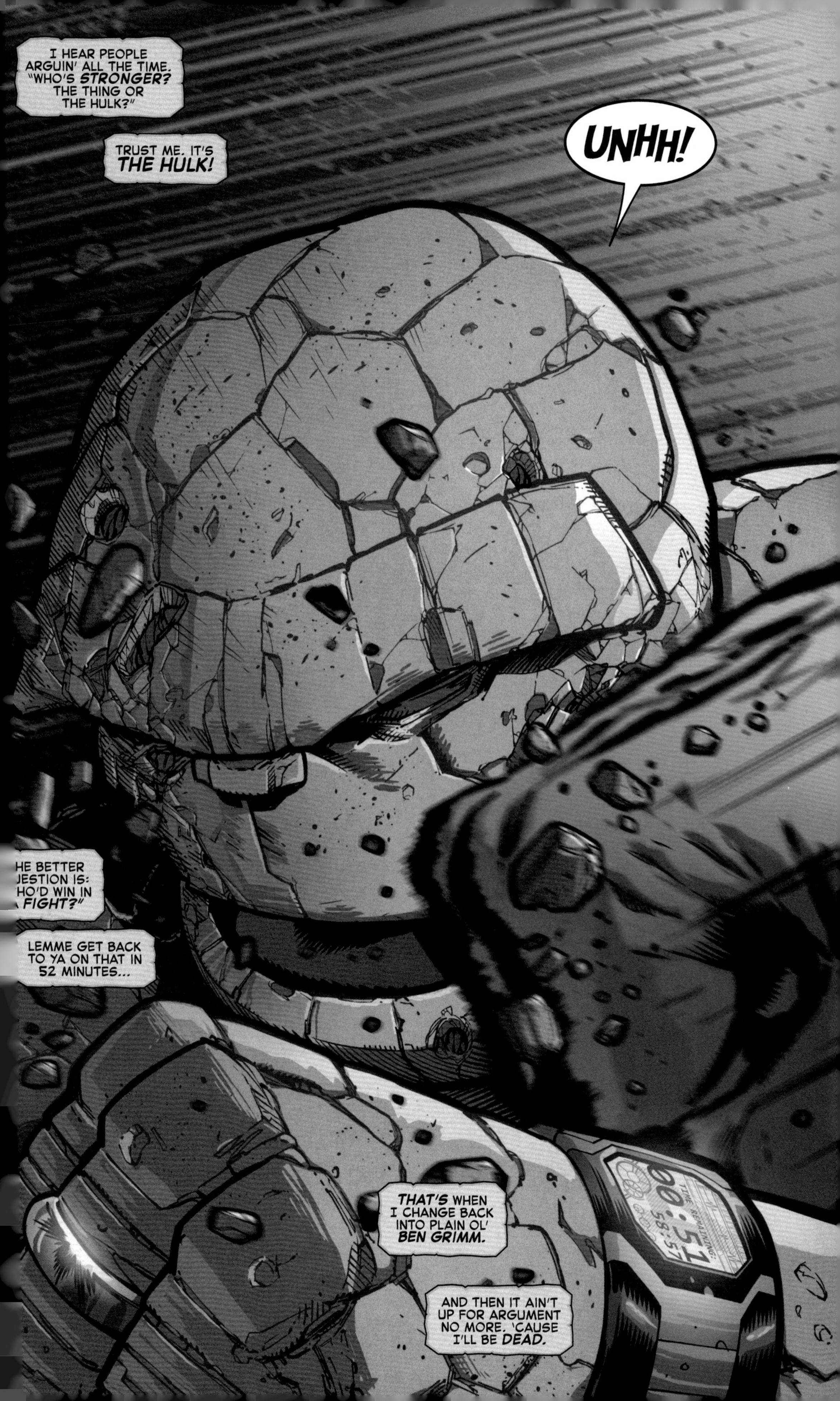
I HEAR PEOPLE ARGUIN' ALL THE TIME. "WHO'S STRONGER? THE THING OR THE HULK?"
TRUST ME. IT'S THE HULK!
UNHH!
HE BETTER JESTION IS: HO'D WIN IN FIGHT?"
LEMME GET BACK TO YA ON THAT IN 52 MINUTES...
THAT'S WHEN I CHANGE BACK INTO PLAIN OL' BEN GRIMM.
AND THEN IT AIN'T UP FOR ARGUMENT NO MORE. 'CAUSE I'LL BE DEAD.

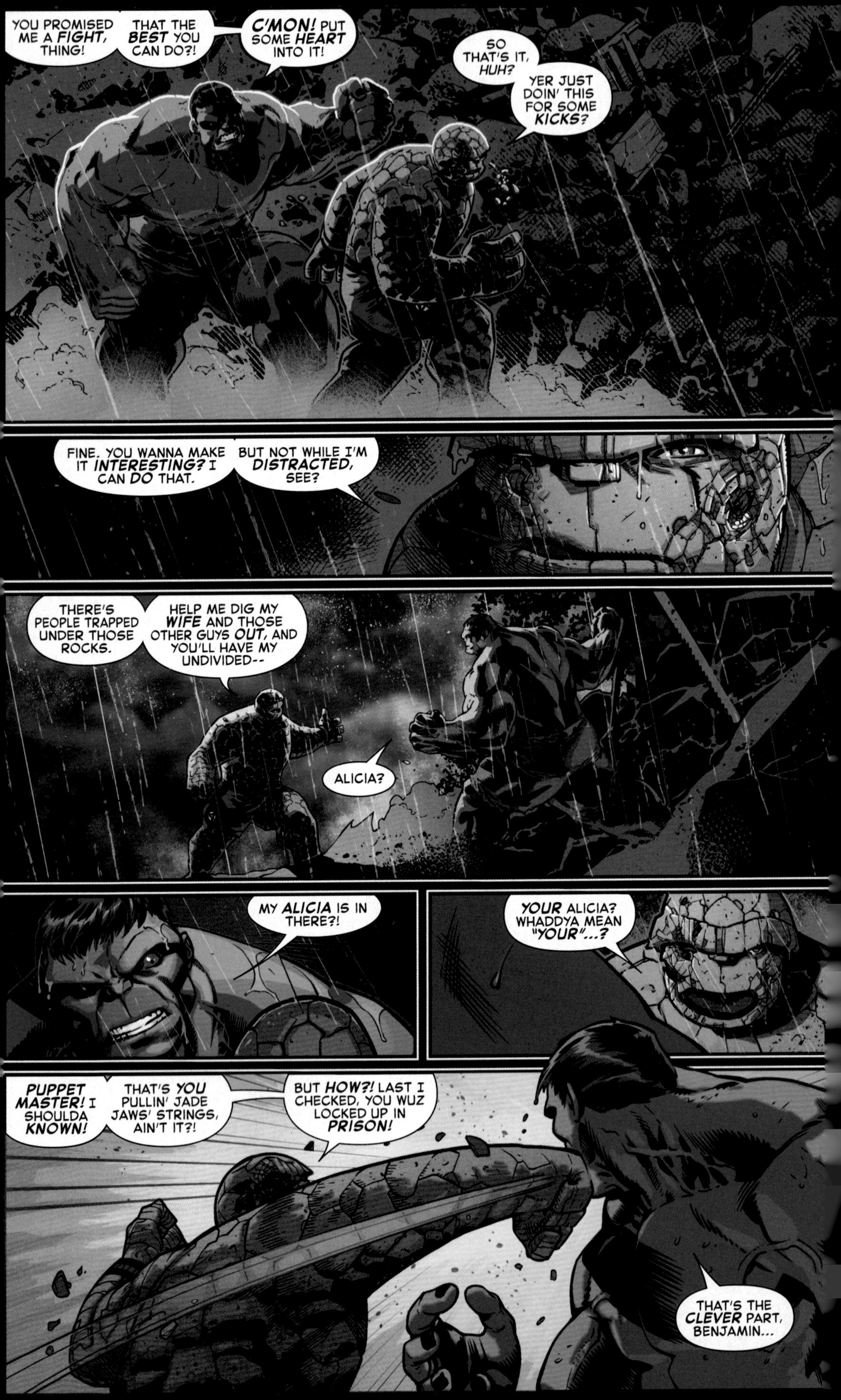

YOU PROMISED ME A FIGHT, THING!
THAT THE BEST YOU CAN DO?!
C'MON! PUT SOME HEART INTO IT!
SO THAT'S IT, HUH?
YER JUST DOIN' THIS FOR SOME KICKS?
FINE. YOU WANNA MAKE IT INTERESTING? I CAN DO THAT.
BUT NOT WHILE I'M DISTRACTED, SEE?
THERE'S PEOPLE TRAPPED UNDER THOSE ROCKS.
HELP ME DIG MY WIFE AND THOSE OTHER GUYS OUT, AND YOU'LL HAVE MY UNDIVIDED--
ALICIA?
MY ALICIA IS IN THERE?!
YOUR ALICIA? WHADDYA MEAN "YOUR"...?
PUPPET MASTER! I SHOULDA KNOWN!
THAT'S YOU PULLIN' JADE JAWS' STRINGS, AIN'T IT?!
BUT HOW?! LAST I CHECKED, YOU WUZ LOCKED UP IN PRISON!
THAT'S THE CLEVER PART, BENJAMIN...

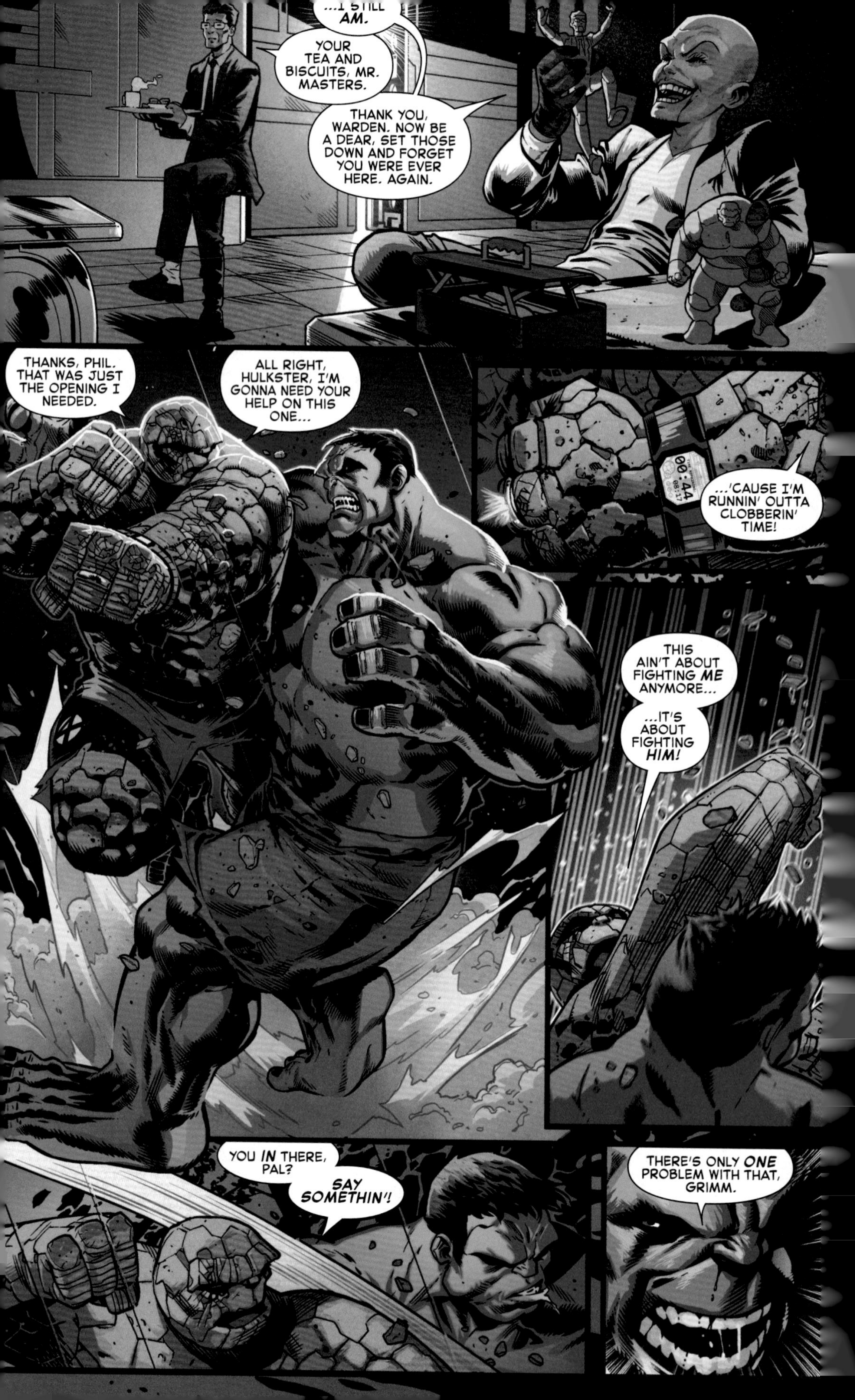
...I STILL AM.
YOUR TEA AND BISCUITS, MR. MASTERS.
THANK YOU, WARDEN. NOW BE A DEAR, SET THOSE DOWN AND FORGET YOU WERE EVER HERE. AGAIN.
THANKS, PHIL. THAT WAS JUST THE OPENING I NEEDED.
ALL RIGHT, HULKSTER, I'M GONNA NEED YOUR HELP ON THIS ONE...
...'CAUSE I'M RUNNIN' OUTTA CLOBBERIN' TIME!
00:44
THIS AIN'T ABOUT FIGHTING ME ANYMORE...
...IT'S ABOUT FIGHTING HIM!
YOU IN THERE, PAL?
SAY SOMETHIN'!
THERE'S ONLY ONE PROBLEM WITH THAT, GRIMM.

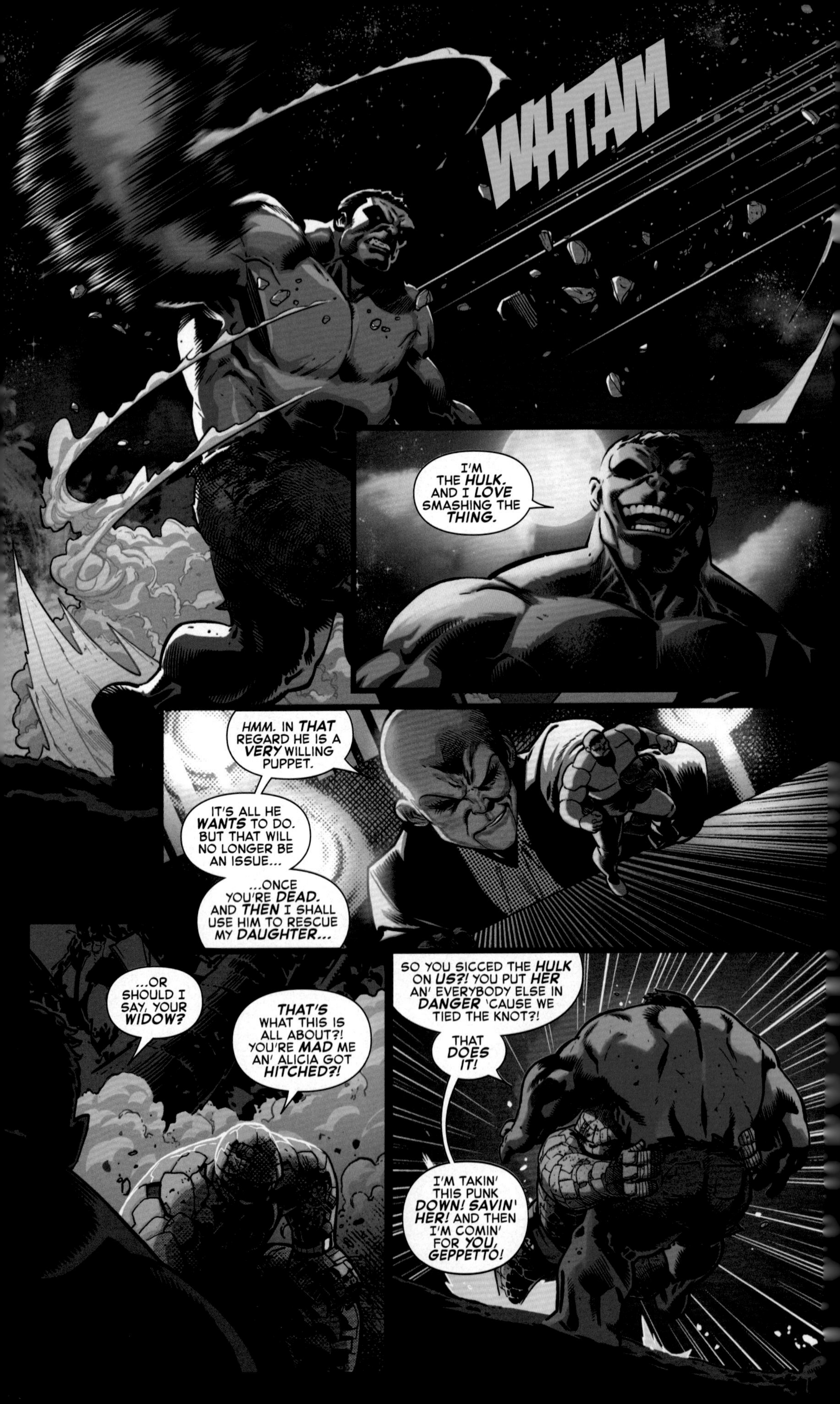
WHTAM
I'M THE HULK. AND I LOVE SMASHING THE THING.
HMM. IN THAT REGARD HE IS A VERY WILLING PUPPET.
IT'S ALL HE WANTS TO DO. BUT THAT WILL NO LONGER BE AN ISSUE...
...ONCE YOU'RE DEAD. AND THEN I SHALL USE HIM TO RESCUE MY DAUGHTER...
...OR SHOULD I SAY, YOUR WIDOW?
THAT'S WHAT THIS IS ALL ABOUT?! YOU'RE MAD ME AN' ALICIA GOT HITCHED?!
SO YOU SICCED THE HULK ON US?! YOU PUT HER AN' EVERYBODY ELSE IN DANGER 'CAUSE WE TIED THE KNOT?!
THAT DOES IT!
I'M TAKIN' THIS PUNK DOWN! SAVIN' HER! AND THEN I'M COMIN' FOR YOU, GEPPETTO!

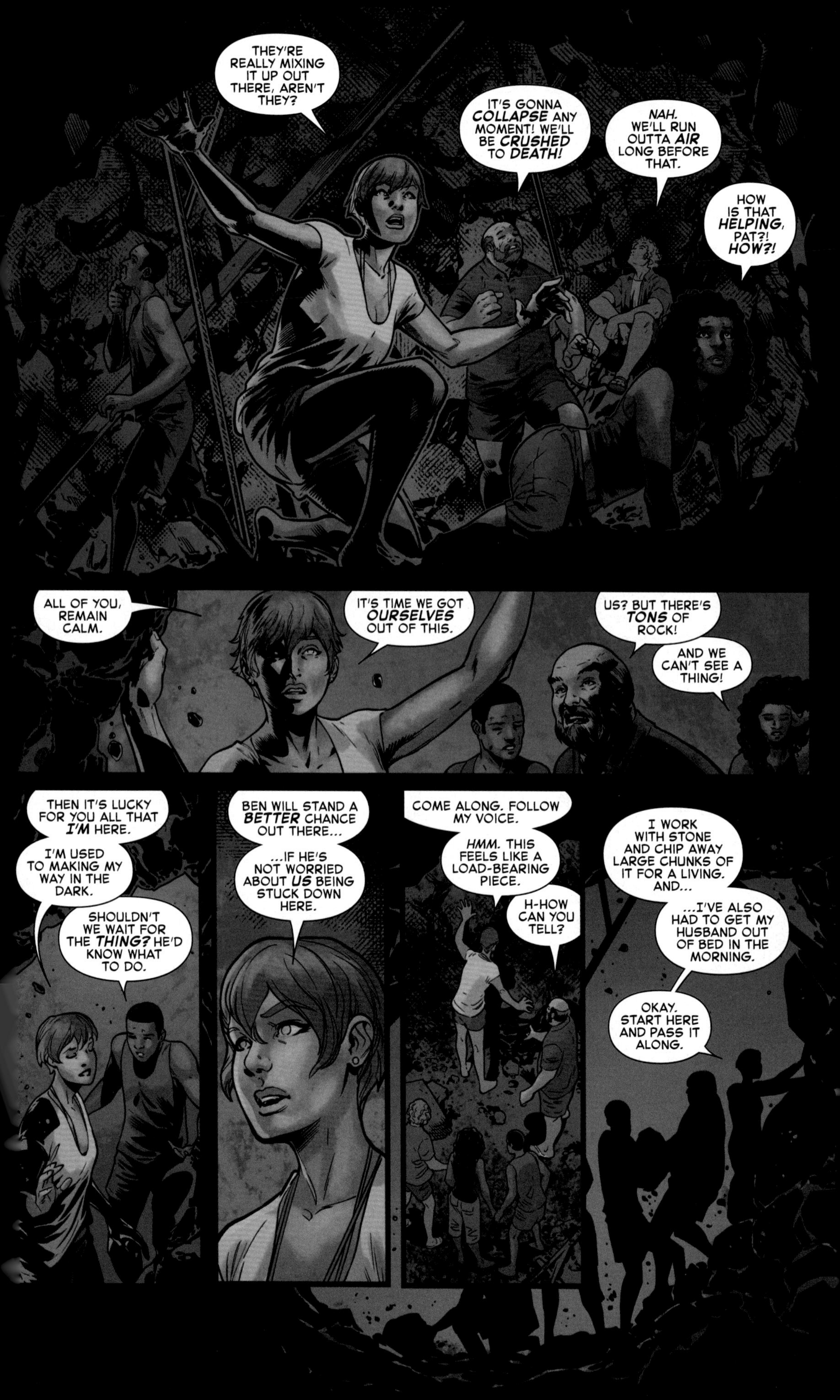
THEY'RE REALLY MIXING IT UP OUT THERE, AREN'T THEY?
IT'S GONNA COLLAPSE ANY MOMENT! WE'LL BE CRUSHED TO DEATH!
NAH. WE'LL RUN OUTTA AIR LONG BEFORE THAT.
HOW IS THAT HELPING, PAT?! HOW?!
ALL OF YOU, REMAIN CALM.
IT'S TIME WE GOT OURSELVES OUT OF THIS.
US? BUT THERE'S TONS OF ROCK!
AND WE CAN'T SEE A THING!
THEN IT'S LUCKY FOR YOU ALL THAT I'M HERE.
I'M USED TO MAKING MY WAY IN THE DARK.
SHOULDN'T WE WAIT FOR THE THING? HE'D KNOW WHAT TO DO.
BEN WILL STAND A BETTER CHANCE OUT THERE...
...IF HE'S NOT WORRIED ABOUT US BEING STUCK DOWN HERE.
COME ALONG. FOLLOW MY VOICE.
HMM. THIS FEELS LIKE A LOAD-BEARING PIECE.
H-HOW CAN YOU TELL?
I WORK WITH STONE AND CHIP AWAY LARGE CHUNKS OF IT FOR A LIVING. AND...
...I'VE ALSO HAD TO GET MY HUSBAND OUT OF BED IN THE MORNING.
OKAY. START HERE AND PASS IT ALONG.

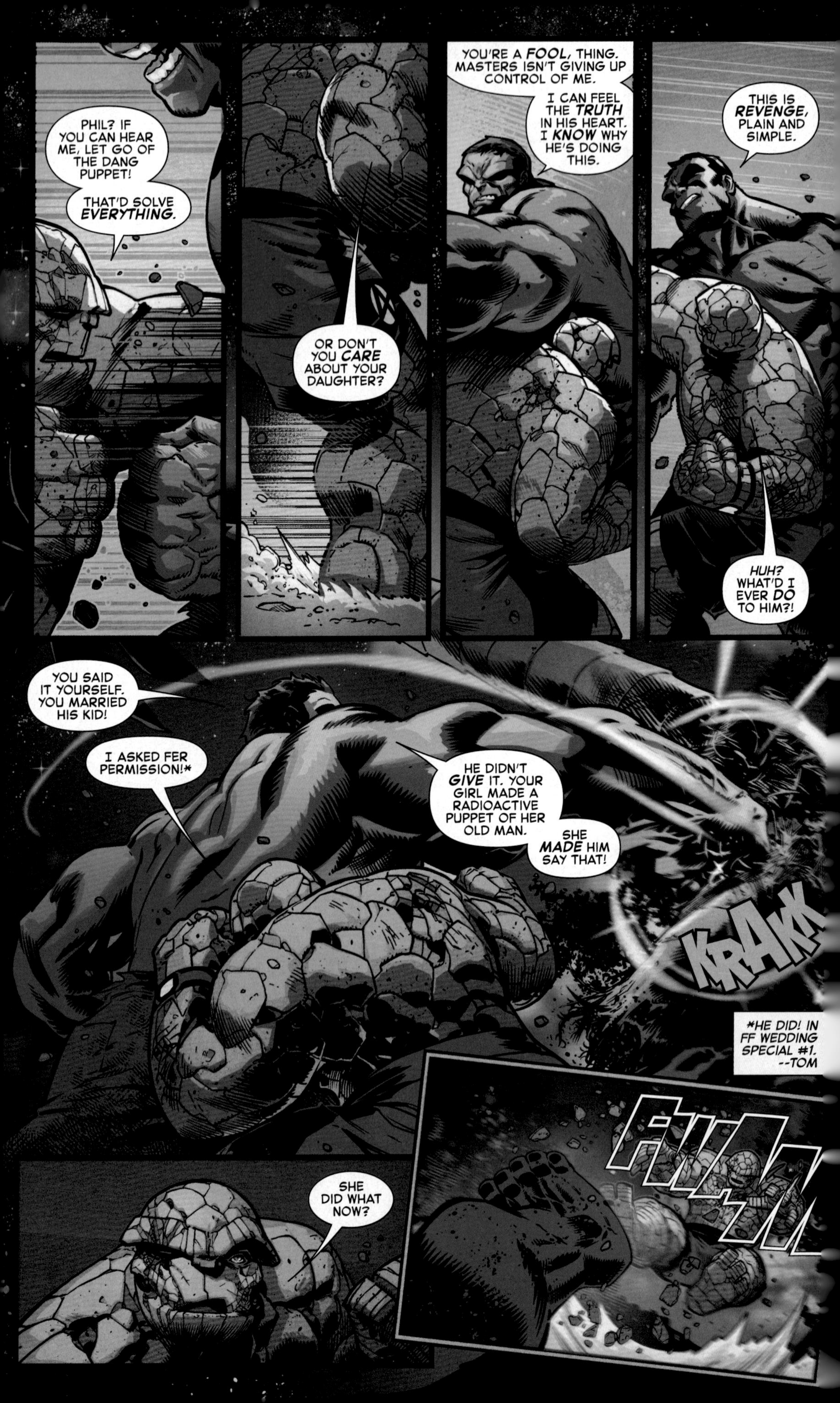
PHIL? IF YOU CAN HEAR ME, LET GO OF THE DANG PUPPET!
THAT'D SOLVE EVERYTHING.
OR DON'T YOU CARE ABOUT YOUR DAUGHTER?
YOU'RE A FOOL, THING. MASTERS ISN'T GIVING UP CONTROL OF ME.
I CAN FEEL THE TRUTH IN HIS HEART. I KNOW WHY HE'S DOING THIS.
THIS IS REVENGE, PLAIN AND SIMPLE.
HUH? WHAT'D I EVER DO TO HIM?!
YOU SAID IT YOURSELF. YOU MARRIED HIS KID!
I ASKED FER PERMISSION!*
HE DIDN'T GIVE IT. YOUR GIRL MADE A RADIOACTIVE PUPPET OF HER OLD MAN.
SHE MADE HIM SAY THAT!
KRAKK
*HE DID! IN FF WEDDING SPECIAL #1. --TOM
SHE DID WHAT NOW?

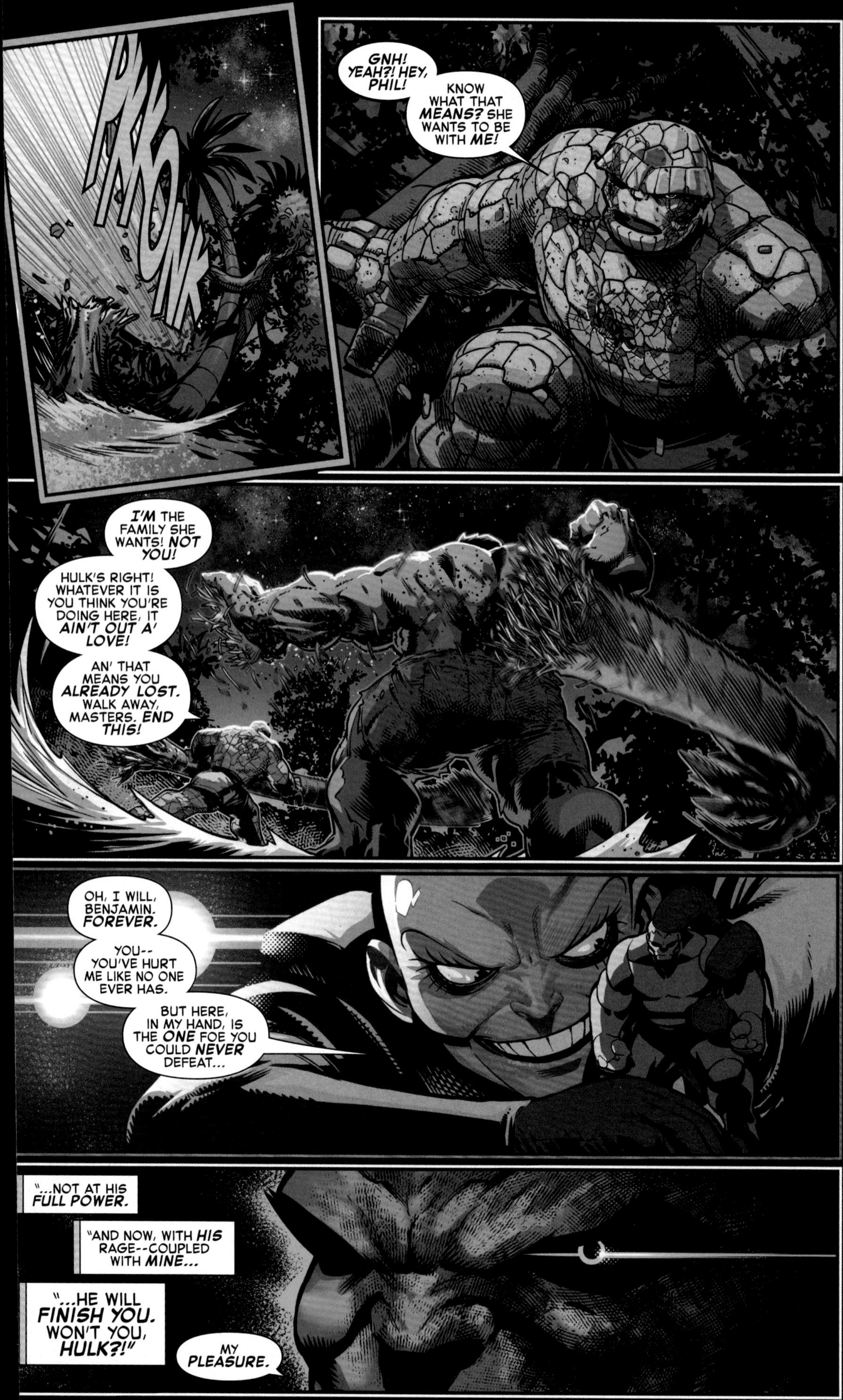
PHONK
GNH! YEAH?! HEY, PHIL!
KNOW WHAT THAT MEANS? SHE WANTS TO BE WITH ME!
I'M THE FAMILY SHE WANTS! NOT YOU!
HULK'S RIGHT! WHATEVER IT IS YOU THINK YOU'RE DOING HERE, IT AIN'T OUT A' LOVE!
AN' THAT MEANS YOU ALREADY LOST. WALK AWAY, MASTERS. END THIS!
OH, I WILL, BENJAMIN. FOREVER.
YOU-- YOU'VE HURT ME LIKE NO ONE EVER HAS.
BUT HERE, IN MY HAND, IS THE ONE FOE YOU COULD NEVER DEFEAT...
"...NOT AT HIS FULL POWER.
"AND NOW, WITH HIS RAGE--COUPLED WITH MINE...
"...HE WILL FINISH YOU. WON'T YOU, HULK?!"
MY PLEASURE.

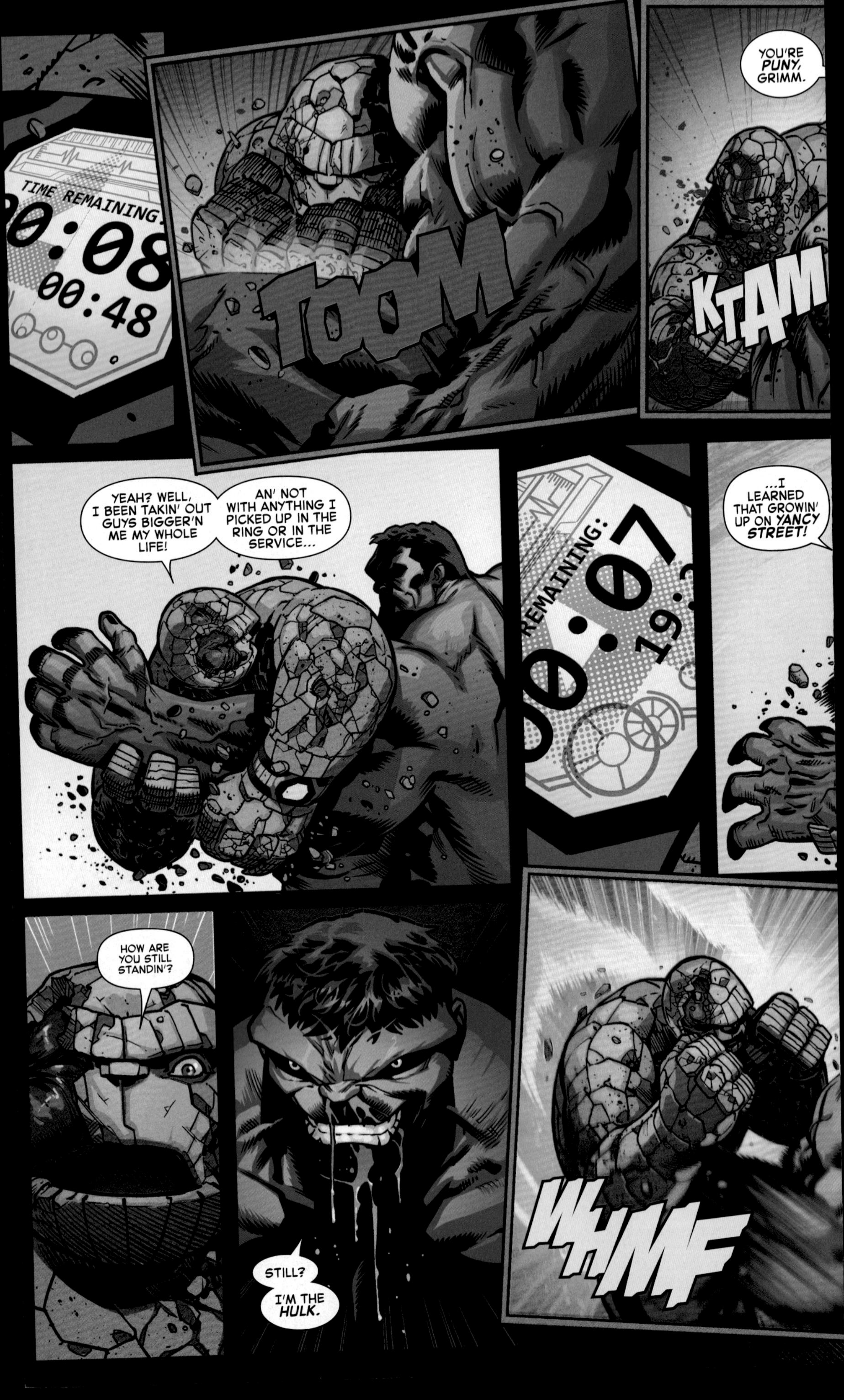
TIME REMAINING:
00:08
00:48
TOOM
YOU'RE PUNY, GRIMM.
KTAM
YEAH? WELL, I BEEN TAKIN' OUT GUYS BIGGER'N ME MY WHOLE LIFE!
AN' NOT WITH ANYTHING I PICKED UP IN THE RING OR IN THE SERVICE...
REMAINING:
00:07
...I LEARNED THAT GROWIN' UP ON YANCY STREET!
HOW ARE YOU STILL STANDIN'?
STILL?
I'M THE HULK.
WHMF

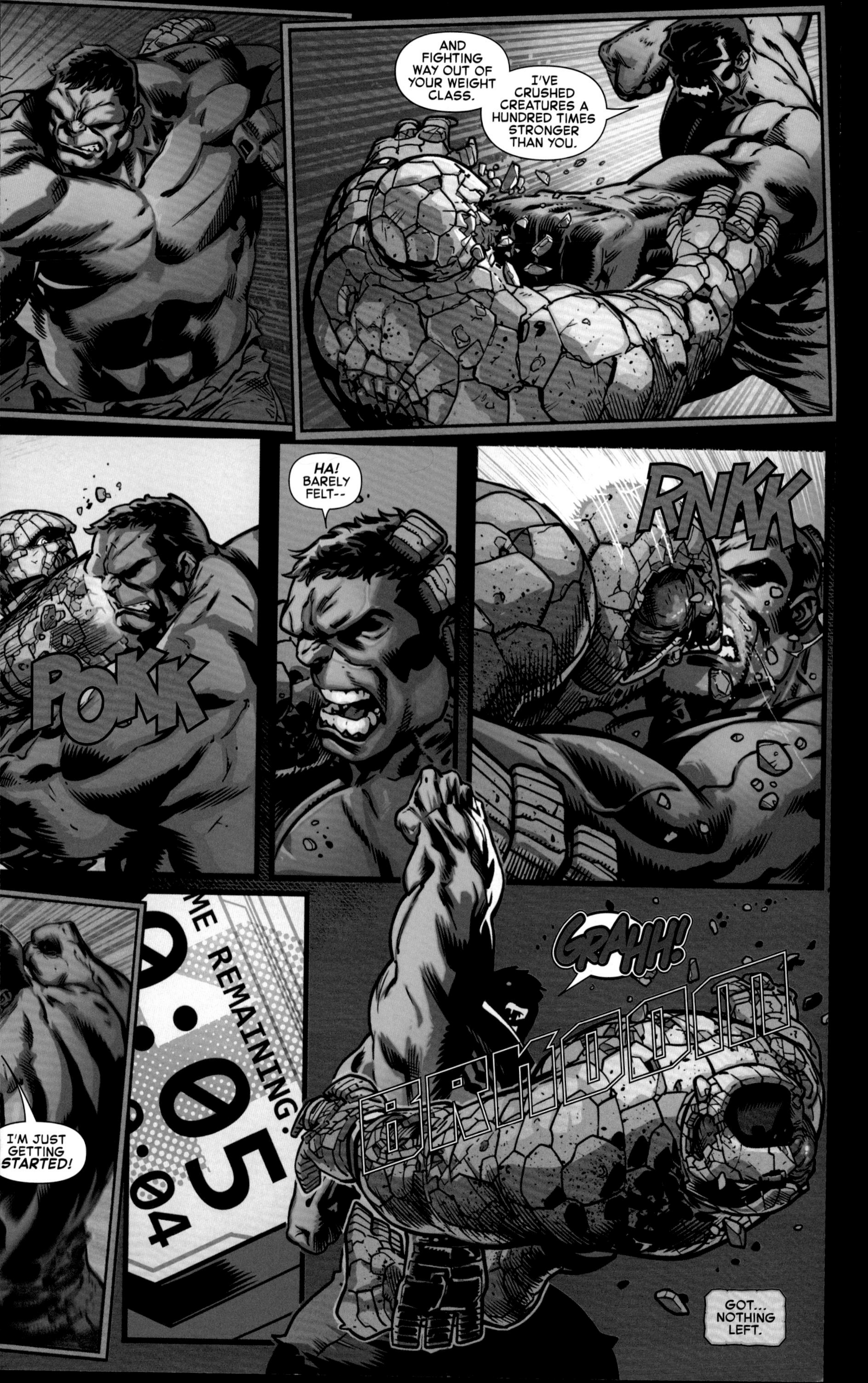
AND FIGHTING WAY OUT OF YOUR WEIGHT CLASS.
I'VE CRUSHED CREATURES A HUNDRED TIMES STRONGER THAN YOU.
POKK
HA! BARELY FELT--
RNKK
REMAINING
I'M JUST GETTING *STARTED!*
GRAHH!
GOT... NOTHING LEFT.

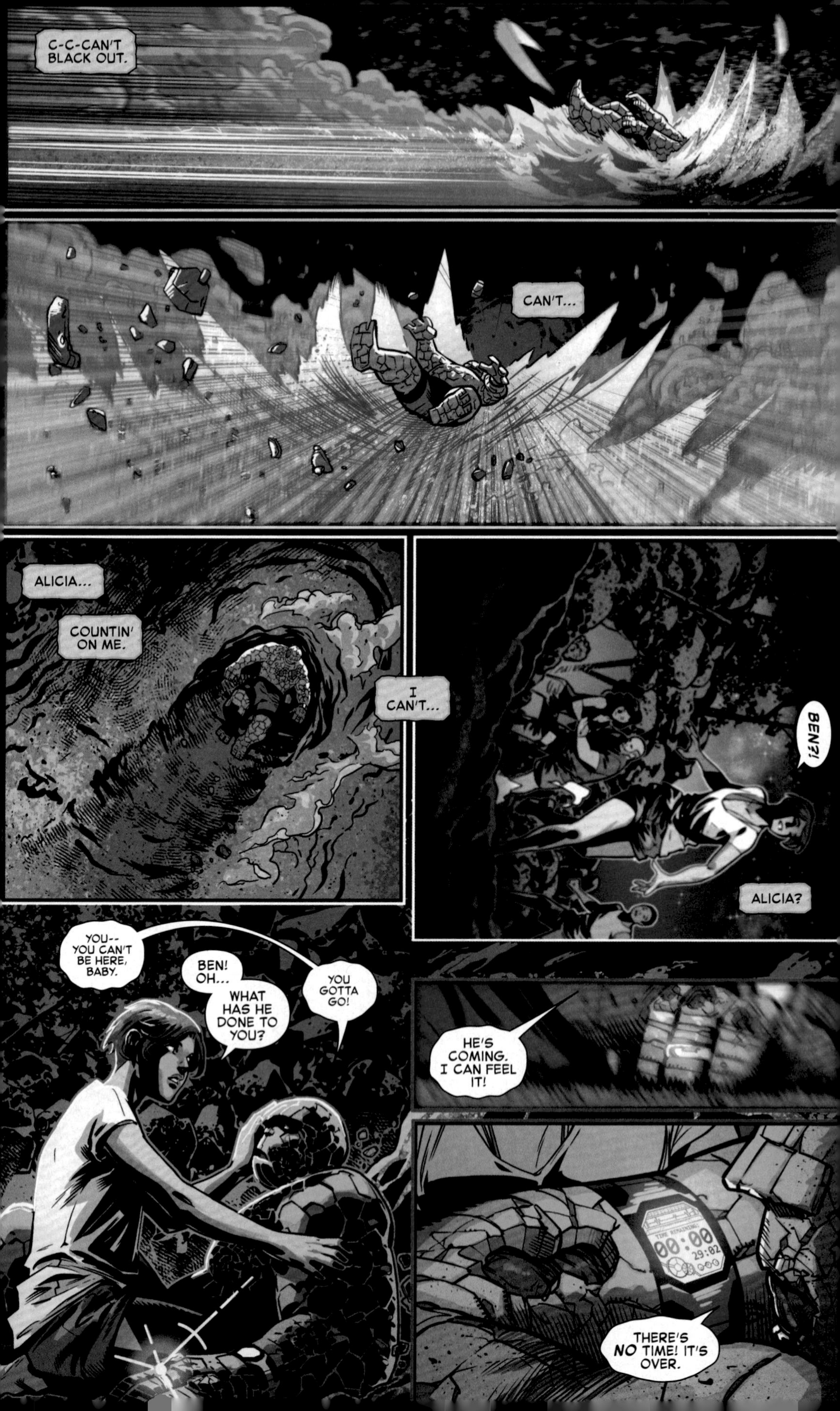
C-C-CAN'T BLACK OUT.
CAN'T...
ALICIA...
COUNTIN' ON ME.
I CAN'T...
BEN?!
ALICIA?
YOU-- YOU CAN'T BE HERE, BABY.
BEN! OH...
WHAT HAS HE DONE TO YOU?
YOU GOTTA GO!
HE'S COMING. I CAN FEEL IT!
THERE'S NO TIME! IT'S OVER.

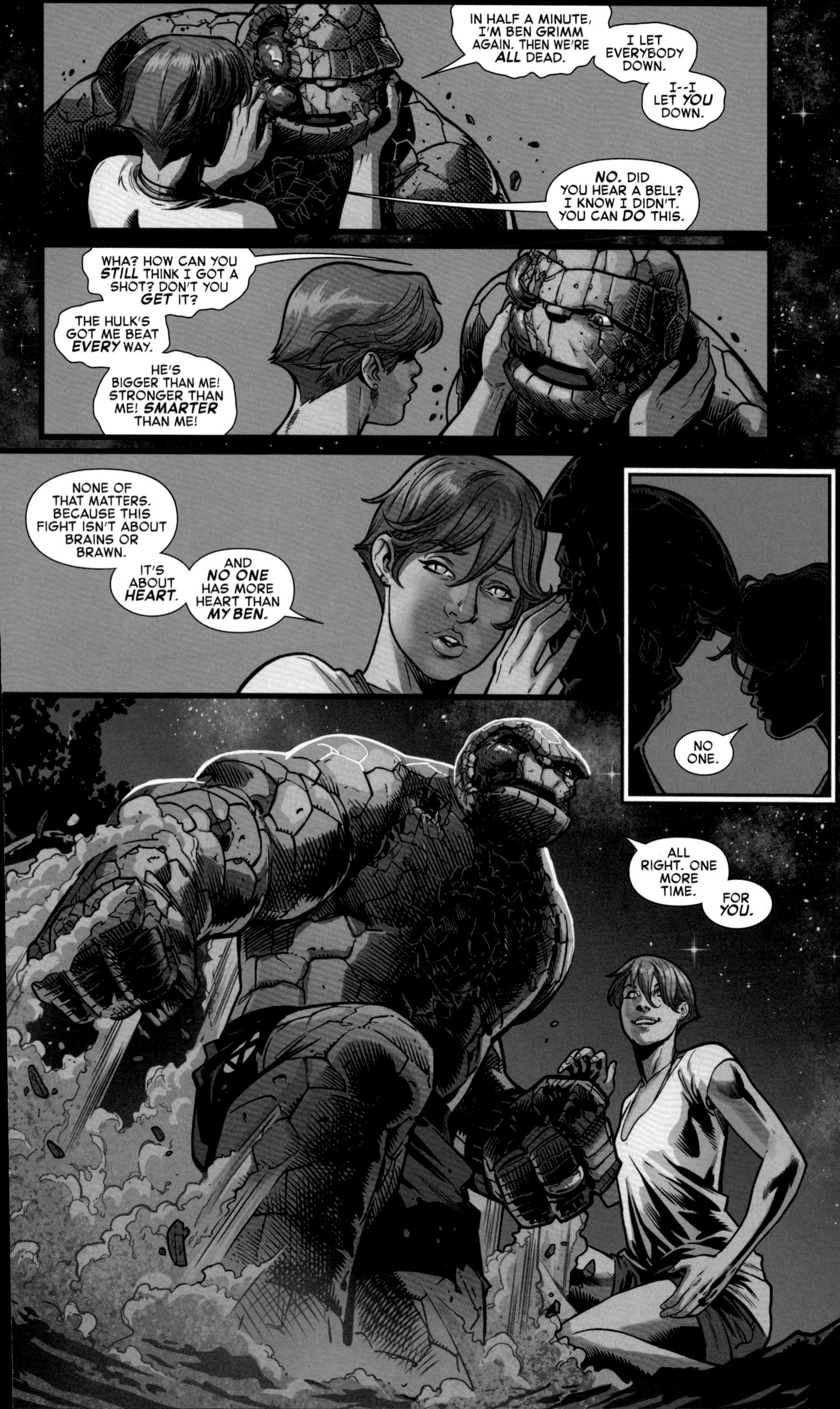
IN HALF A MINUTE, I'M BEN GRIMM AGAIN. THEN WE'RE ALL DEAD.
I LET EVERYBODY DOWN.
I--I LET YOU DOWN.
NO. DID YOU HEAR A BELL? I KNOW I DIDN'T. YOU CAN DO THIS.
WHA? HOW CAN YOU STILL THINK I GOT A SHOT? DON'T YOU GET IT?
THE HULK'S GOT ME BEAT EVERY WAY.
HE'S BIGGER THAN ME! STRONGER THAN ME! SMARTER THAN ME!
NONE OF THAT MATTERS. BECAUSE THIS FIGHT ISN'T ABOUT BRAINS OR BRAWN.
IT'S ABOUT HEART.
AND NO ONE HAS MORE HEART THAN MY BEN.
NO ONE.
ALL RIGHT. ONE MORE TIME.
FOR YOU.

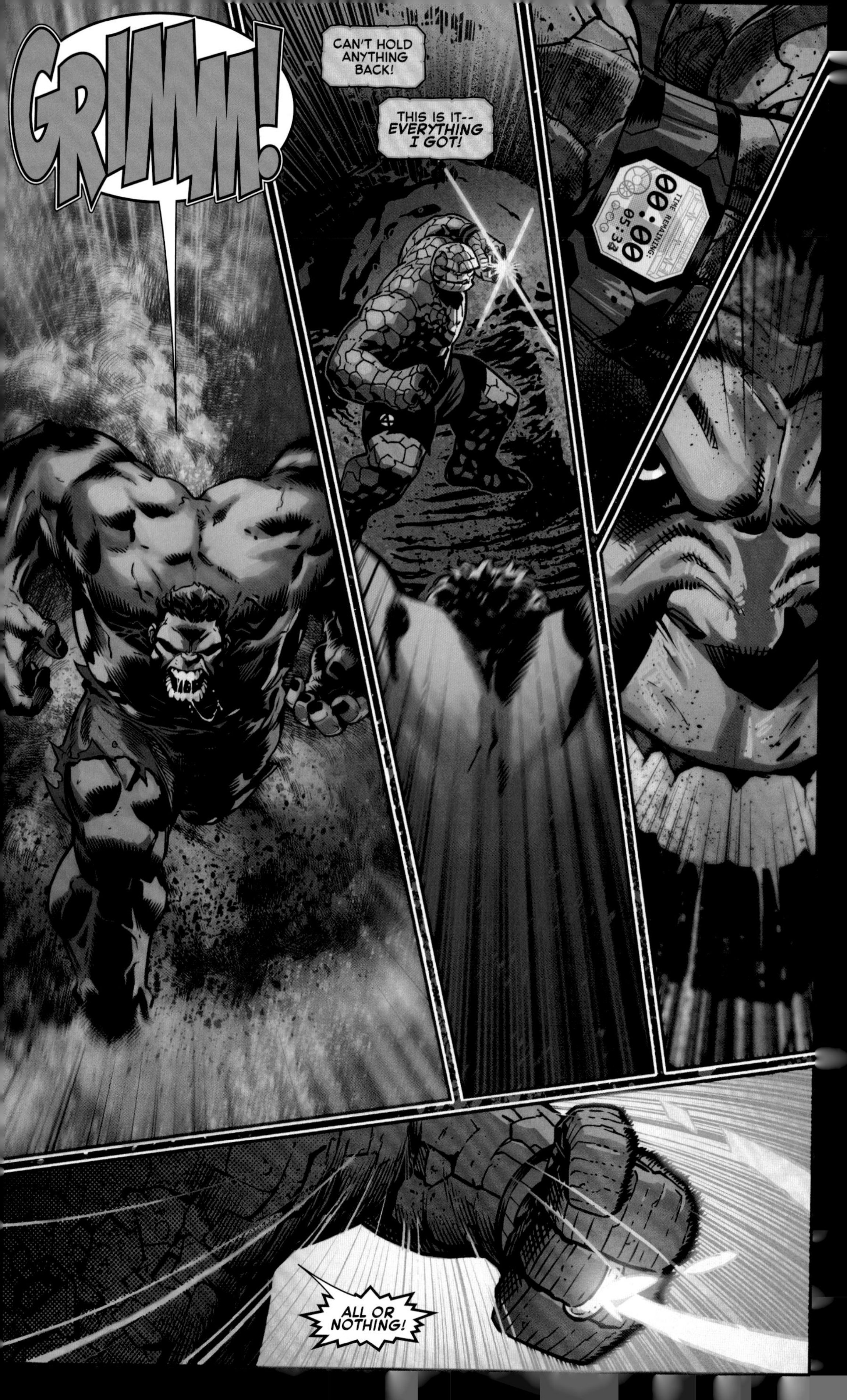
GRIMMM!
CAN'T HOLD ANYTHING BACK!
THIS IS IT-- *EVERYTHING* I GOT!
ALL OR NOTHING!

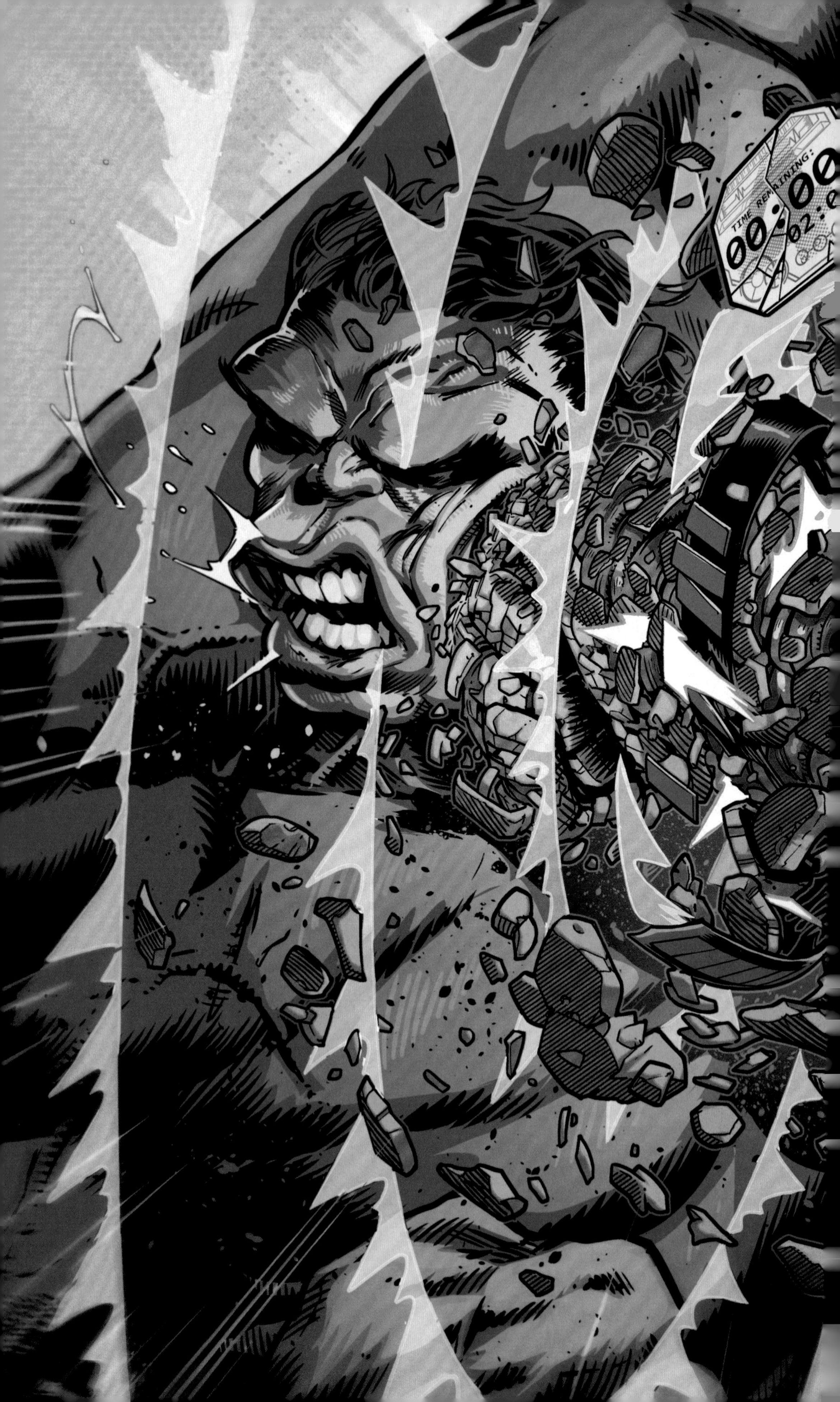
TIME REMAINING:
00:00

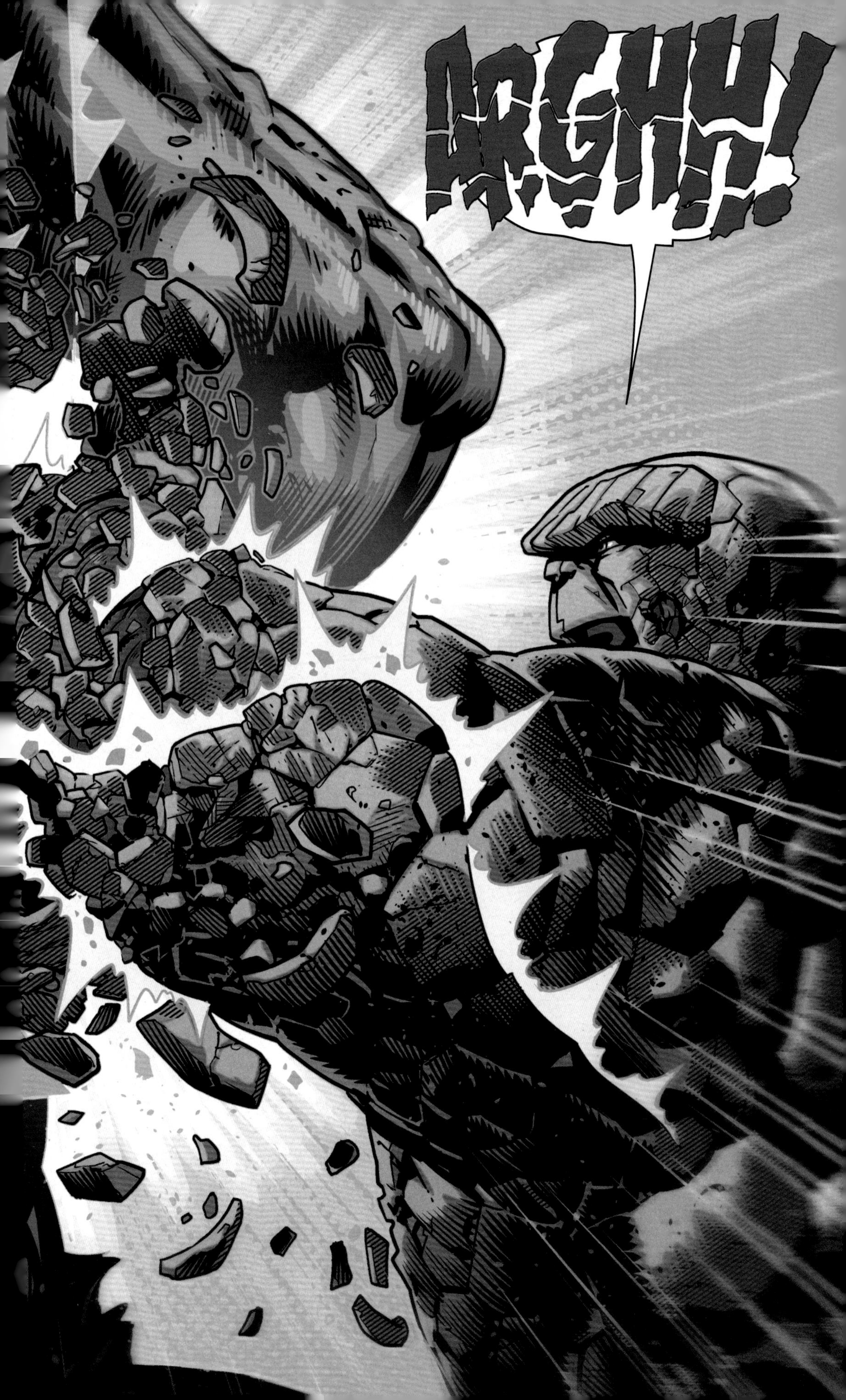
ARGHH!

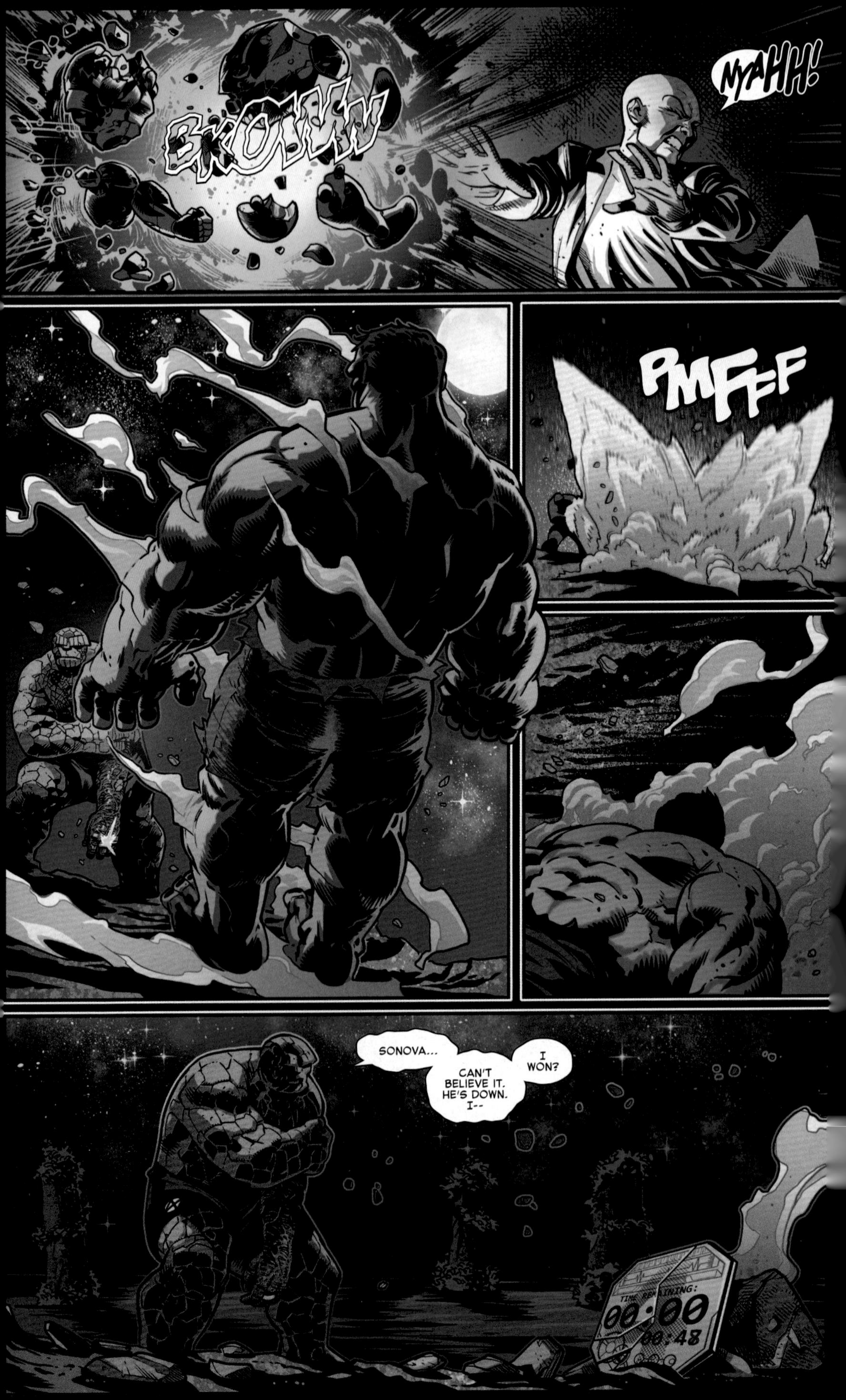
NYAHH!
PMFFF
SONOVA...
CAN'T BELIEVE IT. HE'S DOWN. I--
I WON?
00:00

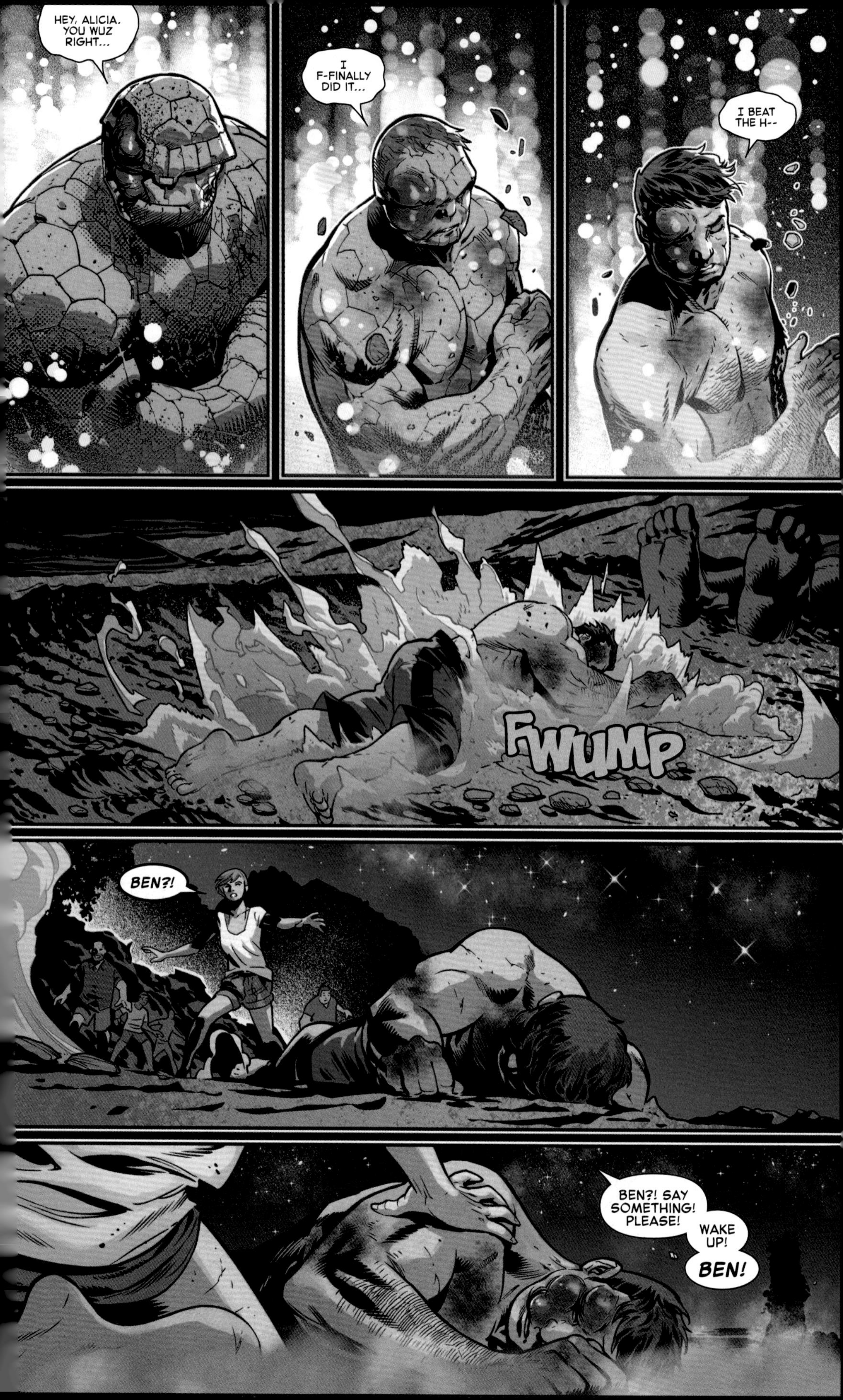
HEY, ALICIA. YOU WUZ RIGHT...
I F-FINALLY DID IT...
I BEAT THE H--
FWUMP
BEN?!
BEN?! SAY SOMETHING! PLEASE!
WAKE UP!
BEN!

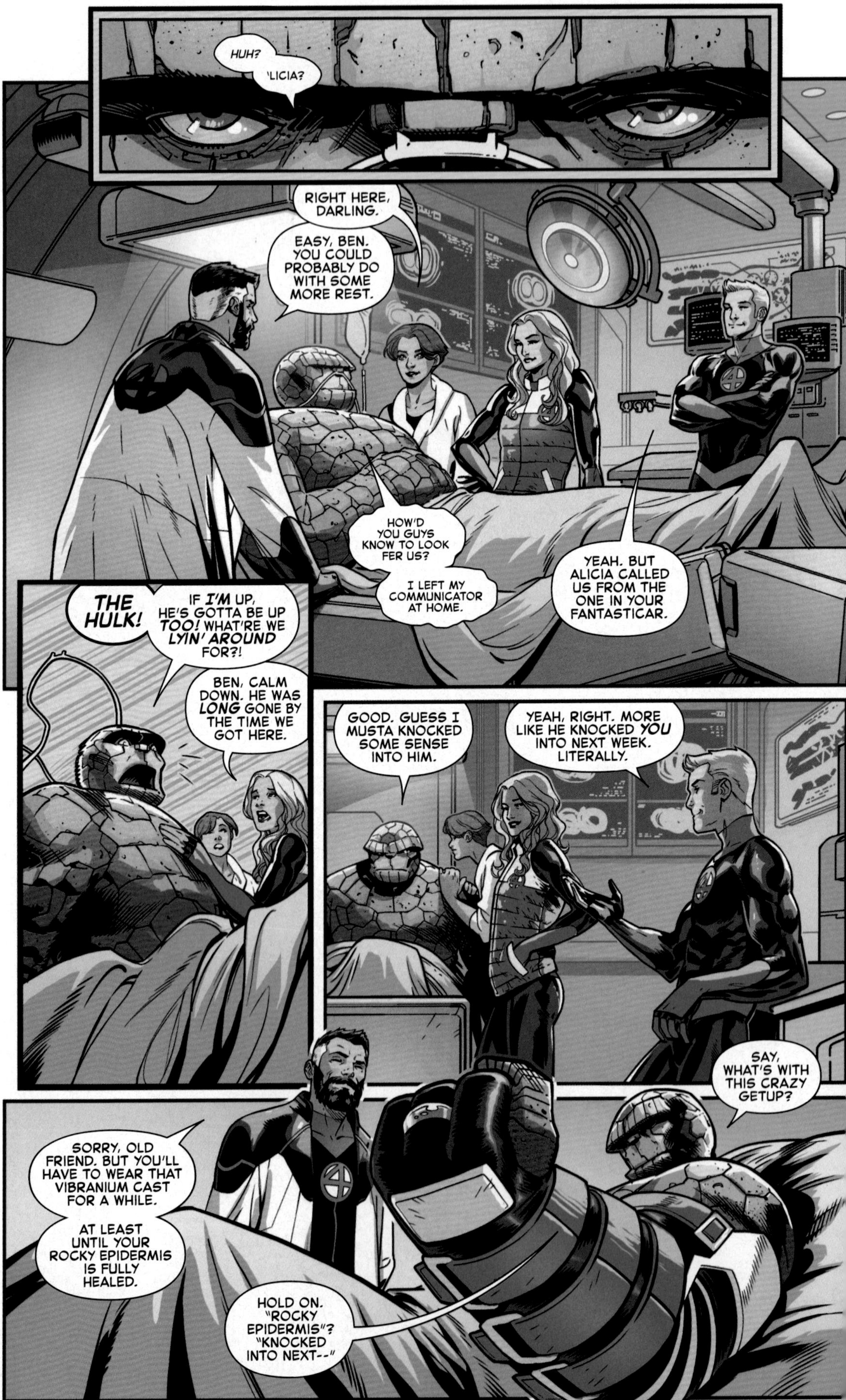

HUH?
'LICIA?
RIGHT HERE, DARLING.
EASY, BEN. YOU COULD PROBABLY DO WITH SOME MORE REST.
HOW'D YOU GUYS KNOW TO LOOK FER US?
I LEFT MY COMMUNICATOR AT HOME.
YEAH. BUT ALICIA CALLED US FROM THE ONE IN YOUR FANTASTICAR.
THE HULK!
IF I'M UP, HE'S GOTTA BE UP TOO! WHAT'RE WE LYIN' AROUND FOR?!
BEN, CALM DOWN. HE WAS LONG GONE BY THE TIME WE GOT HERE.
GOOD. GUESS I MUSTA KNOCKED SOME SENSE INTO HIM.
YEAH, RIGHT. MORE LIKE HE KNOCKED YOU INTO NEXT WEEK. LITERALLY.
SAY, WHAT'S WITH THIS CRAZY GETUP?
SORRY, OLD FRIEND. BUT YOU'LL HAVE TO WEAR THAT VIBRANIUM CAST FOR A WHILE.
AT LEAST UNTIL YOUR ROCKY EPIDERMIS IS FULLY HEALED.
HOLD ON. "ROCKY EPIDERMIS"? "KNOCKED INTO NEXT--"

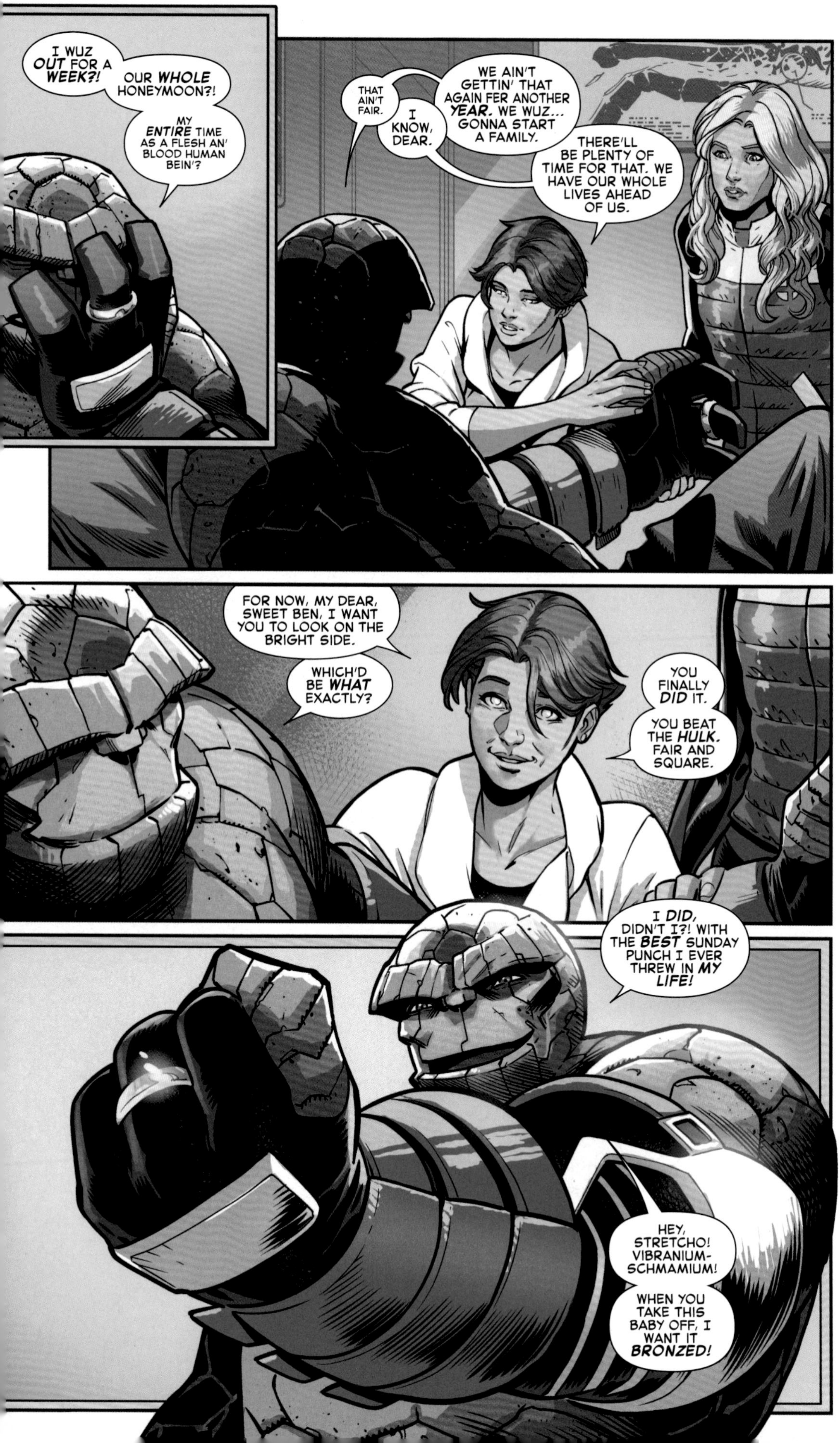
I WUZ OUT FOR A WEEK?!
OUR WHOLE HONEYMOON?!
MY ENTIRE TIME AS A FLESH AN' BLOOD HUMAN BEIN'?
THAT AIN'T FAIR.
I KNOW, DEAR.
WE AIN'T GETTIN' THAT AGAIN FER ANOTHER YEAR. WE WUZ... GONNA START A FAMILY.
THERE'LL BE PLENTY OF TIME FOR THAT. WE HAVE OUR WHOLE LIVES AHEAD OF US.
FOR NOW, MY DEAR, SWEET BEN, I WANT YOU TO LOOK ON THE BRIGHT SIDE.
WHICH'D BE WHAT EXACTLY?
YOU FINALLY DID IT.
YOU BEAT THE HULK. FAIR AND SQUARE.
I DID, DIDN'T I?! WITH THE BEST SUNDAY PUNCH I EVER THREW IN MY LIFE!
HEY, STRETCHO! VIBRANIUM-SCHMAMIUM!
WHEN YOU TAKE THIS BABY OFF, I WANT IT BRONZED!

EPILOGUE

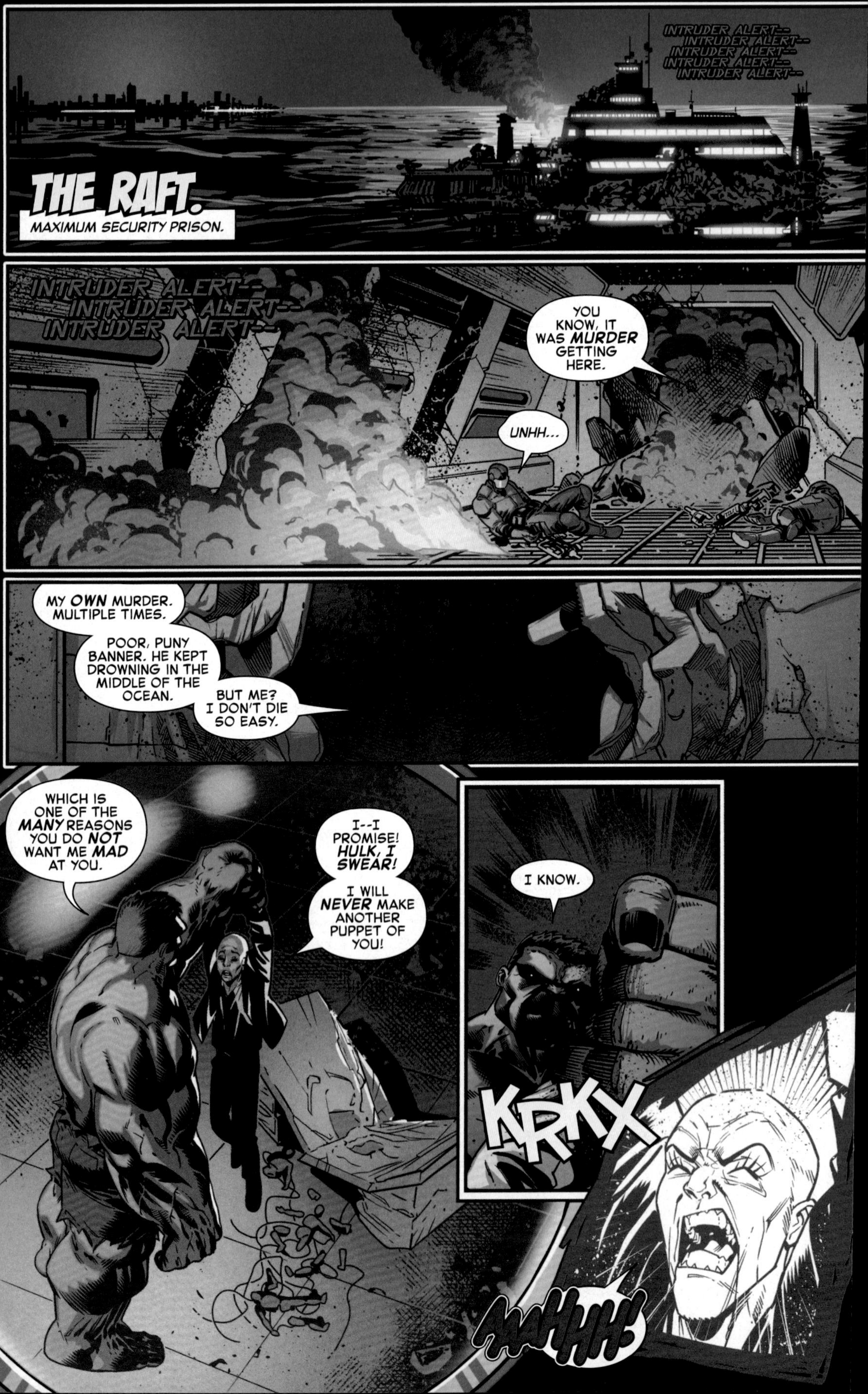

INTRUDER ALERT-- INTRUDER ALERT-- INTRUDER ALERT-- INTRUDER ALERT-- INTRUDER ALERT--
THE RAFT.
MAXIMUM SECURITY PRISON.
INTRUDER ALERT-- INTRUDER ALERT-- INTRUDER ALERT--
YOU KNOW, IT WAS MURDER GETTING HERE.
UNHH...
MY OWN MURDER. MULTIPLE TIMES.
POOR, PUNY BANNER. HE KEPT DROWNING IN THE MIDDLE OF THE OCEAN.
BUT ME? I DON'T DIE SO EASY.
WHICH IS ONE OF THE MANY REASONS YOU DO NOT WANT ME MAD AT YOU.
I--I PROMISE! HULK, I SWEAR!
I WILL NEVER MAKE ANOTHER PUPPET OF YOU!
I KNOW.
KRKX
AAAHHHH!

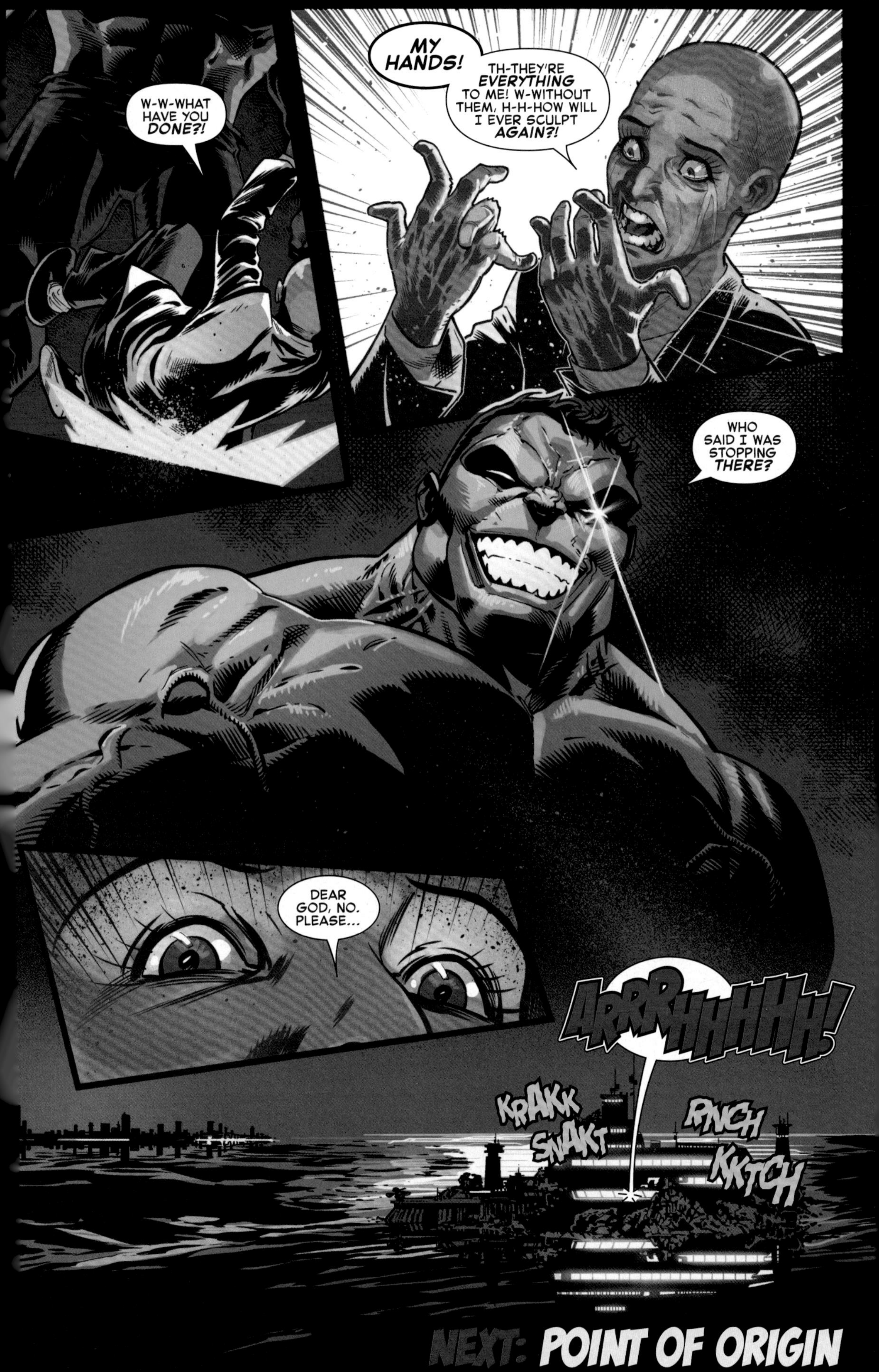
W-W-WHAT HAVE YOU DONE?!
MY HANDS!
TH-THEY'RE EVERYTHING TO ME! W-WITHOUT THEM, H-H-HOW WILL I EVER SCULPT AGAIN?!
WHO SAID I WAS STOPPING THERE?
DEAR GOD, NO. PLEASE...
ARRRHHHHHH!
KRAKK
SNAKT
RNCH
KKTCH
NEXT: POINT OF ORIGIN

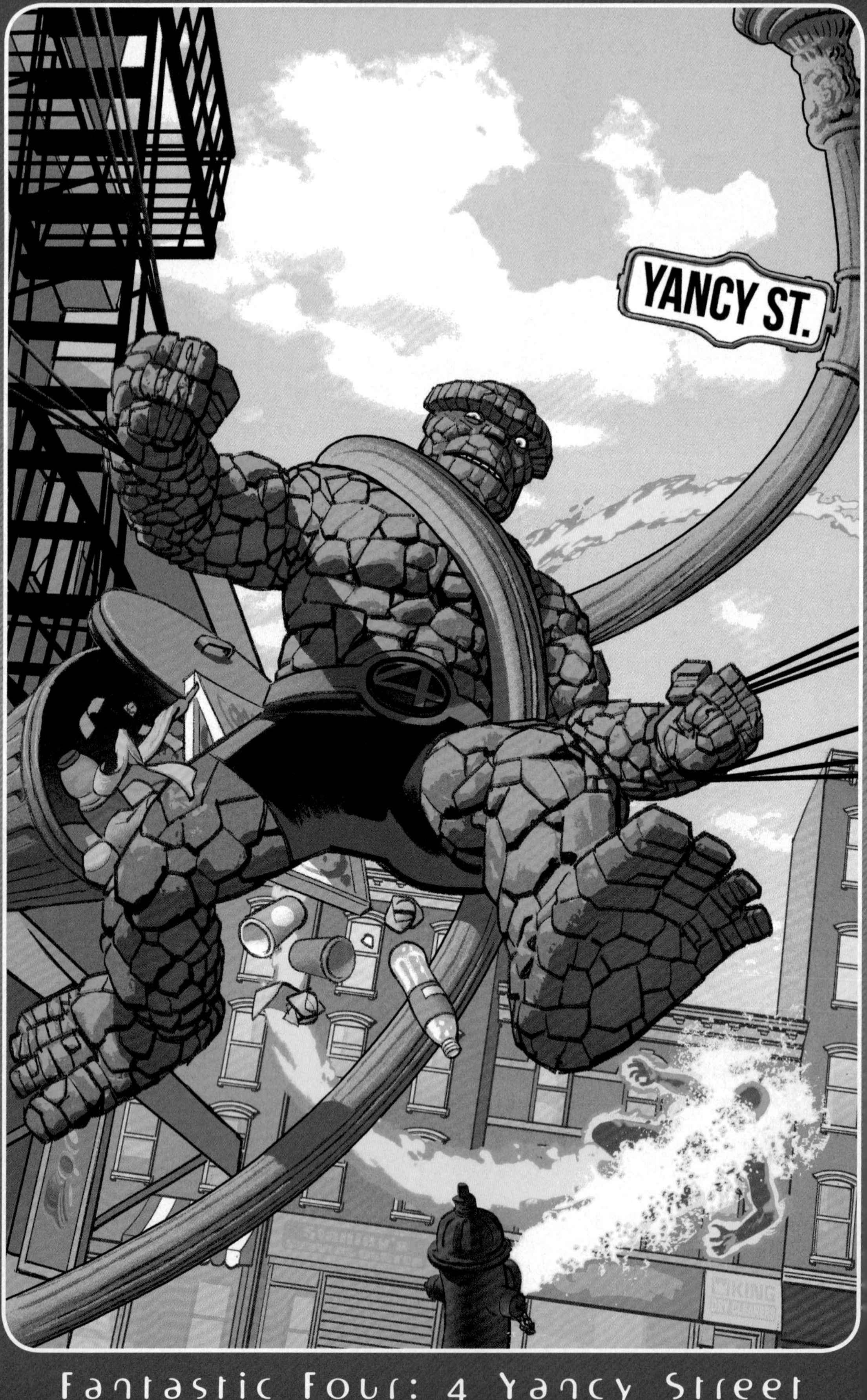
YANCY ST.

Fantastic Four: 4 Yancy Street

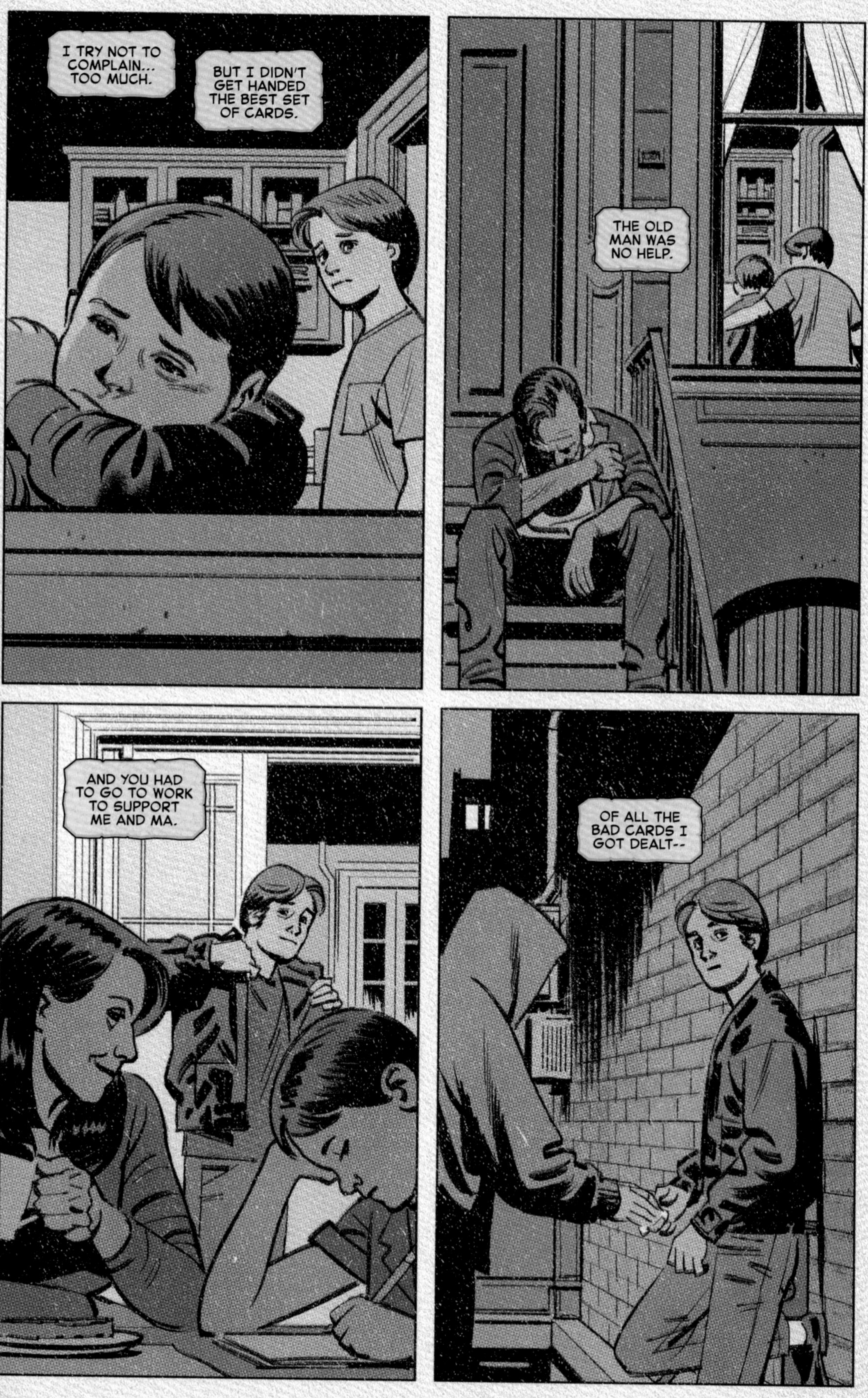
I TRY NOT TO COMPLAIN... TOO MUCH.
BUT I DIDN'T GET HANDED THE BEST SET OF CARDS.
THE OLD MAN WAS NO HELP.
AND YOU HAD TO GO TO WORK TO SUPPORT ME AND MA.
OF ALL THE BAD CARDS I GOT DEALT--

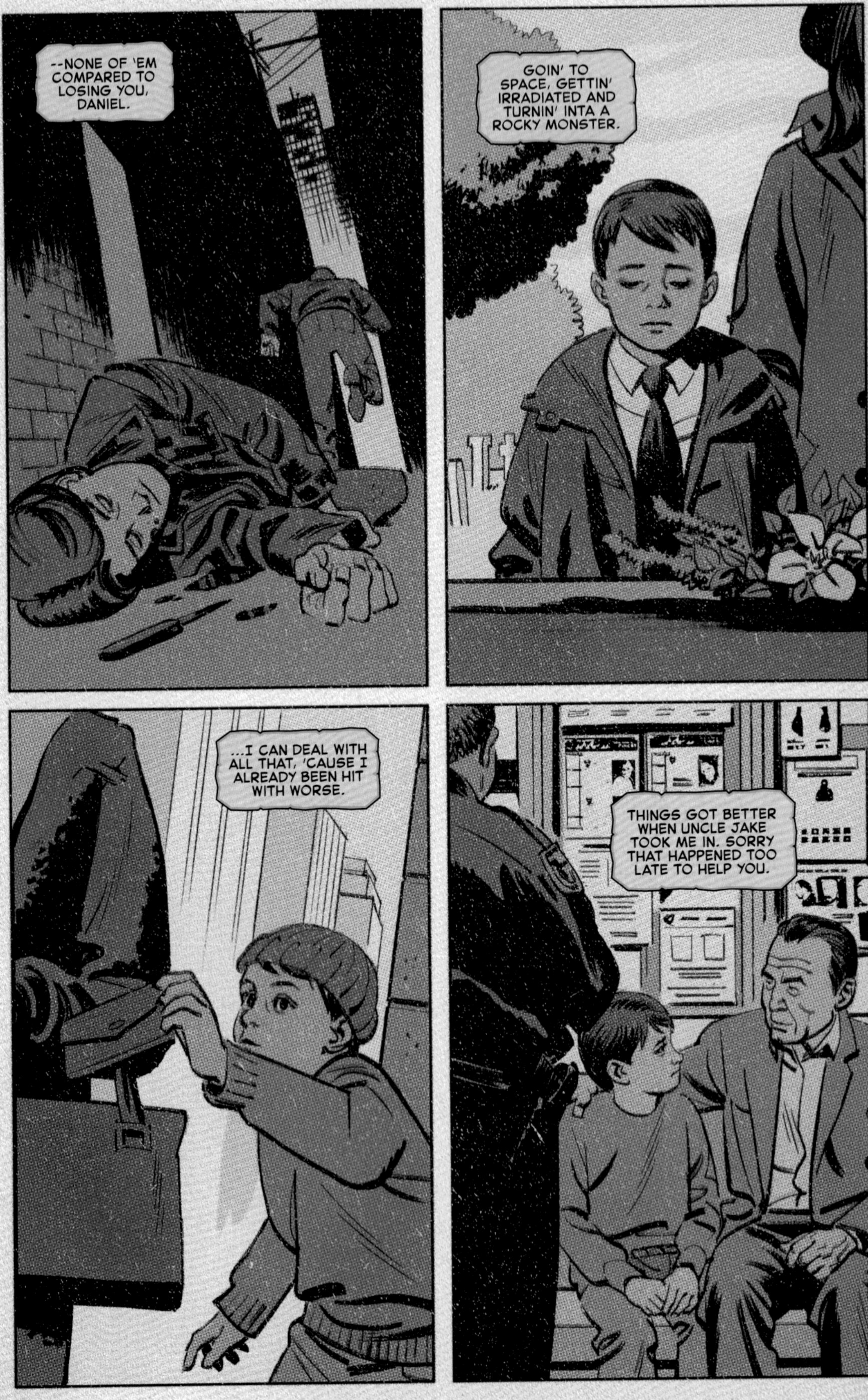
--NONE OF 'EM COMPARED TO LOSING YOU, DANIEL.
GOIN' TO SPACE, GETTIN' IRRADIATED AND TURNIN' INTA A ROCKY MONSTER.
...I CAN DEAL WITH ALL THAT, 'CAUSE I ALREADY BEEN HIT WITH WORSE.
THINGS GOT BETTER WHEN UNCLE JAKE TOOK ME IN. SORRY THAT HAPPENED TOO LATE TO HELP YOU.

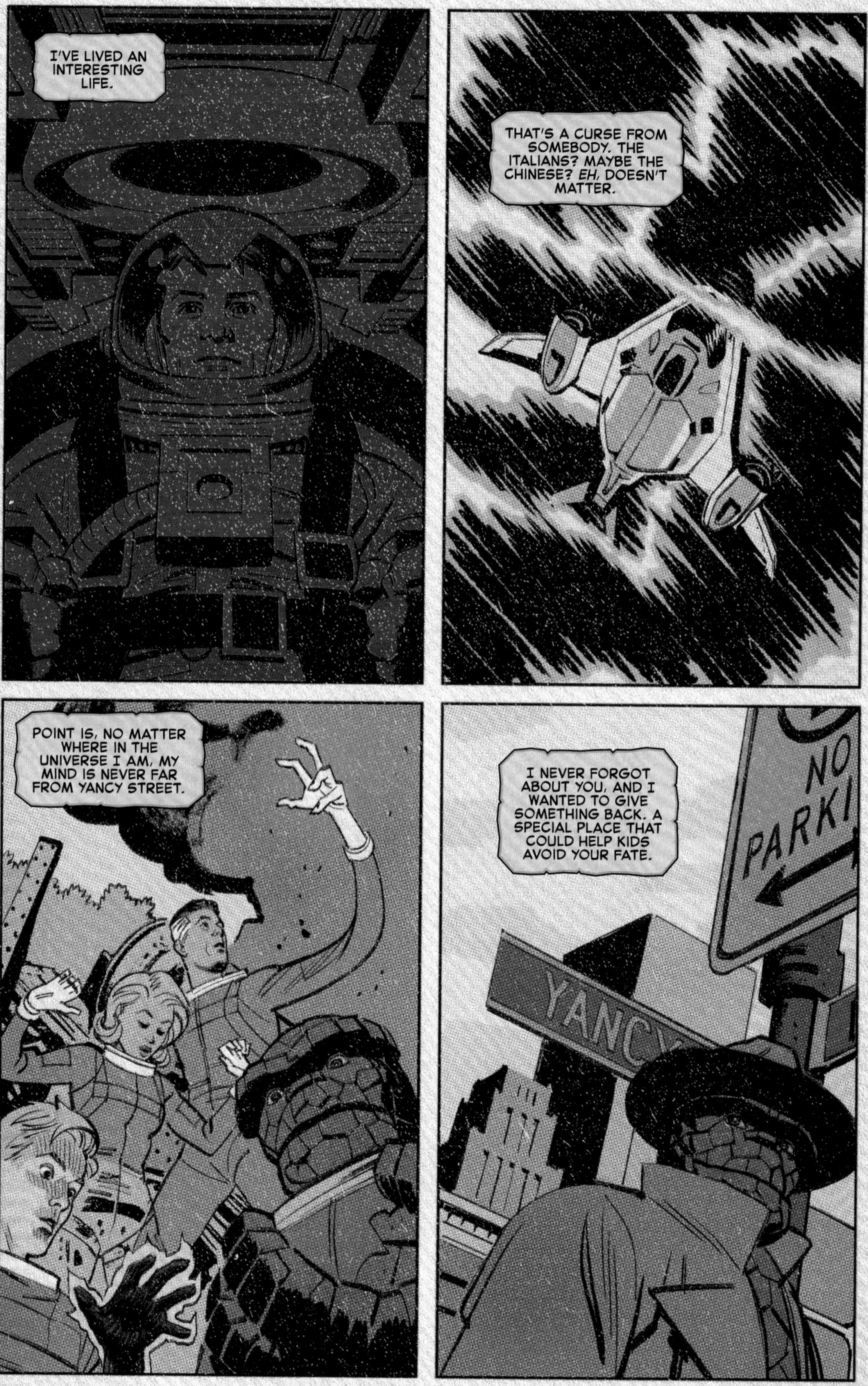
I'VE LIVED AN INTERESTING LIFE.
THAT'S A CURSE FROM SOMEBODY. THE ITALIANS? MAYBE THE CHINESE? *EH,* DOESN'T MATTER.
POINT IS, NO MATTER WHERE IN THE UNIVERSE I AM, MY MIND IS NEVER FAR FROM YANCY STREET.
I NEVER FORGOT ABOUT YOU, AND I WANTED TO GIVE SOMETHING BACK. A SPECIAL PLACE THAT COULD HELP KIDS AVOID YOUR FATE.
NO PARKI
YANCY

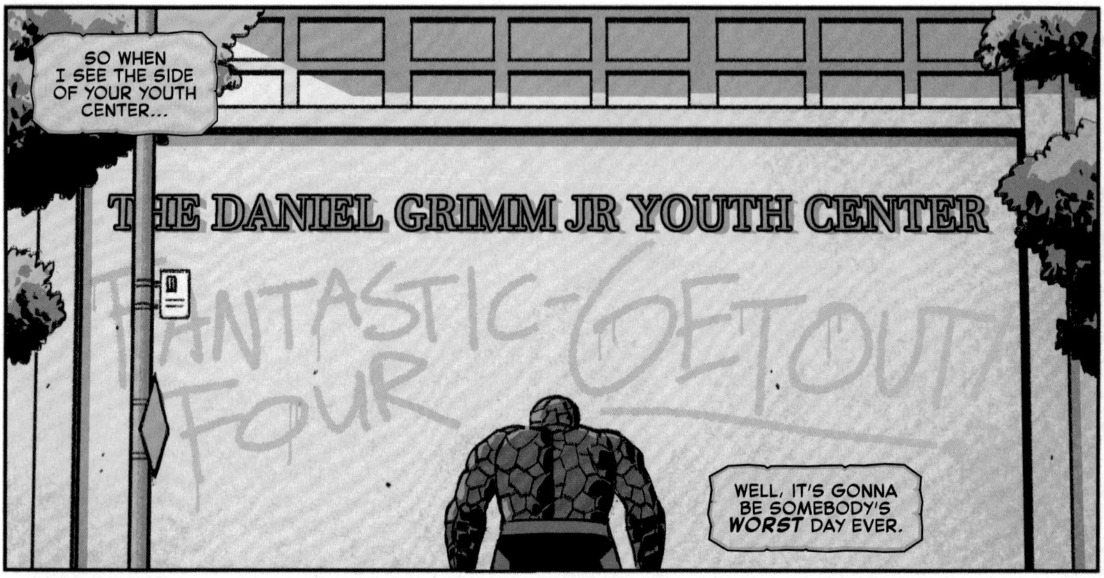
SO WHEN I SEE THE SIDE OF YOUR YOUTH CENTER...
THE DANIEL GRIMM JR YOUTH CENTER
FANTASTIC FOUR - GET OUT
WELL, IT'S GONNA BE SOMEBODY'S WORST DAY EVER.

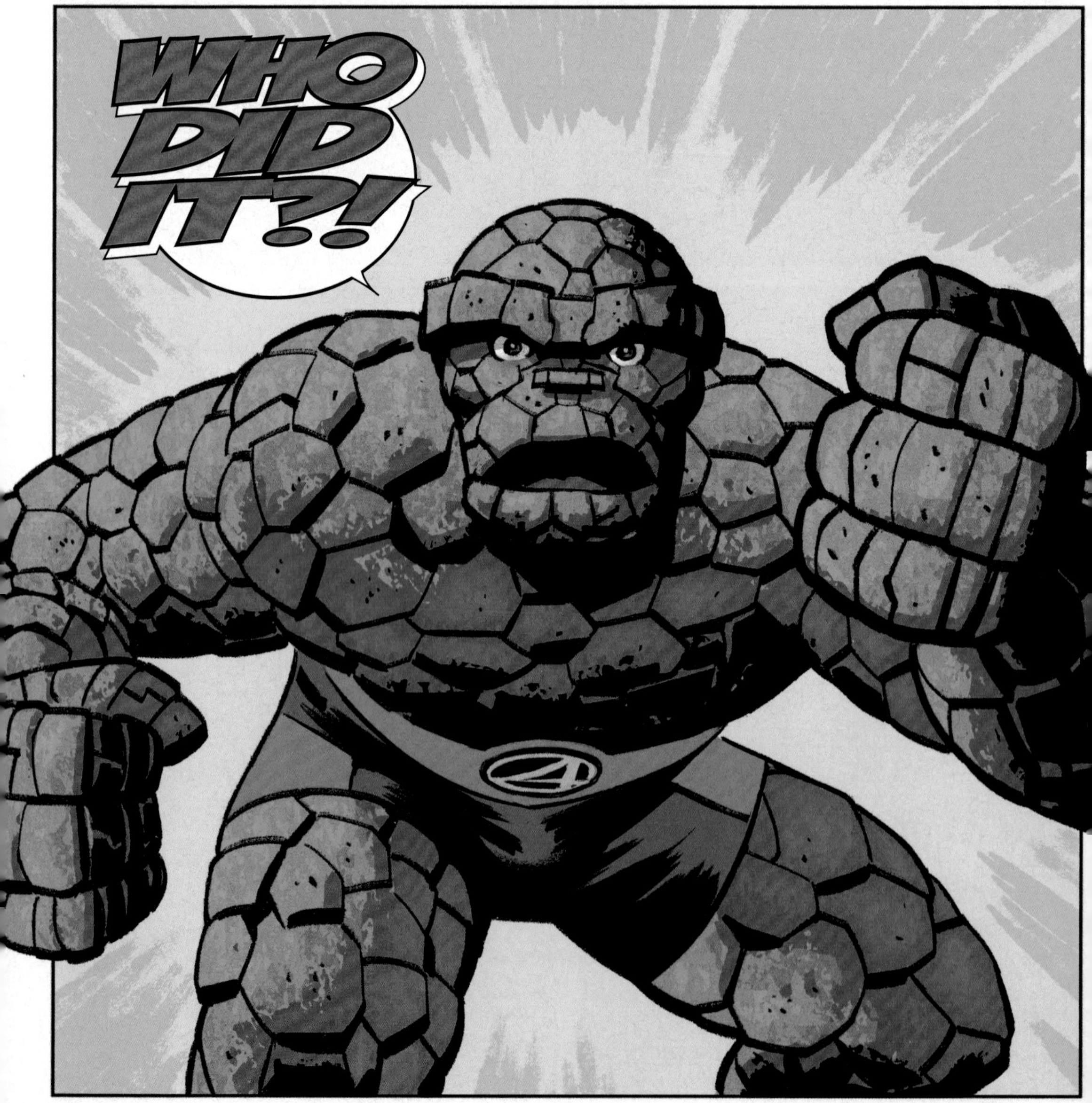
WHO DID IT?!

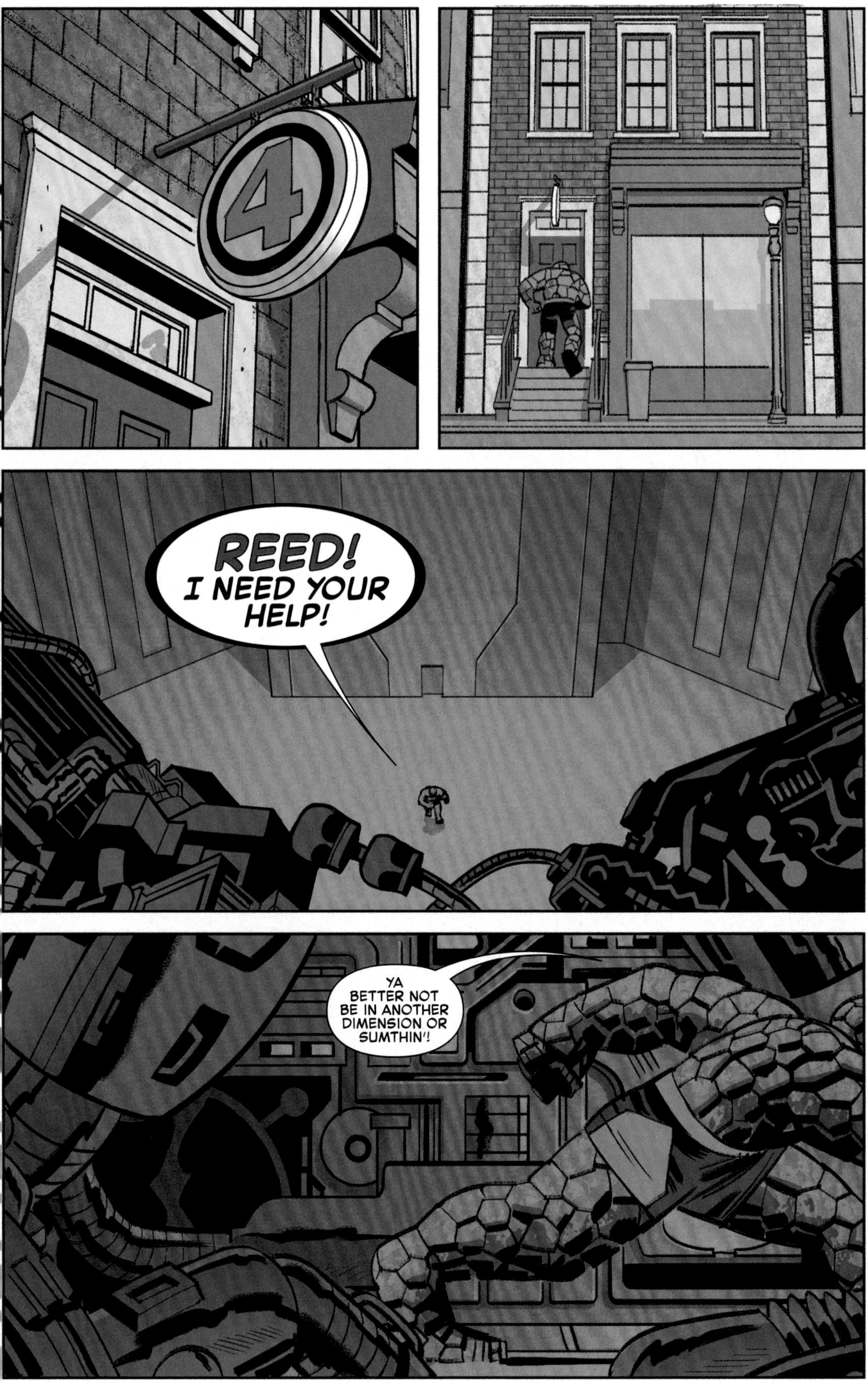
4
REED! I NEED YOUR HELP!
YA BETTER NOT BE IN ANOTHER DIMENSION OR SUMTHIN'!

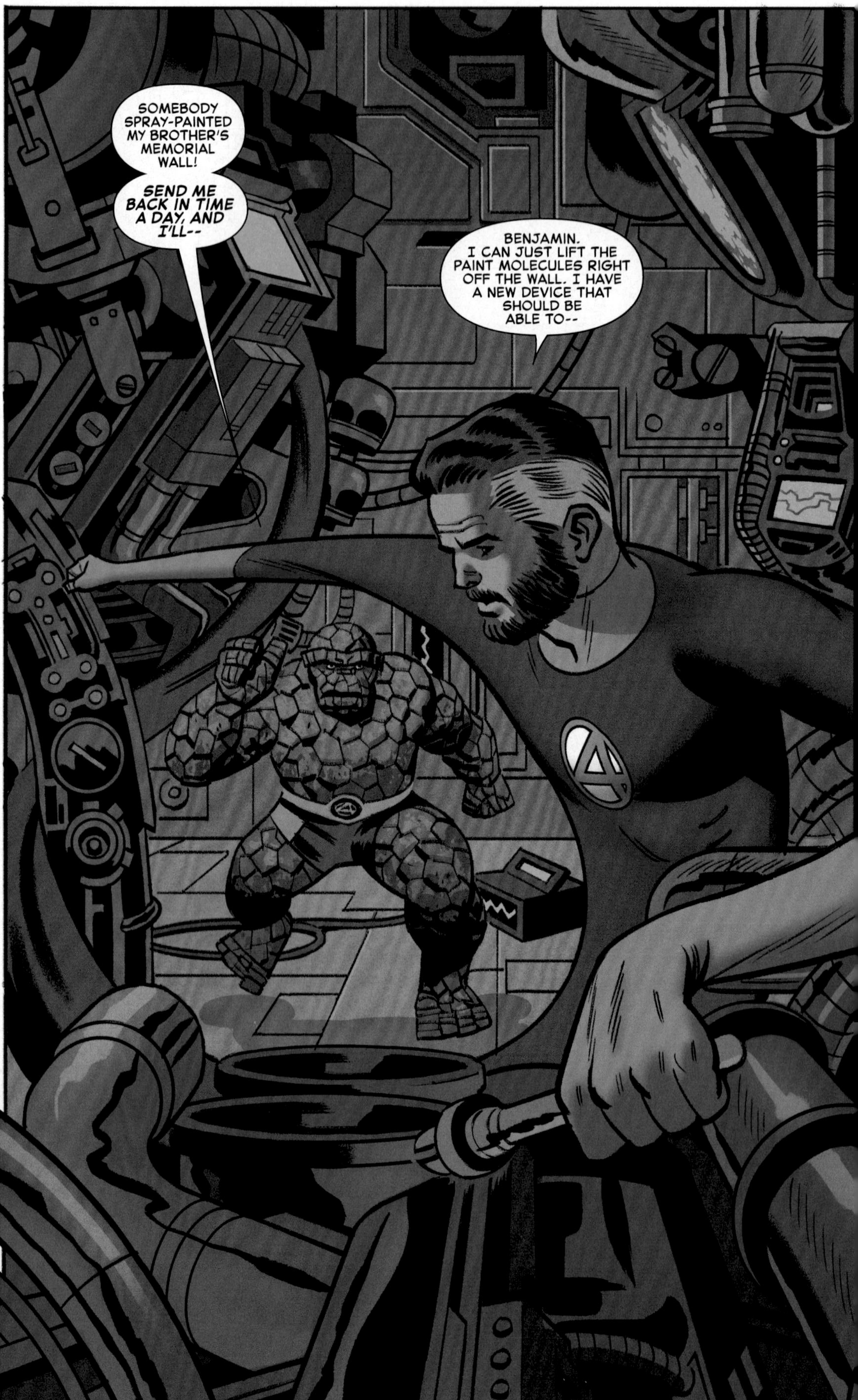

SOMEBODY SPRAY-PAINTED MY BROTHER'S MEMORIAL WALL!
SEND ME BACK IN TIME A DAY, AND I'LL--
BENJAMIN. I CAN JUST LIFT THE PAINT MOLECULES RIGHT OFF THE WALL. I HAVE A NEW DEVICE THAT SHOULD BE ABLE TO--

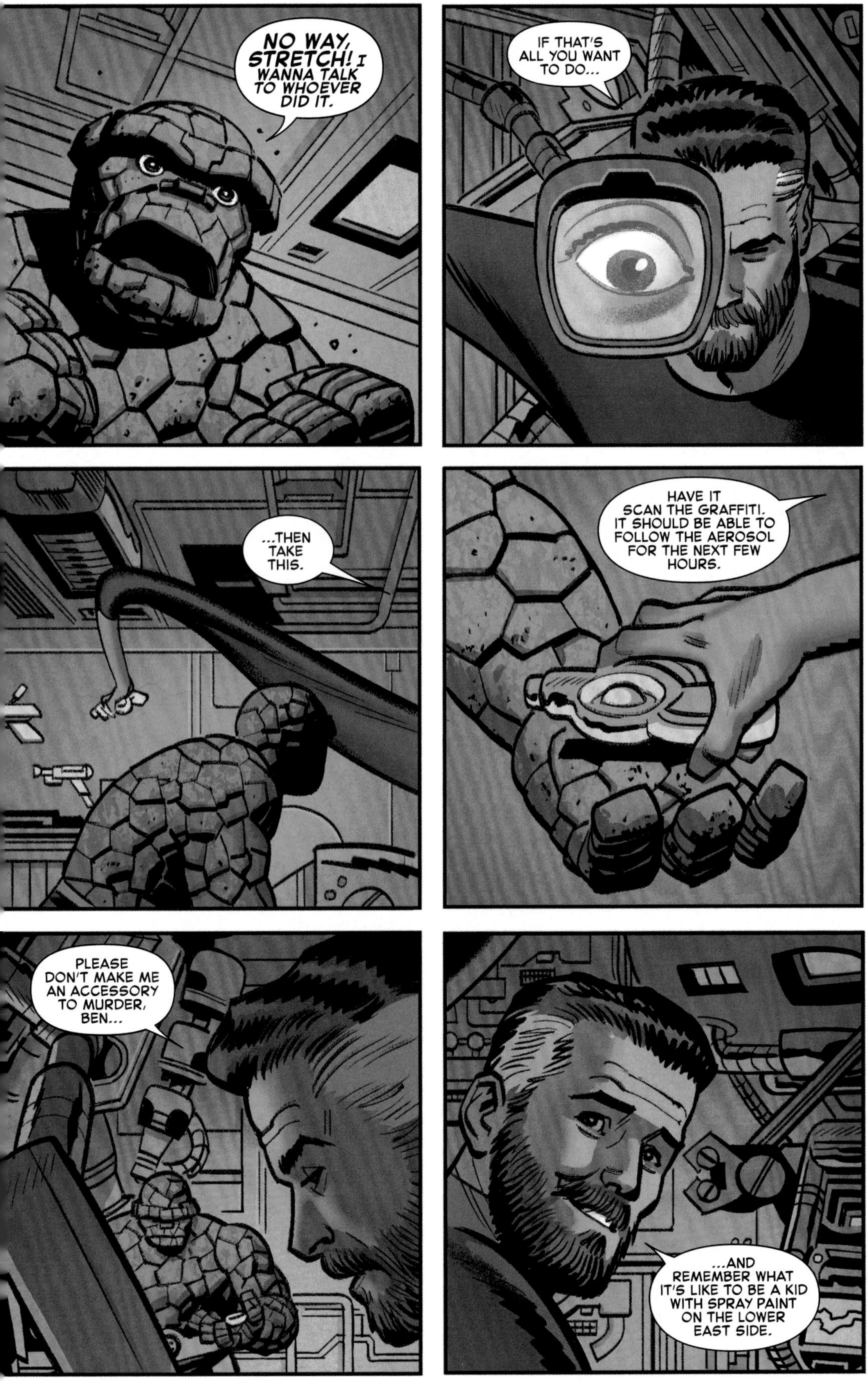
NO WAY, STRETCH! I WANNA TALK TO WHOEVER DID IT.
IF THAT'S ALL YOU WANT TO DO...
...THEN TAKE THIS.
HAVE IT SCAN THE GRAFFITI. IT SHOULD BE ABLE TO FOLLOW THE AEROSOL FOR THE NEXT FEW HOURS.
PLEASE DON'T MAKE ME AN ACCESSORY TO MURDER, BEN...
...AND REMEMBER WHAT IT'S LIKE TO BE A KID WITH SPRAY PAINT ON THE LOWER EAST SIDE.

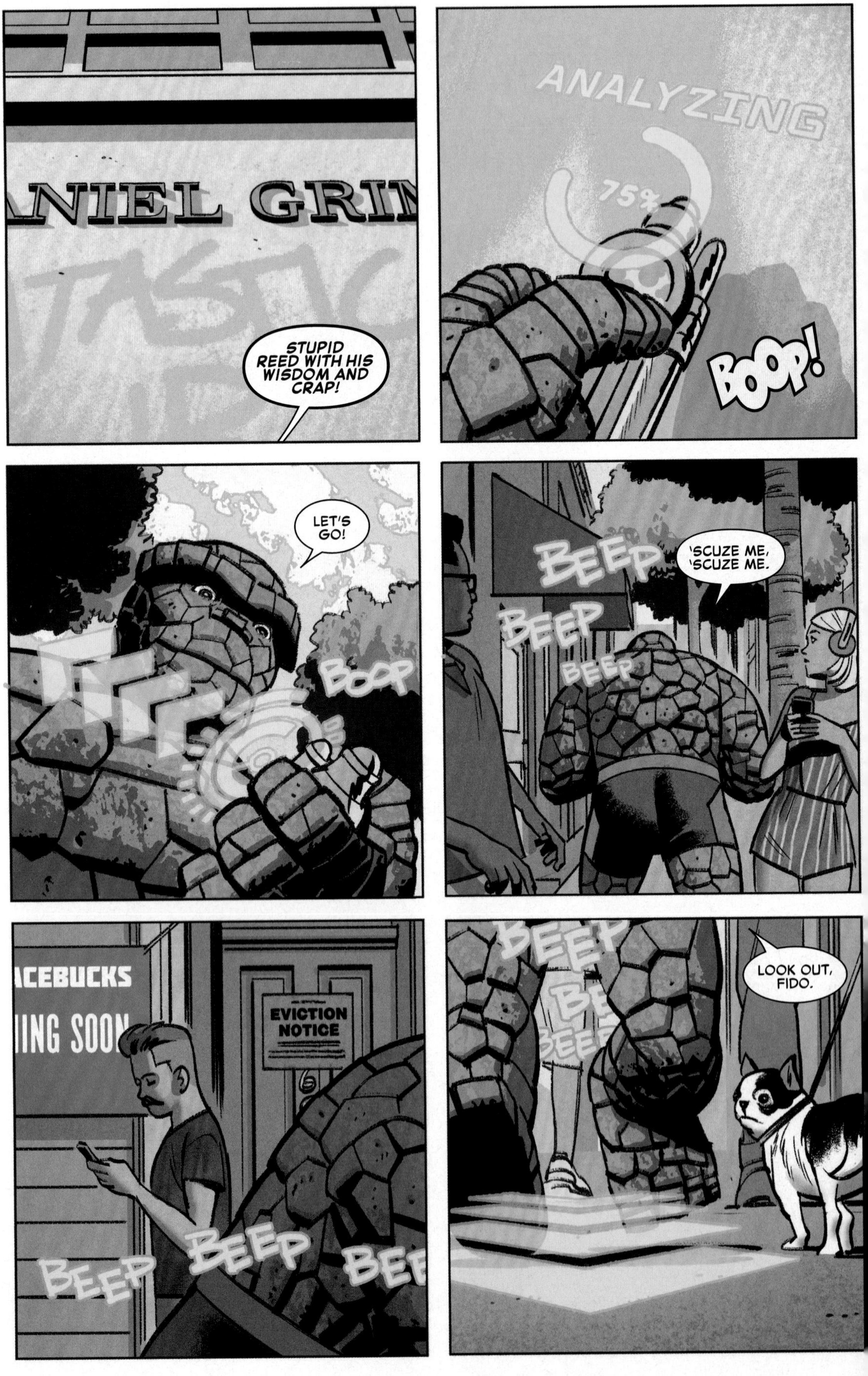
ANIEL GRIM
STUPID REED WITH HIS WISDOM AND CRAP!
ANALYZING
75%
BOOP!
LET'S GO!
BOOP
BEEP
'SCUZE ME, 'SCUZE ME.
BEEP
BEEP
ACEBUCKS
IING SOON
EVICTION NOTICE
BEEP
BEEP
LOOK OUT, FIDO.

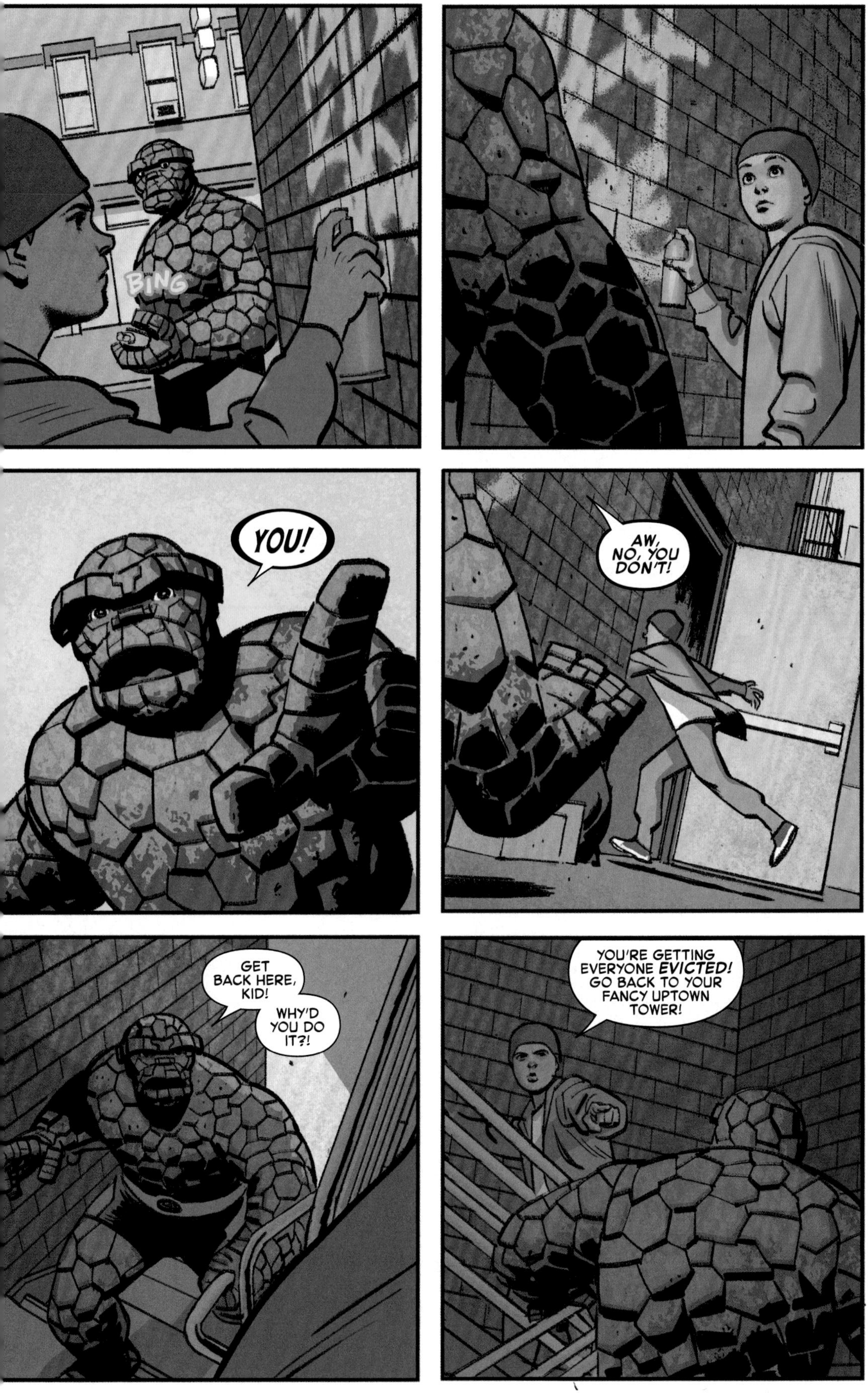
BING
YOU!
AW, NO, YOU DON'T!
GET BACK HERE, KID!
WHY'D YOU DO IT?!
YOU'RE GETTING EVERYONE EVICTED! GO BACK TO YOUR FANCY UPTOWN TOWER!

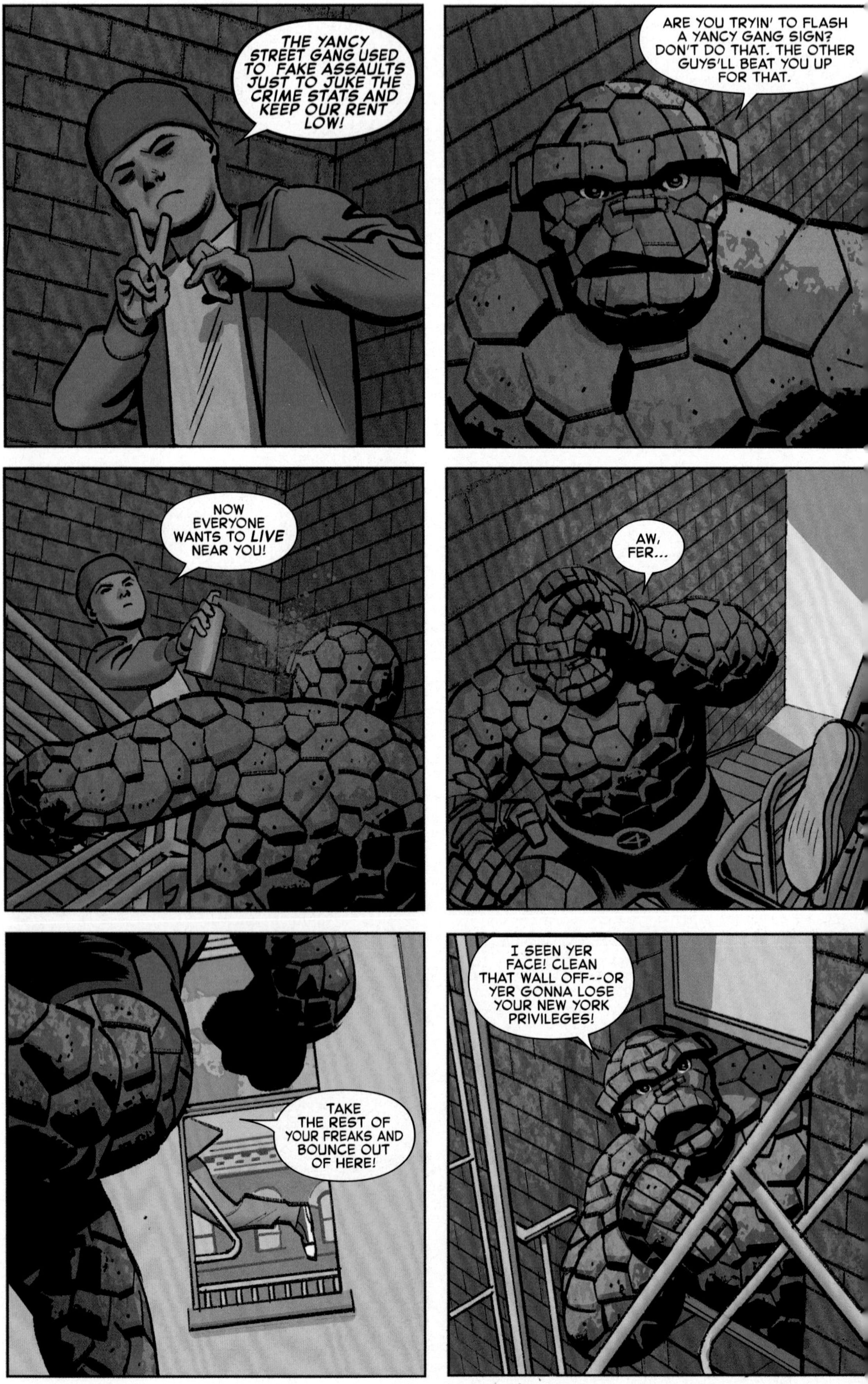
THE YANCY STREET GANG USED TO FAKE ASSAULTS JUST TO JUKE THE CRIME STATS AND KEEP OUR RENT LOW!
ARE YOU TRYIN' TO FLASH A YANCY GANG SIGN? DON'T DO THAT. THE OTHER GUYS'LL BEAT YOU UP FOR THAT.
NOW EVERYONE WANTS TO *LIVE* NEAR YOU!
AW, FER...
TAKE THE REST OF YOUR FREAKS AND BOUNCE OUT OF HERE!
I SEEN YER FACE! CLEAN THAT WALL OFF--OR YER GONNA LOSE YOUR NEW YORK PRIVILEGES!

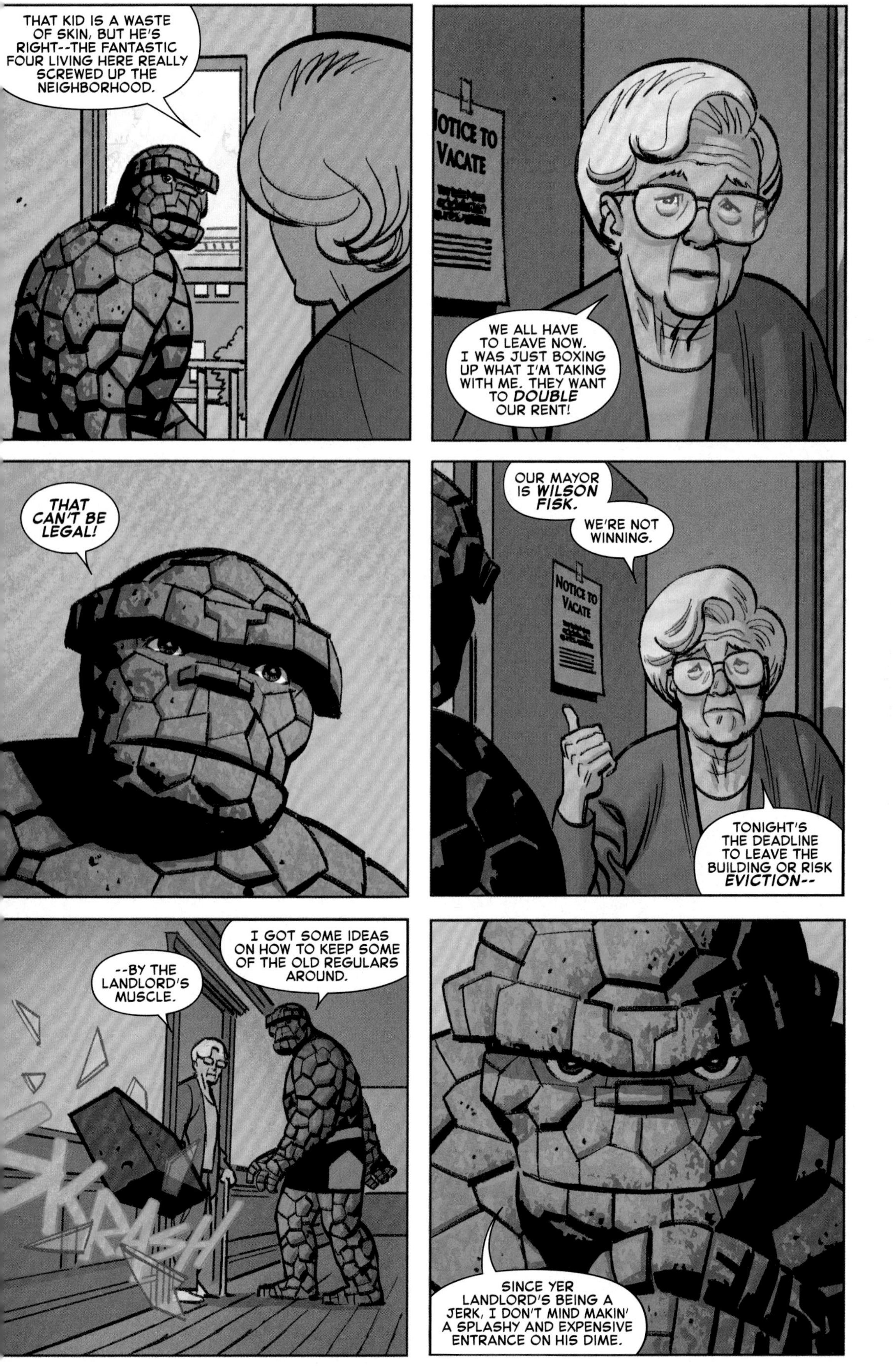
THAT KID IS A WASTE OF SKIN, BUT HE'S RIGHT--THE FANTASTIC FOUR LIVING HERE REALLY SCREWED UP THE NEIGHBORHOOD.
NOTICE TO VACATE
WE ALL HAVE TO LEAVE NOW. I WAS JUST BOXING UP WHAT I'M TAKING WITH ME. THEY WANT TO DOUBLE OUR RENT!
THAT CAN'T BE LEGAL!
OUR MAYOR IS WILSON FISK.
WE'RE NOT WINNING.
NOTICE TO VACATE
TONIGHT'S THE DEADLINE TO LEAVE THE BUILDING OR RISK EVICTION--
--BY THE LANDLORD'S MUSCLE.
I GOT SOME IDEAS ON HOW TO KEEP SOME OF THE OLD REGULARS AROUND.
KRASH
SINCE YER LANDLORD'S BEING A JERK, I DON'T MIND MAKIN' A SPLASHY AND EXPENSIVE ENTRANCE ON HIS DIME.

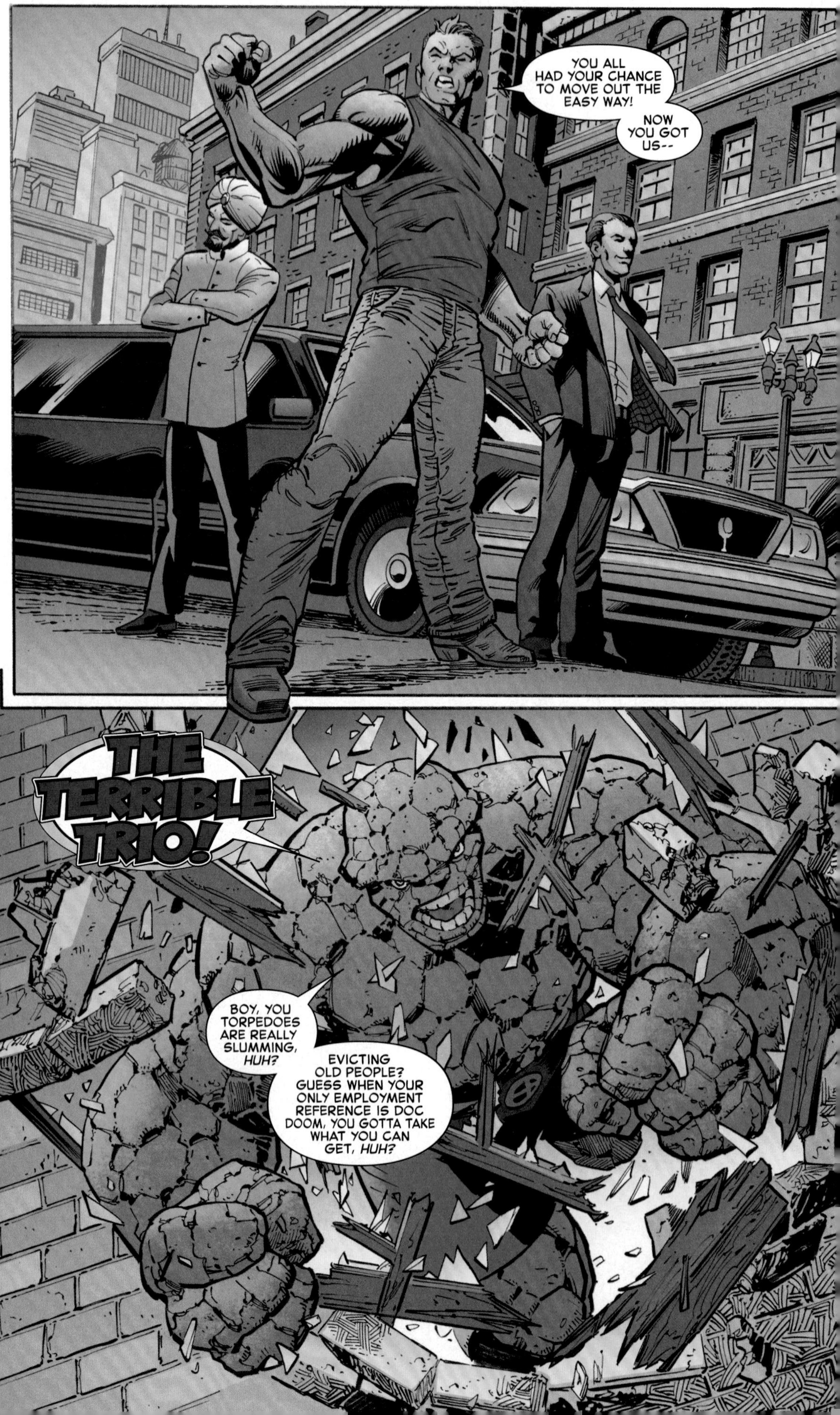
YOU ALL HAD YOUR CHANCE TO MOVE OUT THE EASY WAY!
NOW YOU GOT US--
THE TERRIBLE TRIO!
BOY, YOU TORPEDOES ARE REALLY SLUMMING, *HUH?*
EVICTING OLD PEOPLE? GUESS WHEN YOUR ONLY EMPLOYMENT REFERENCE IS DOC DOOM, YOU GOTTA TAKE WHAT YOU CAN GET, *HUH?*

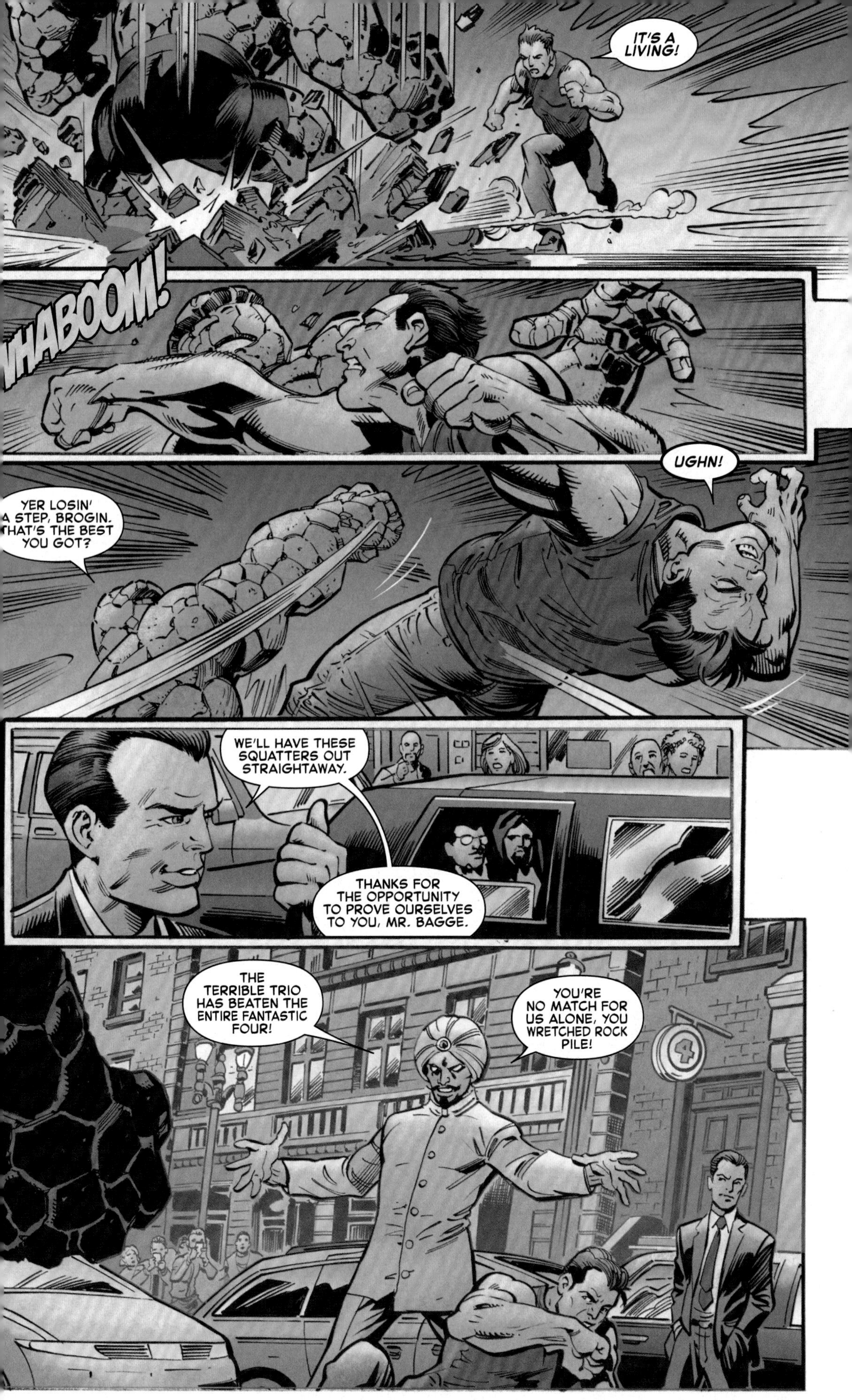
IT'S A LIVING!
WHABOOM!
UGHN!
YER LOSIN' A STEP, BROGIN. THAT'S THE BEST YOU GOT?
WE'LL HAVE THESE SQUATTERS OUT STRAIGHTAWAY.
THANKS FOR THE OPPORTUNITY TO PROVE OURSELVES TO YOU, MR. BAGGE.
THE TERRIBLE TRIO HAS BEATEN THE ENTIRE FANTASTIC FOUR!
YOU'RE NO MATCH FOR US ALONE, YOU WRETCHED ROCK PILE!

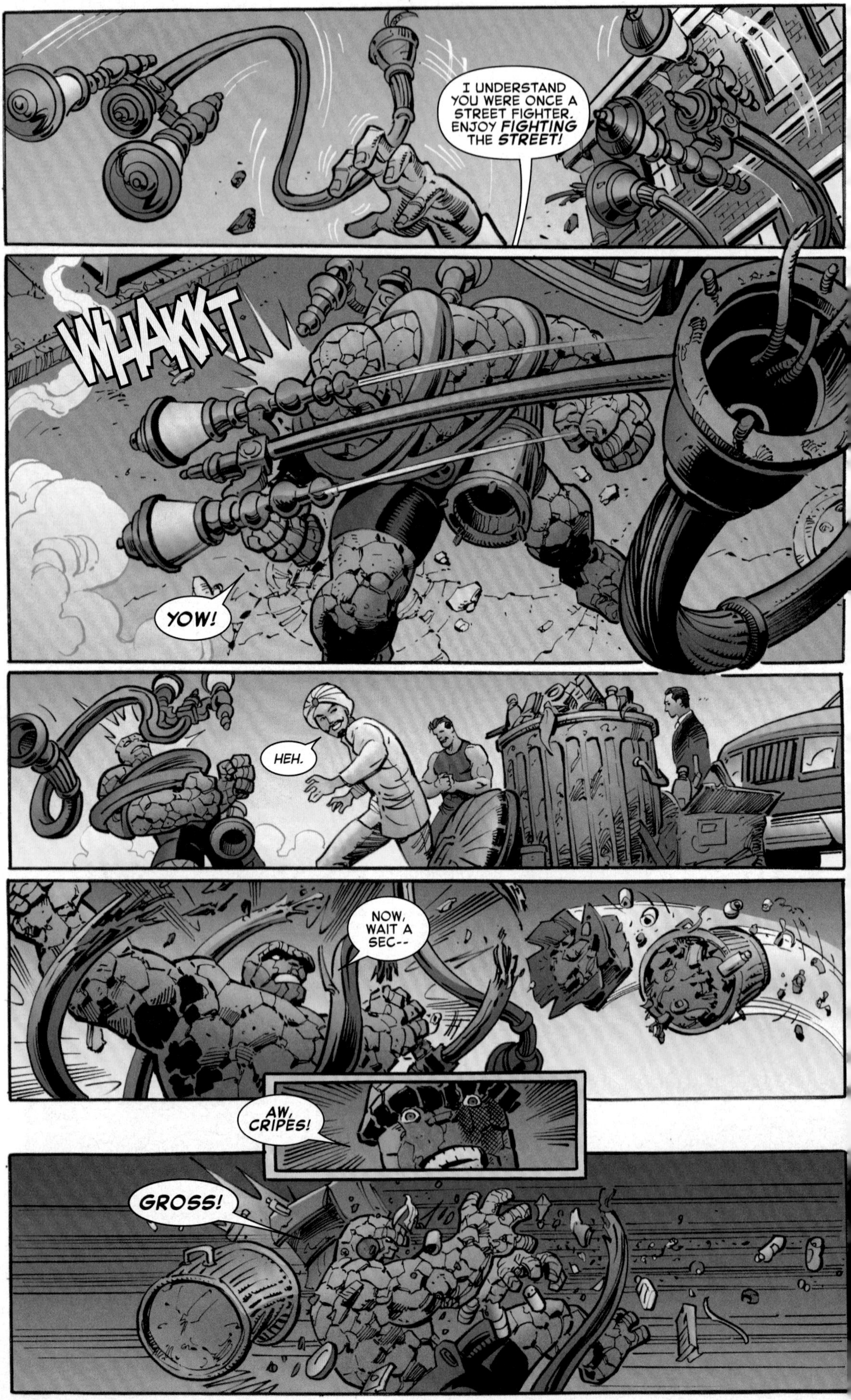
I UNDERSTAND YOU WERE ONCE A STREET FIGHTER. ENJOY FIGHTING THE STREET!
WHAKKT
YOW!
HEH.
NOW, WAIT A SEC--
AW, CRIPES!
GROSS!

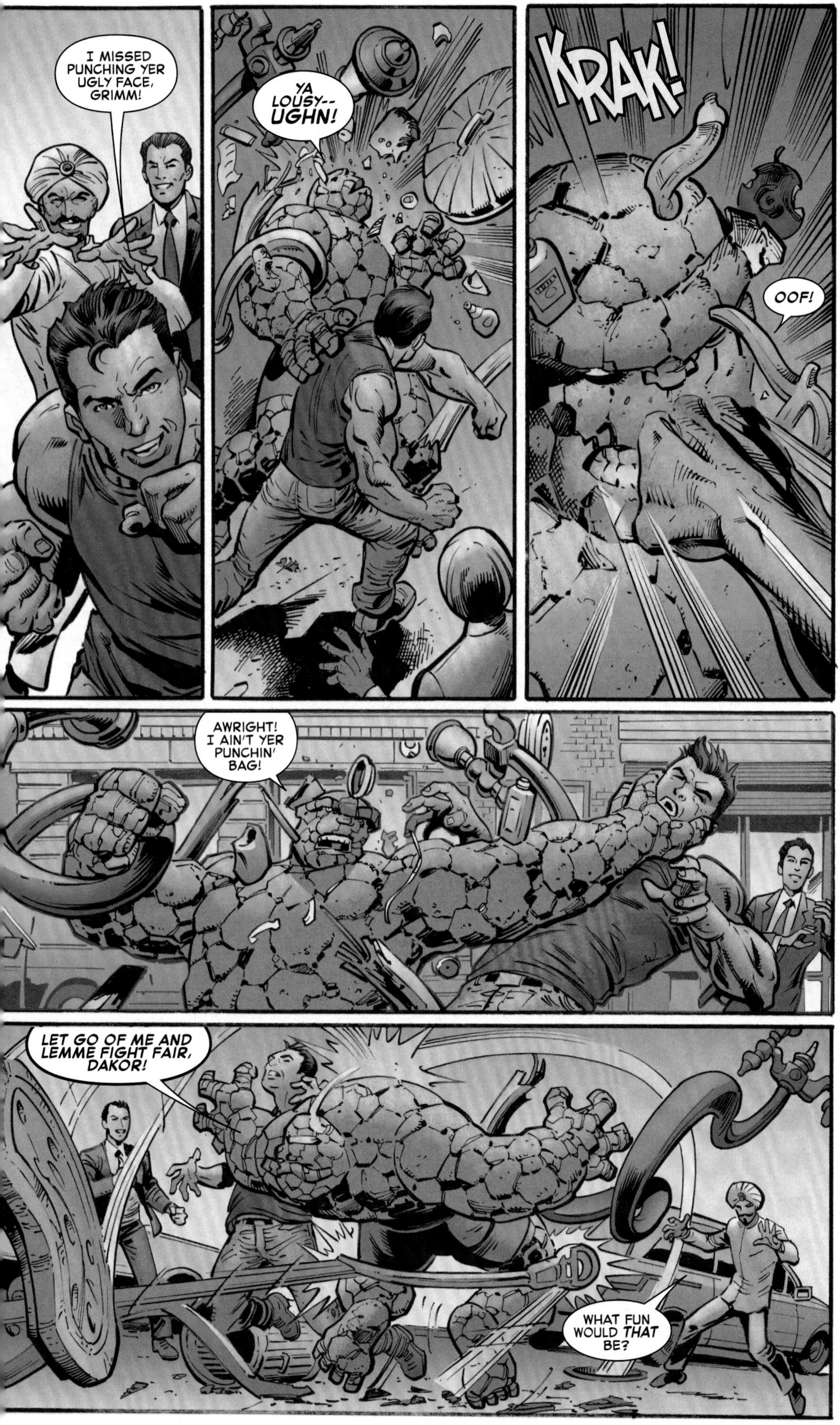
I MISSED PUNCHING YER UGLY FACE, GRIMM!
YA LOUSY-- UGHN!
KRAK!
OOF!
AWRIGHT! I AIN'T YER PUNCHIN' BAG!
LET GO OF ME AND LEMME FIGHT FAIR, DAKOR!
WHAT FUN WOULD *THAT* BE?

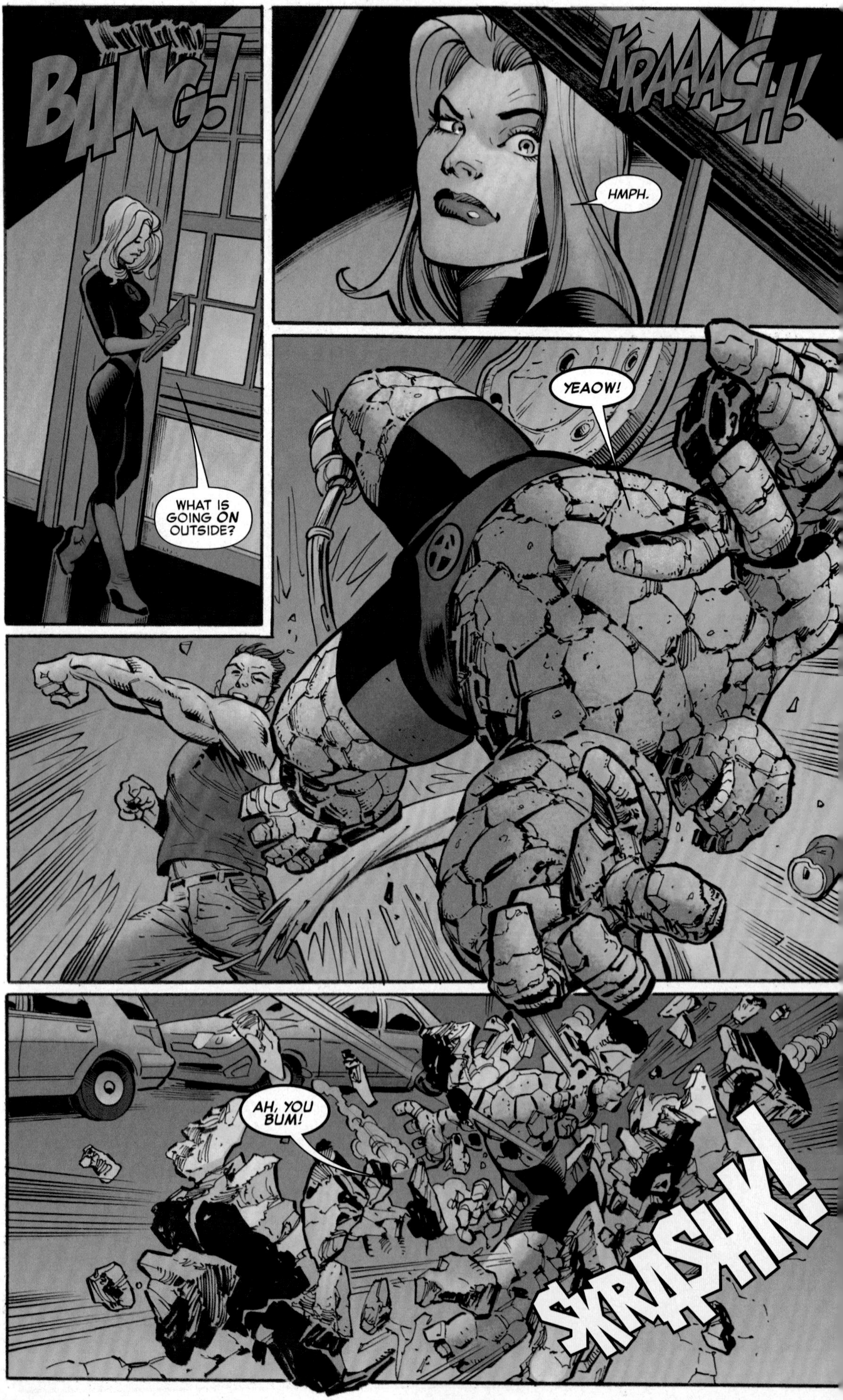
BANG!
WHAT IS GOING ON OUTSIDE?
KRAAASH!
HMPH.
YEAOW!
AH, YOU BUM!
SKRASHK!

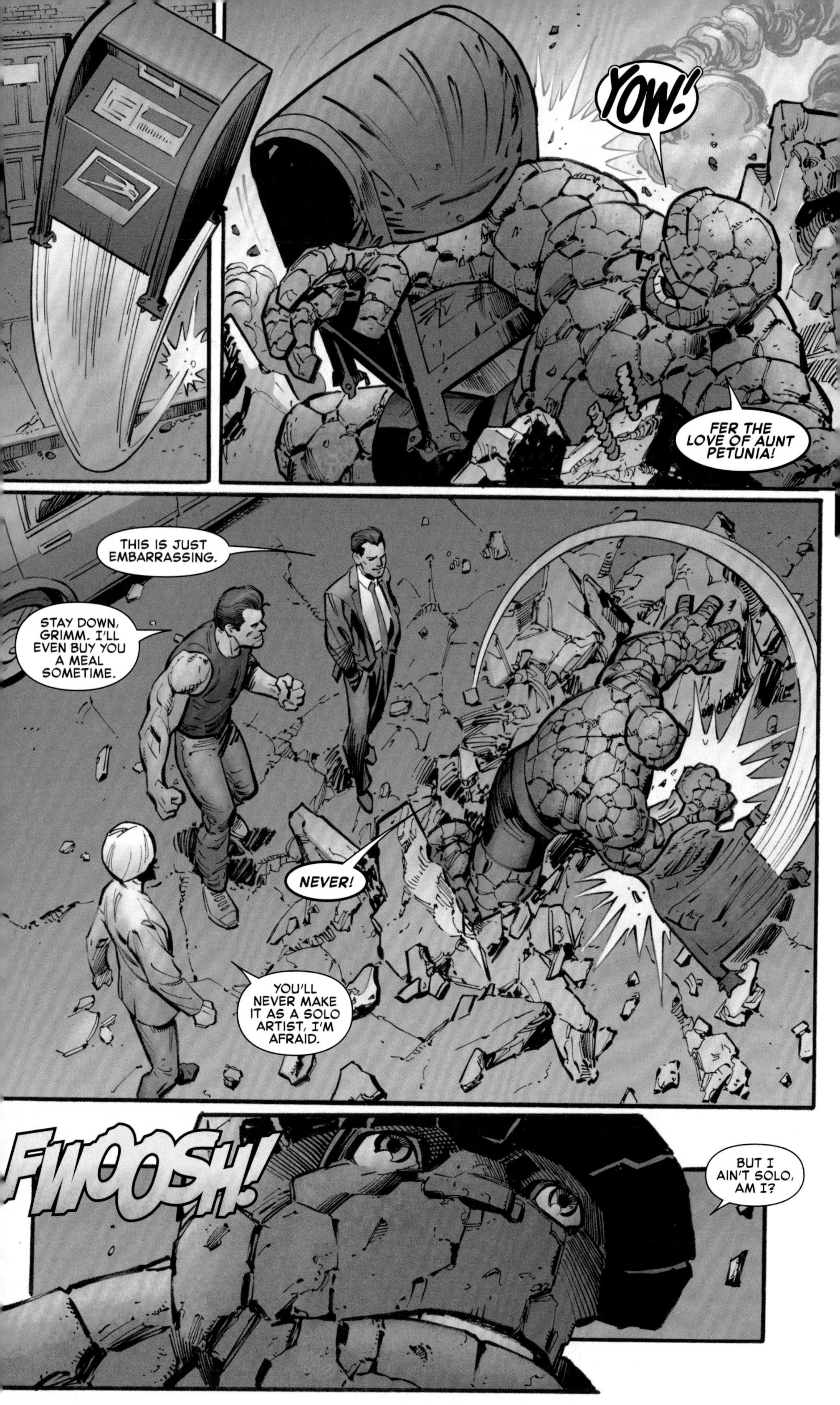
YOW!
FER THE LOVE OF AUNT PETUNIA!
THIS IS JUST EMBARRASSING.
STAY DOWN, GRIMM. I'LL EVEN BUY YOU A MEAL SOMETIME.
NEVER!
YOU'LL NEVER MAKE IT AS A SOLO ARTIST, I'M AFRAID.
FWOOSH!
BUT I AIN'T SOLO, AM I?

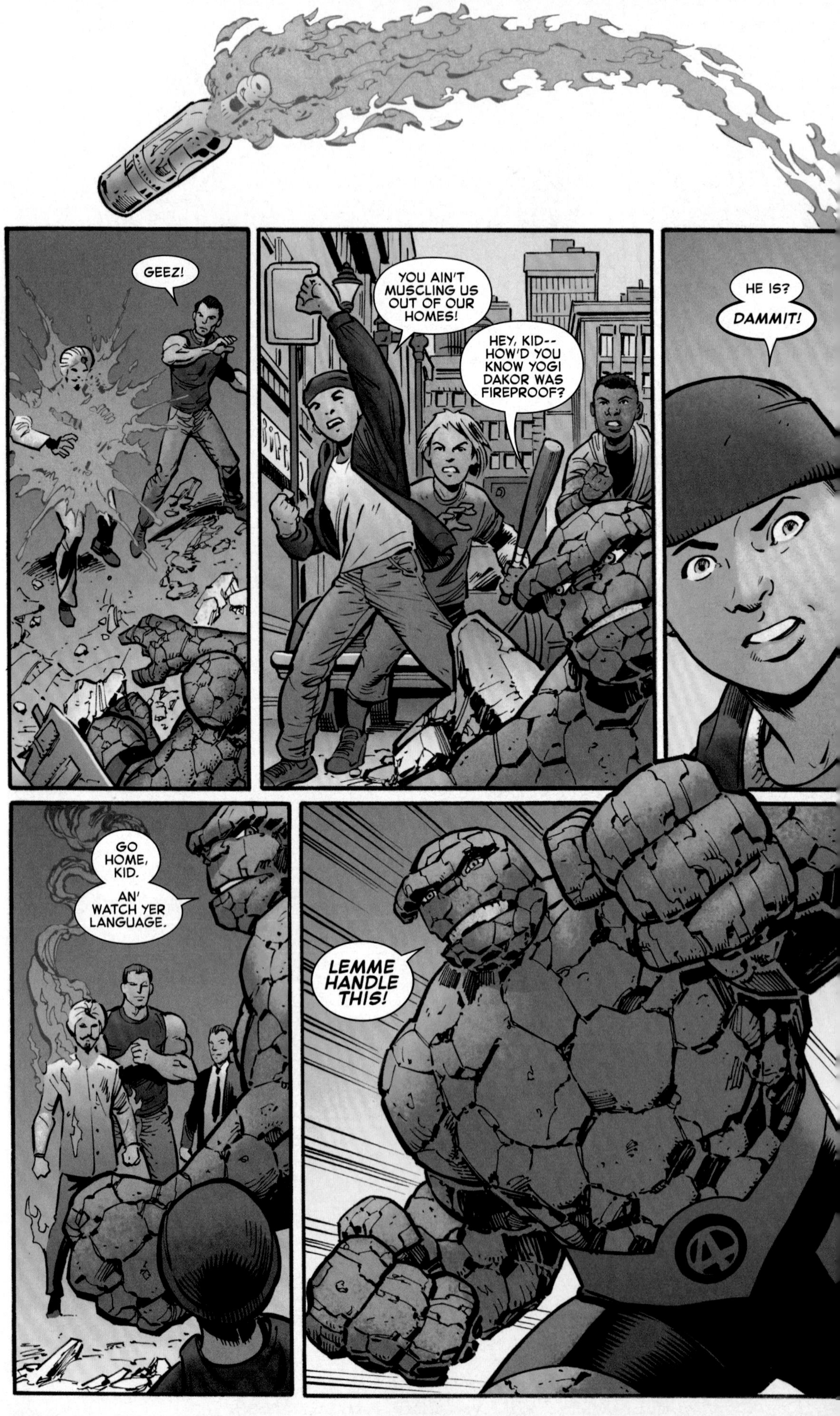
GEEZ!
YOU AIN'T MUSCLING US OUT OF OUR HOMES!
HEY, KID-- HOW'D YOU KNOW YOGI DAKOR WAS FIREPROOF?
HE IS?
DAMMIT!
GO HOME, KID.
AN' WATCH YER LANGUAGE.
LEMME HANDLE THIS!

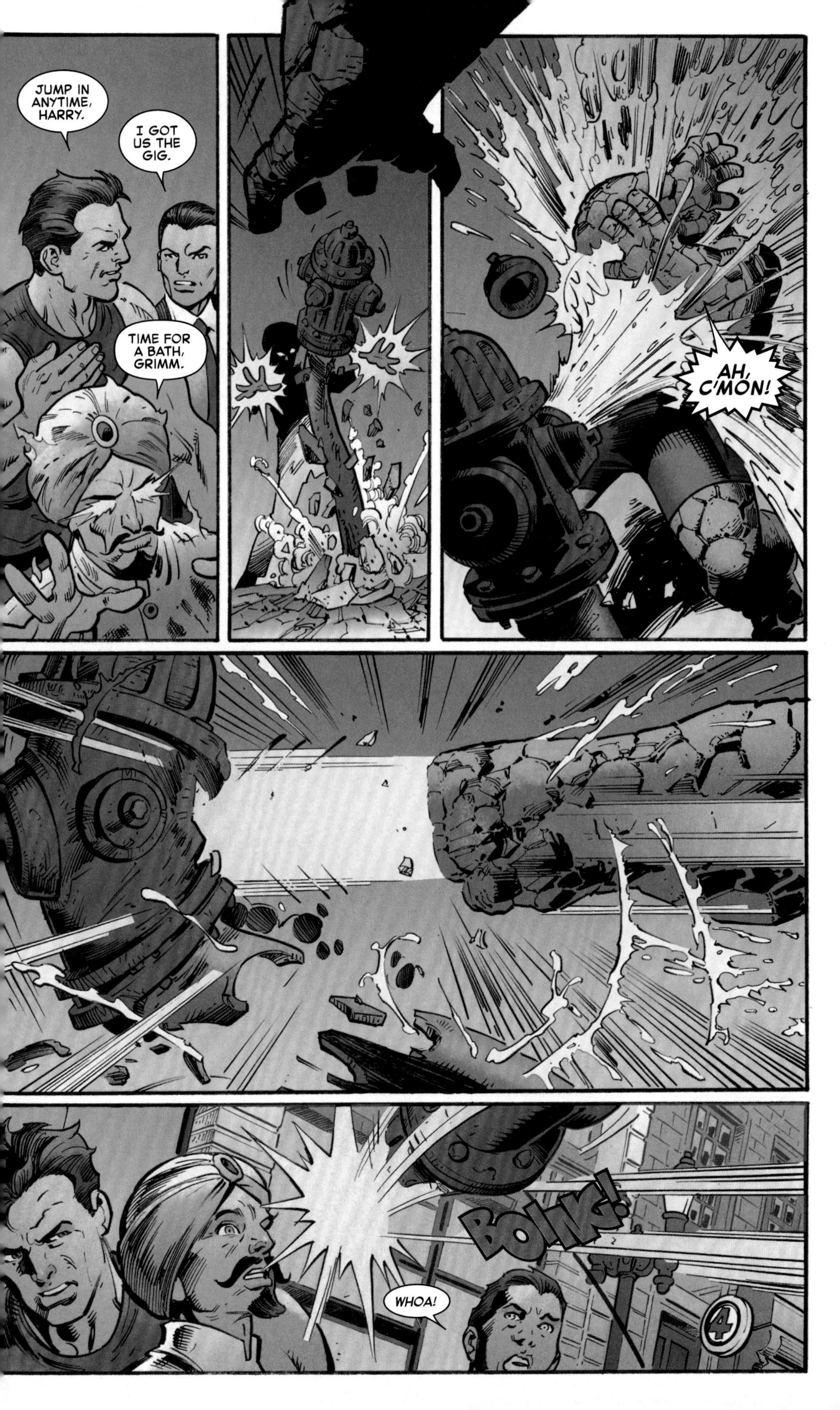
JUMP IN ANYTIME, HARRY.
I GOT US THE GIG.
TIME FOR A BATH, GRIMM.
AH, C'MON!
BOING!
WHOA!
4

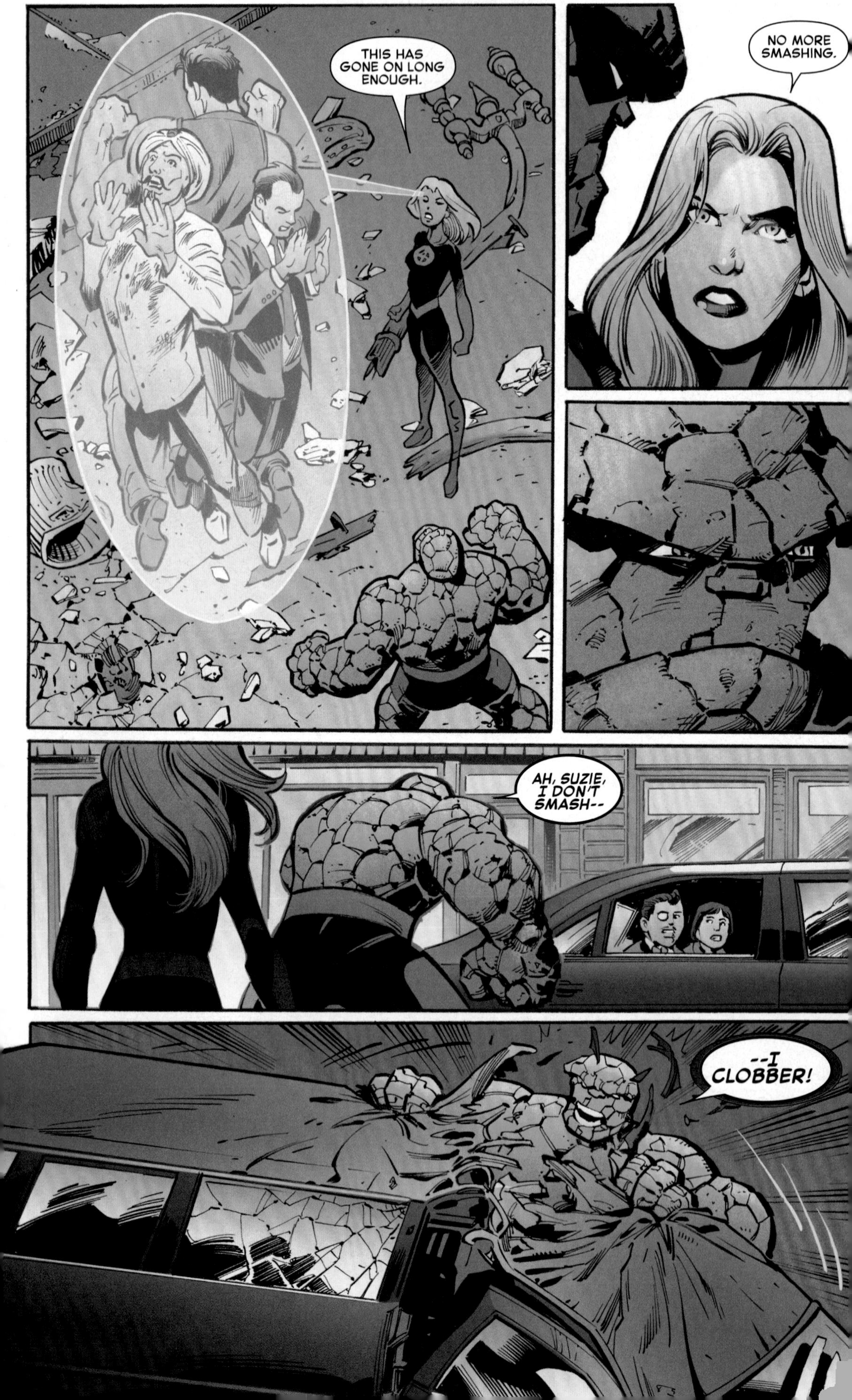
THIS HAS GONE ON LONG ENOUGH.
NO MORE SMASHING.
AH, SUZIE, I DON'T SMASH--
--I CLOBBER!

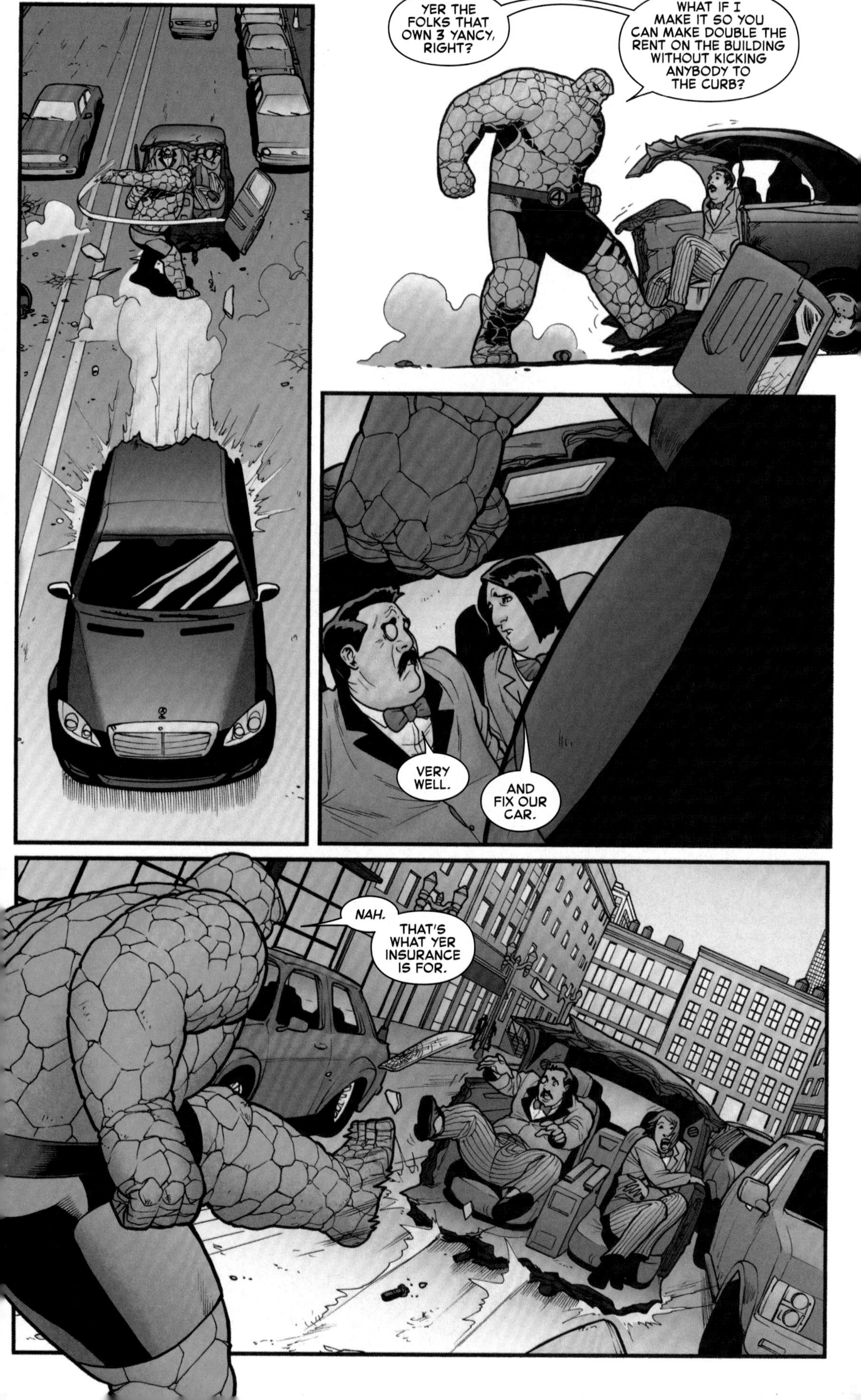
YER THE FOLKS THAT OWN 3 YANCY, RIGHT?
WHAT IF I MAKE IT SO YOU CAN MAKE DOUBLE THE RENT ON THE BUILDING WITHOUT KICKING ANYBODY TO THE CURB?
VERY WELL.
AND FIX OUR CAR.
NAH.
THAT'S WHAT YER INSURANCE IS FOR.

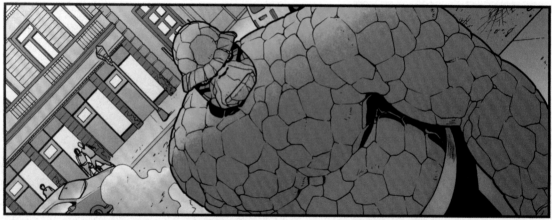

I'M SORRY, SISTER--"HANDSOME HARRY" PHILLIPS CONVINCED ME HE AND HIS FRIENDS WERE THE RIGHT MEN FOR THE JOB, AND HIS RESUME WAS QUITE IMPRESSIVE.

SAVE IT.

LOOK. UH...

SORRY I TAGGED THE WALL. I DIDN'T KNOW IT WAS SPECIAL. I WAS JUST DOING MY REGULAR THING, SPREADING THE WORD ABOUT YOU JERKS.

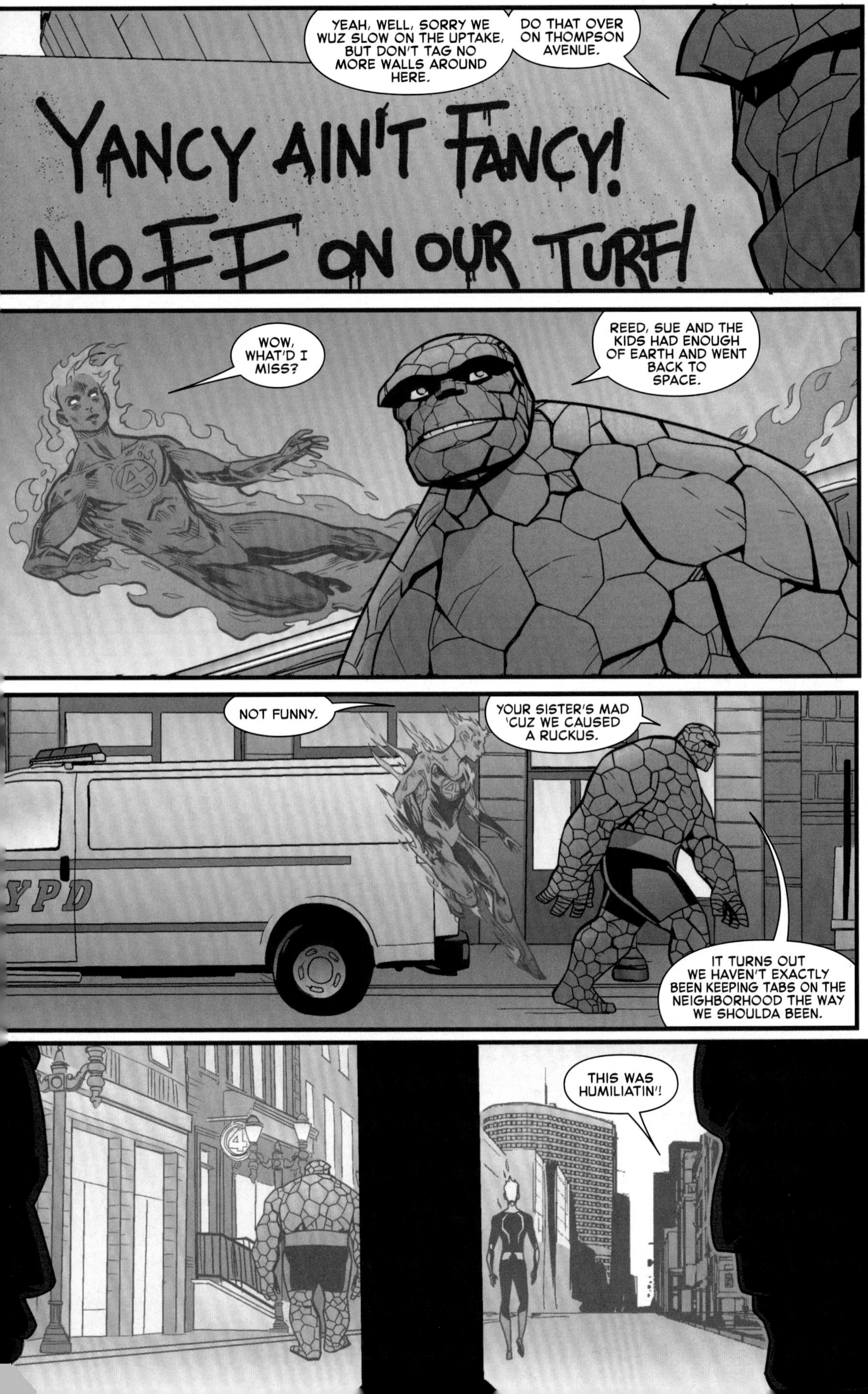
YEAH, WELL, SORRY WE WUZ SLOW ON THE UPTAKE, BUT DON'T TAG NO MORE WALLS AROUND HERE.
DO THAT OVER ON THOMPSON AVENUE.
YANCY AIN'T FANCY! NO FF ON OUR TURF!
WOW, WHAT'D I MISS?
REED, SUE AND THE KIDS HAD ENOUGH OF EARTH AND WENT BACK TO SPACE.
NOT FUNNY.
YOUR SISTER'S MAD 'CUZ WE CAUSED A RUCKUS.
YPD
IT TURNS OUT WE HAVEN'T EXACTLY BEEN KEEPING TABS ON THE NEIGHBORHOOD THE WAY WE SHOULDA BEEN.
THIS WAS HUMILIATIN'!

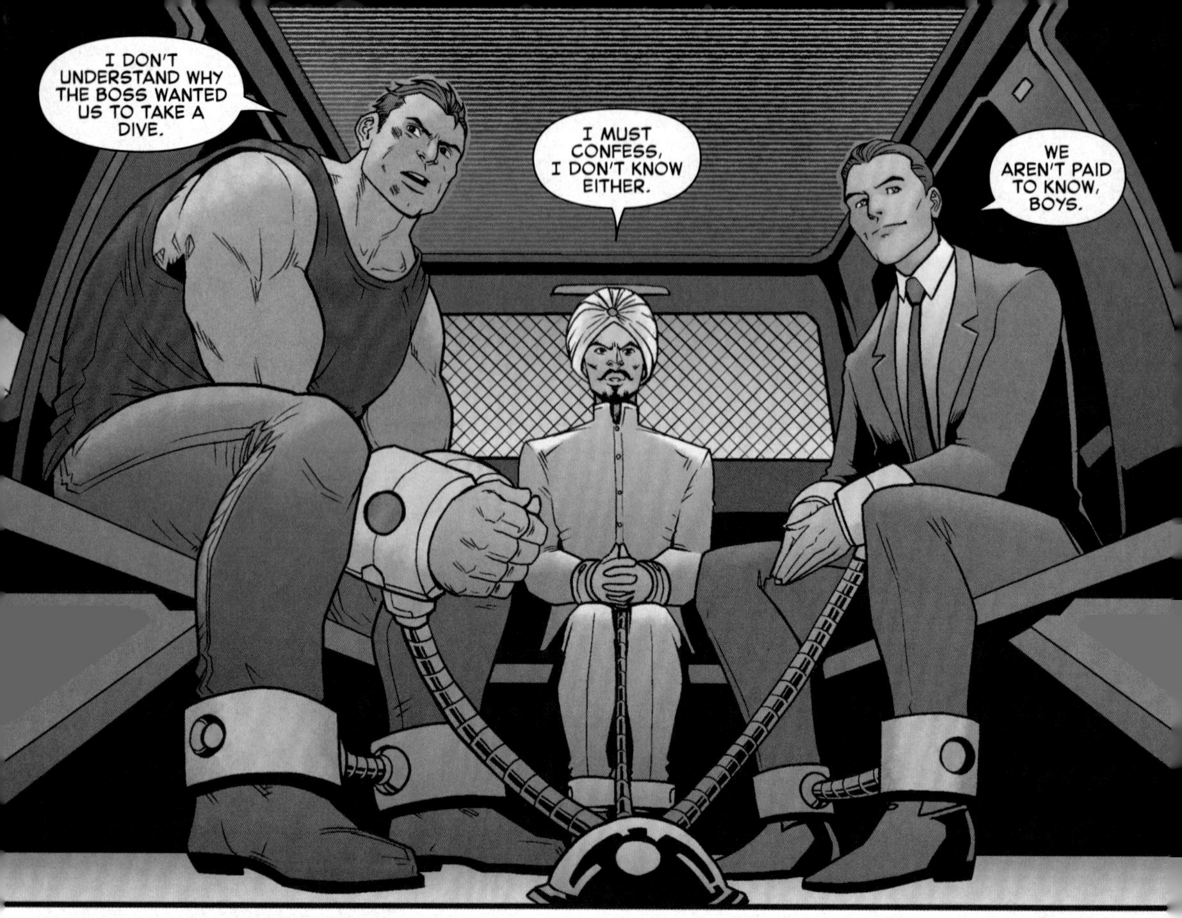
I DON'T UNDERSTAND WHY THE BOSS WANTED US TO TAKE A DIVE.
I MUST CONFESS, I DON'T KNOW EITHER.
WE AREN'T PAID TO KNOW, BOYS.

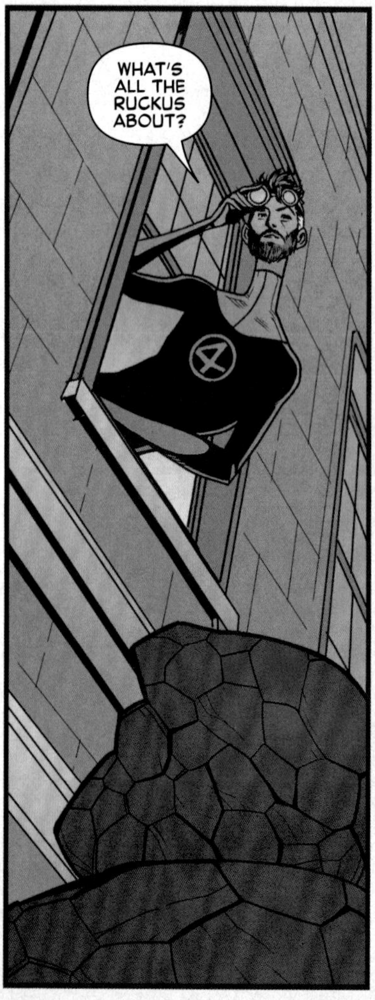
WHAT'S ALL THE RUCKUS ABOUT?

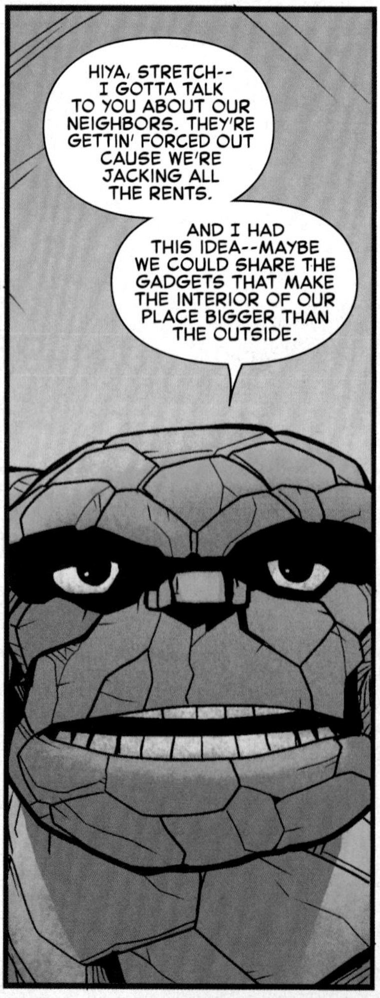
HIYA, STRETCH-- I GOTTA TALK TO YOU ABOUT OUR NEIGHBORS. THEY'RE GETTIN' FORCED OUT CAUSE WE'RE JACKING ALL THE RENTS.
AND I HAD THIS IDEA--MAYBE WE COULD SHARE THE GADGETS THAT MAKE THE INTERIOR OF OUR PLACE BIGGER THAN THE OUTSIDE.

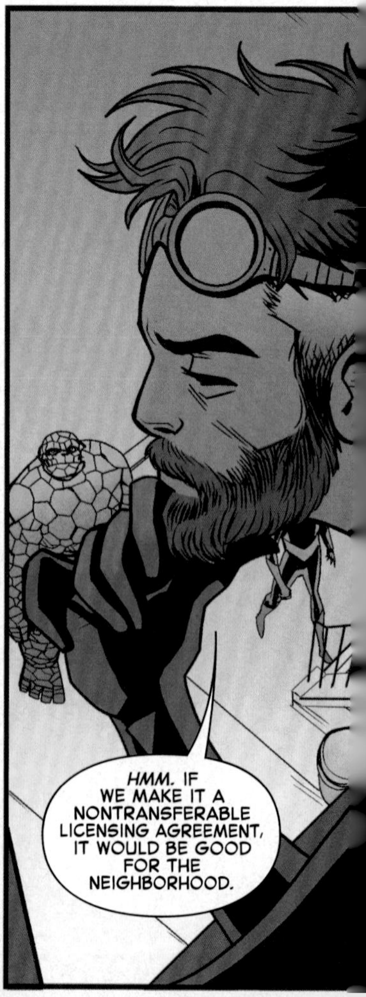
HMM. IF WE MAKE IT A NONTRANSFERABLE LICENSING AGREEMENT, IT WOULD BE GOOD FOR THE NEIGHBORHOOD.

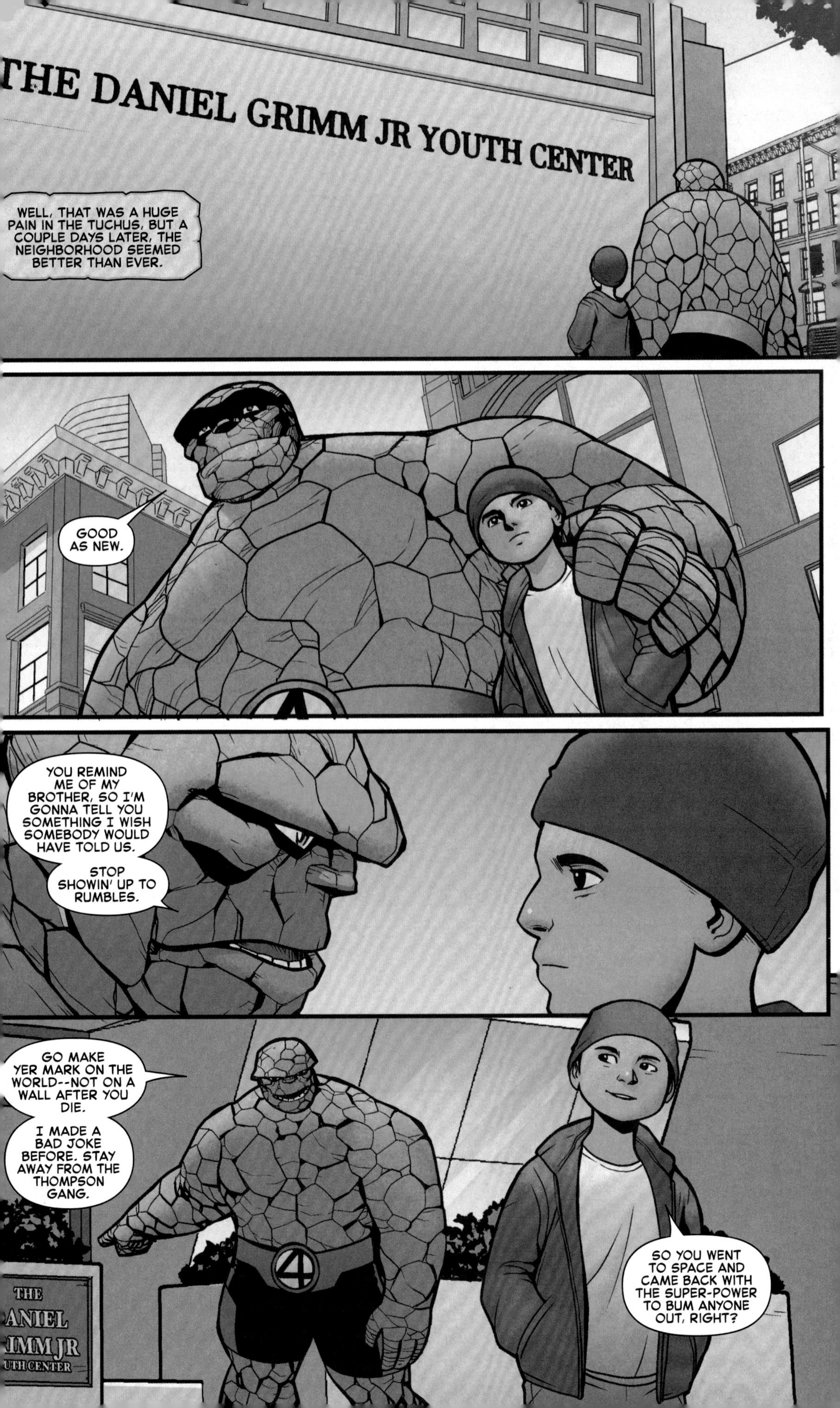
THE DANIEL GRIMM JR YOUTH CENTER
WELL, THAT WAS A HUGE PAIN IN THE TUCHUS, BUT A COUPLE DAYS LATER, THE NEIGHBORHOOD SEEMED BETTER THAN EVER.
GOOD AS NEW.
YOU REMIND ME OF MY BROTHER, SO I'M GONNA TELL YOU SOMETHING I WISH SOMEBODY WOULD HAVE TOLD US.
STOP SHOWIN' UP TO RUMBLES.
GO MAKE YER MARK ON THE WORLD--NOT ON A WALL AFTER YOU DIE.
I MADE A BAD JOKE BEFORE. STAY AWAY FROM THE THOMPSON GANG.
SO YOU WENT TO SPACE AND CAME BACK WITH THE SUPER-POWER TO BUM ANYONE OUT, RIGHT?

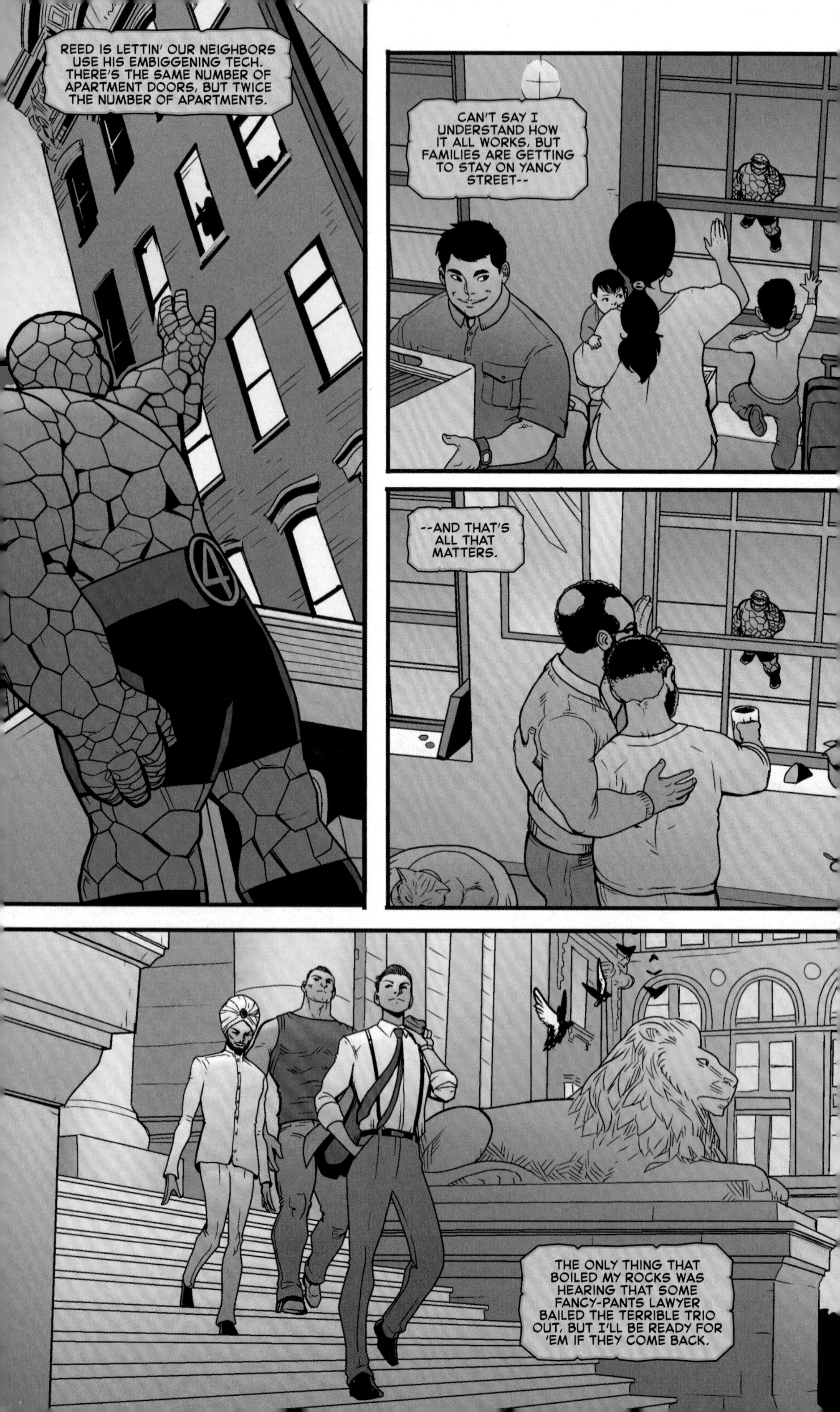
REED IS LETTIN' OUR NEIGHBORS USE HIS EMBIGGENING TECH. THERE'S THE SAME NUMBER OF APARTMENT DOORS, BUT TWICE THE NUMBER OF APARTMENTS.
CAN'T SAY I UNDERSTAND HOW IT ALL WORKS, BUT FAMILIES ARE GETTING TO STAY ON YANCY STREET--
--AND THAT'S ALL THAT MATTERS.
THE ONLY THING THAT BOILED MY ROCKS WAS HEARING THAT SOME FANCY-PANTS LAWYER BAILED THE TERRIBLE TRIO OUT, BUT I'LL BE READY FOR 'EM IF THEY COME BACK.

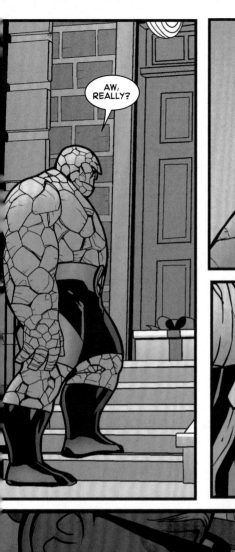

AW, REALLY?

To Ben,
from your friend
at 3B.

WILL WONDERS NEVER CEASE?

I CAN'T BELIEVE IT WASN'T A PIE IN THE FACE.

GRIMM
1

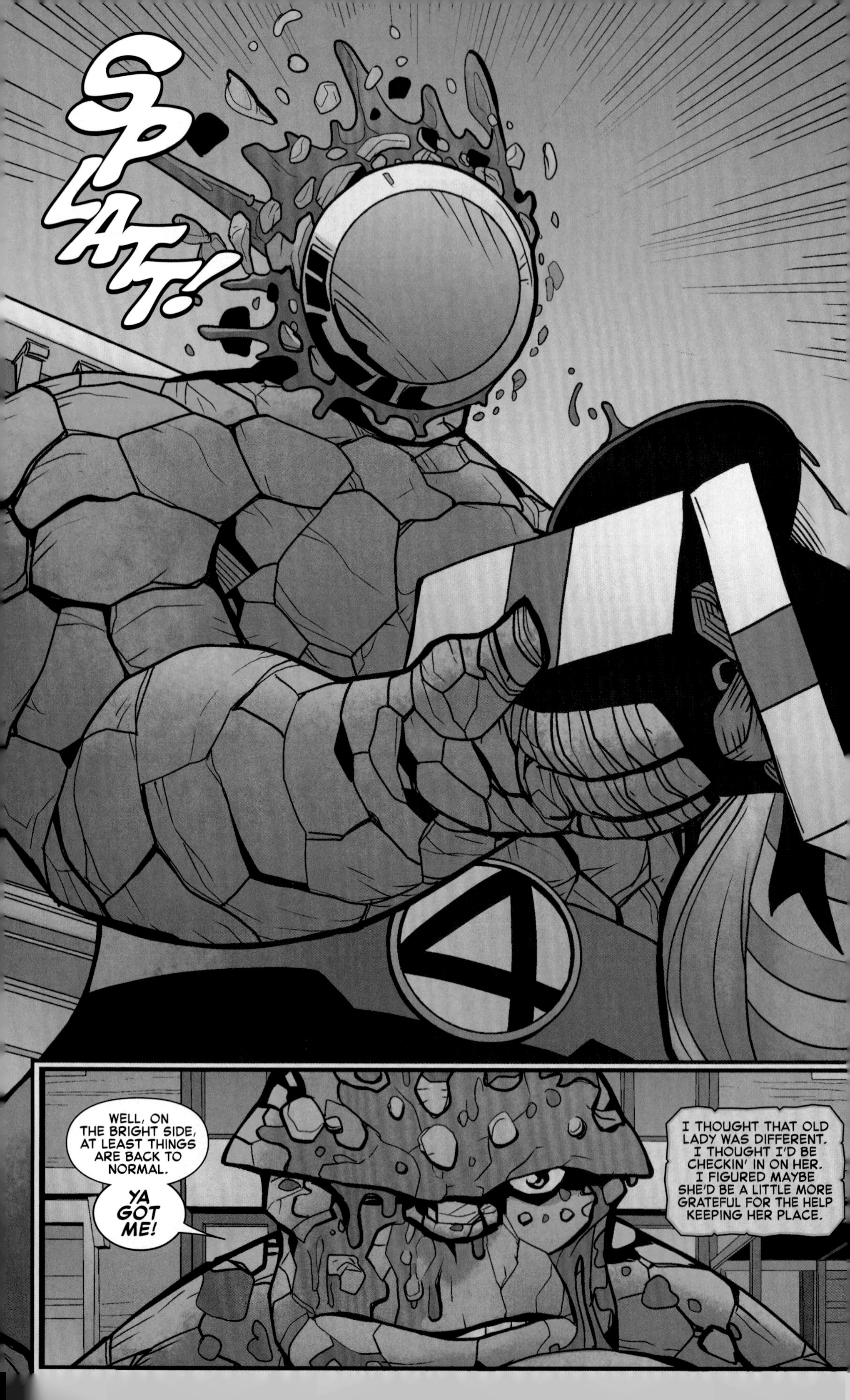
SPLATT!
WELL, ON THE BRIGHT SIDE, AT LEAST THINGS ARE BACK TO NORMAL.
YA GOT ME!
I THOUGHT THAT OLD LADY WAS DIFFERENT. I THOUGHT I'D BE CHECKIN' IN ON HER. I FIGURED MAYBE SHE'D BE A LITTLE MORE GRATEFUL FOR THE HELP KEEPING HER PLACE.

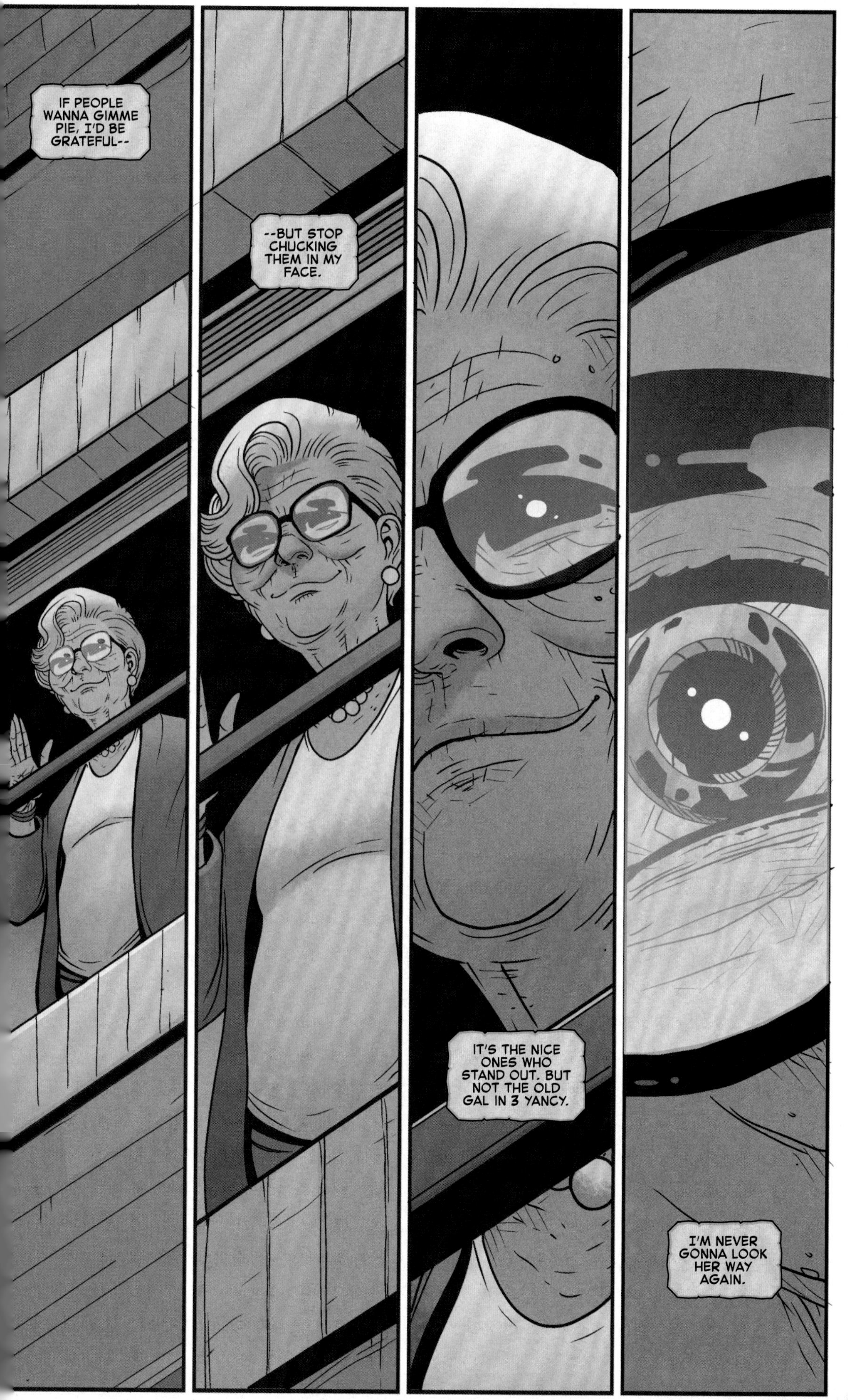
IF PEOPLE WANNA GIMME PIE, I'D BE GRATEFUL--
--BUT STOP CHUCKING THEM IN MY FACE.
IT'S THE NICE ONES WHO STAND OUT. BUT NOT THE OLD GAL IN 3 YANCY.
I'M NEVER GONNA LOOK HER WAY AGAIN.

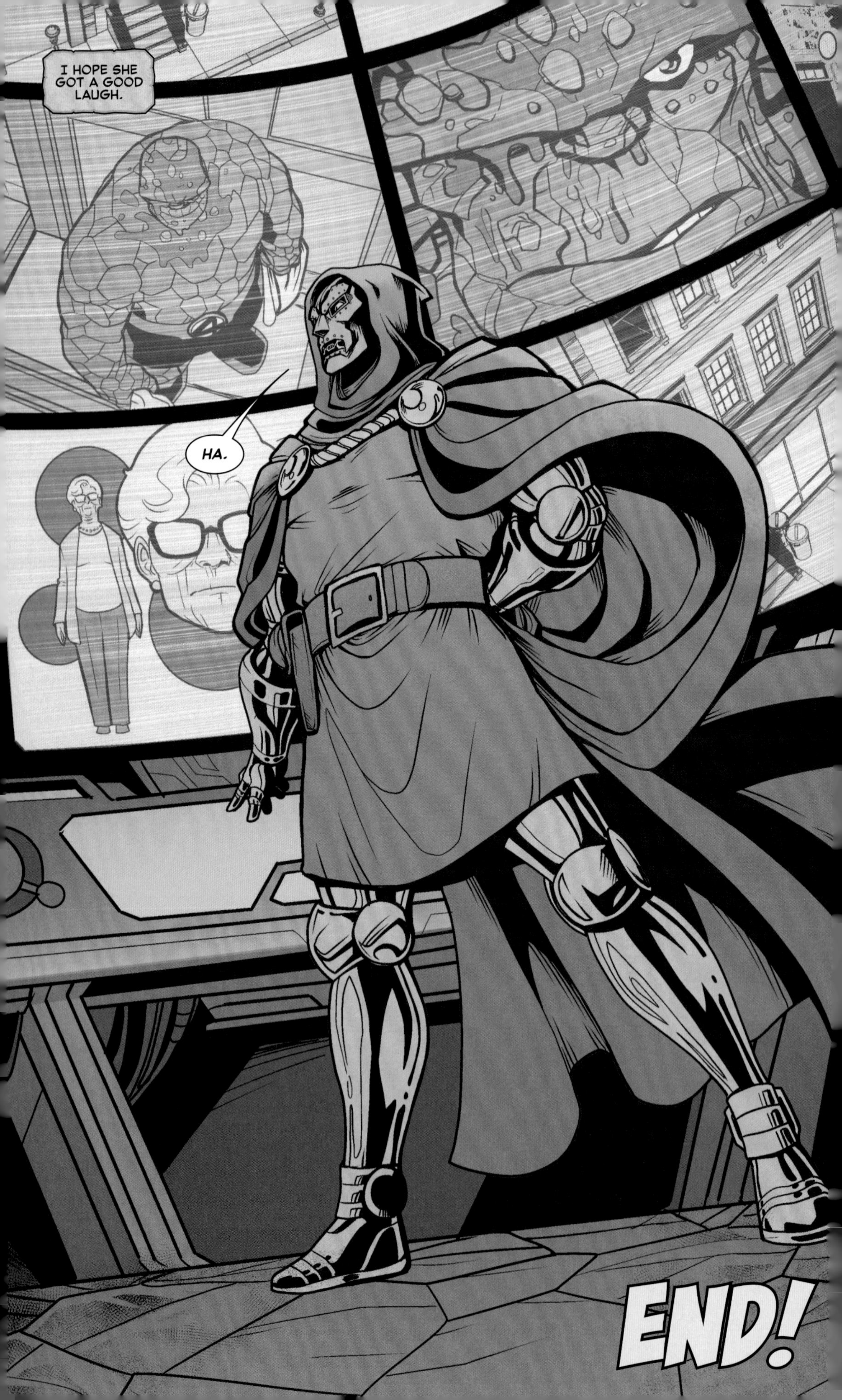
I HOPE SHE GOT A GOOD LAUGH.
HA.
END!

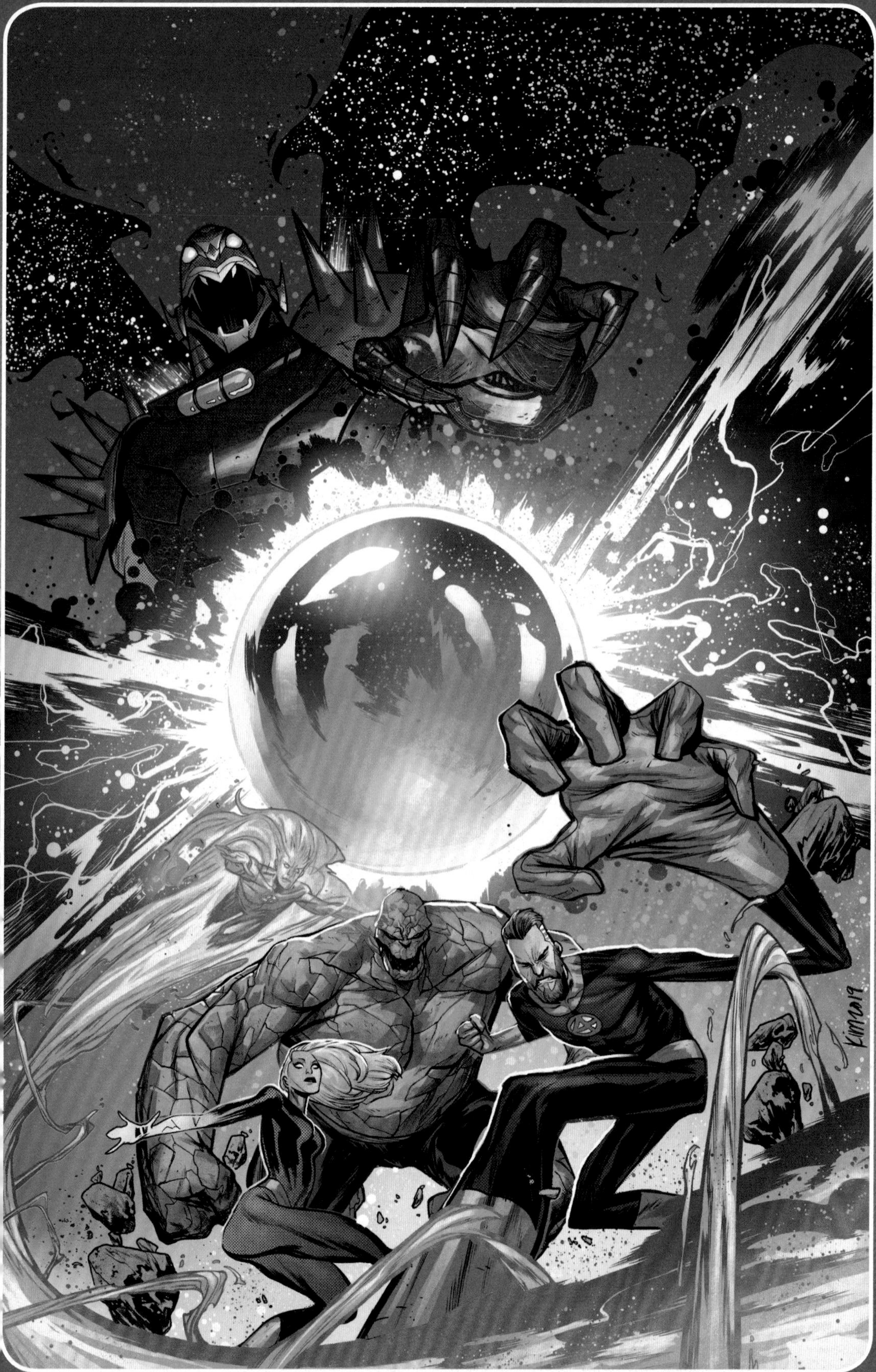

Fantastic Four: Negative Zone

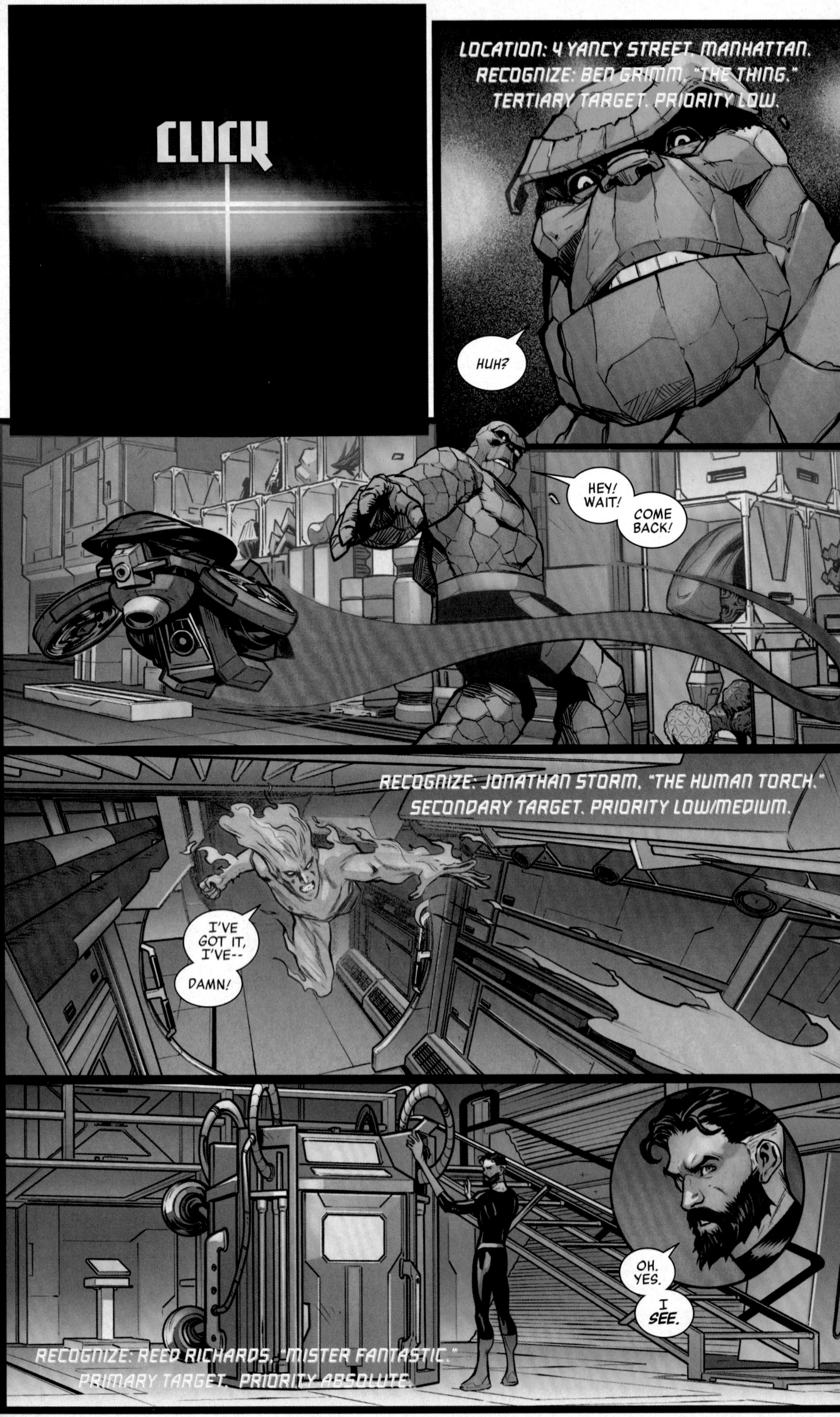
CLICK
LOCATION: 4 YANCY STREET, MANHATTAN.
RECOGNIZE: BEN GRIMM, "THE THING."
TERTIARY TARGET. PRIORITY LOW.
HUH?
HEY! WAIT!
COME BACK!
RECOGNIZE: JONATHAN STORM, "THE HUMAN TORCH."
SECONDARY TARGET. PRIORITY LOW/MEDIUM.
I'VE GOT IT, I'VE--
DAMN!
OH. YES.
I SEE.
RECOGNIZE: REED RICHARDS, "MISTER FANTASTIC."
PRIMARY TARGET. PRIORITY ABSOLUTE.

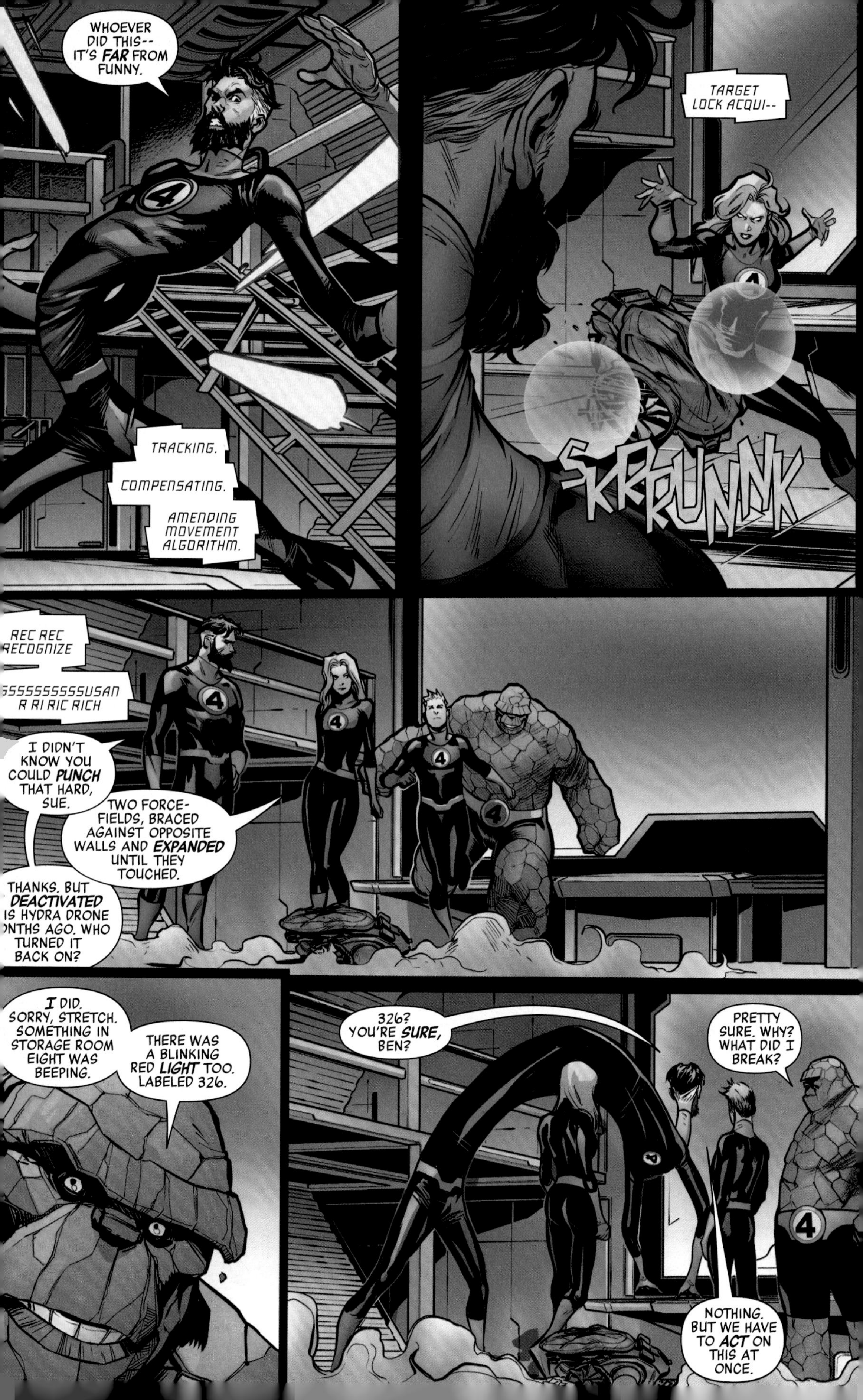
WHOEVER DID THIS-- IT'S FAR FROM FUNNY.
TRACKING.
COMPENSATING.
AMENDING MOVEMENT ALGORITHM.
TARGET LOCK ACQUI--
SKRRUNNK
REC REC RECOGNIZE
SSSSSSSSSSUSAN R RI RIC RICH
I DIDN'T KNOW YOU COULD PUNCH THAT HARD, SUE.
TWO FORCE-FIELDS, BRACED AGAINST OPPOSITE WALLS AND EXPANDED UNTIL THEY TOUCHED.
THANKS. BUT DEACTIVATED IS HYDRA DRONE ONTHS AGO. WHO TURNED IT BACK ON?
I DID. SORRY, STRETCH. SOMETHING IN STORAGE ROOM EIGHT WAS BEEPING.
THERE WAS A BLINKING RED LIGHT TOO. LABELED 326.
326? YOU'RE SURE, BEN?
PRETTY SURE. WHY? WHAT DID I BREAK?
NOTHING. BUT WE HAVE TO ACT ON THIS AT ONCE.

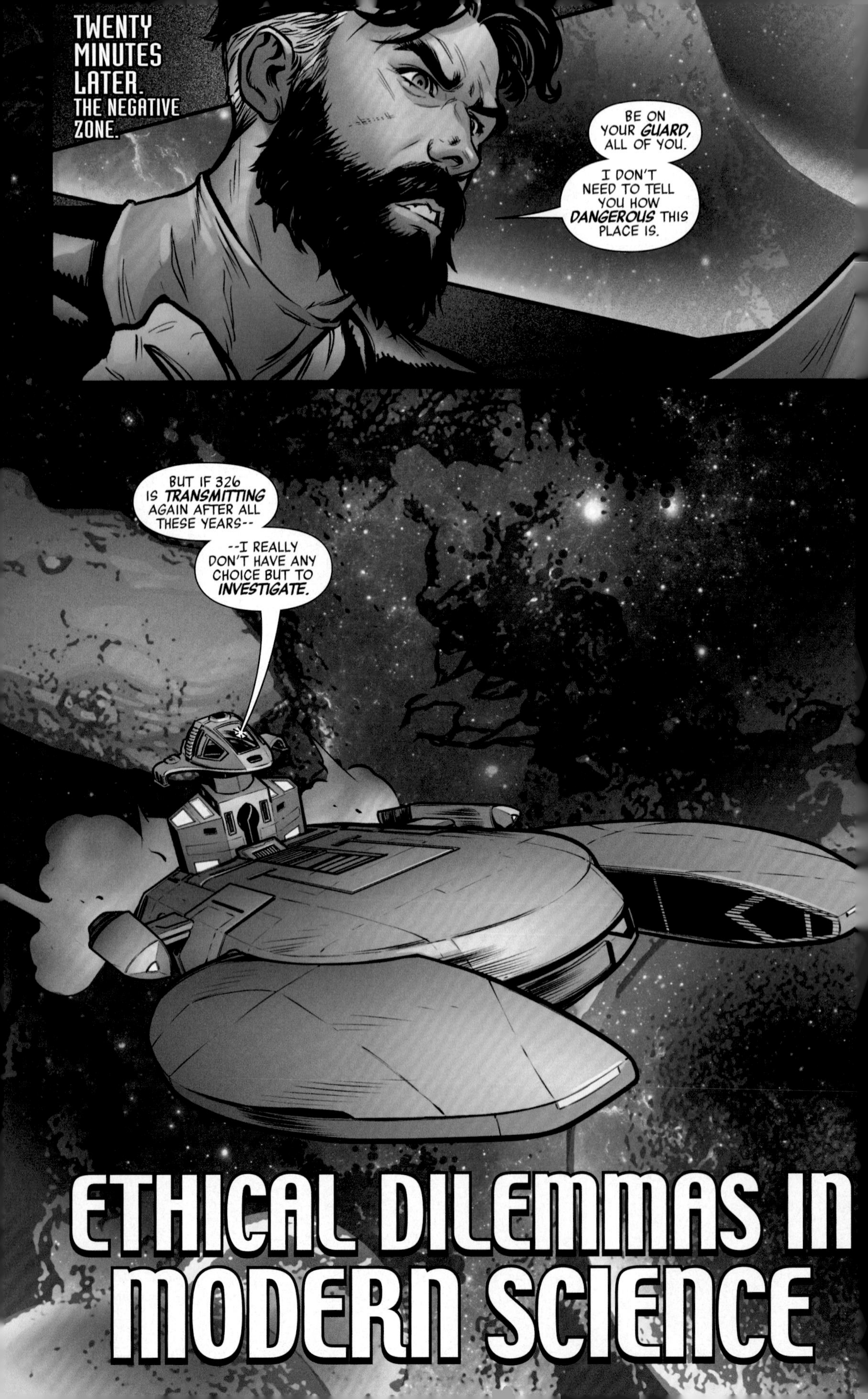
TWENTY MINUTES LATER. THE NEGATIVE ZONE.
BE ON YOUR GUARD, ALL OF YOU.
I DON'T NEED TO TELL YOU HOW DANGEROUS THIS PLACE IS.
BUT IF 326 IS TRANSMITTING AGAIN AFTER ALL THESE YEARS--
--I REALLY DON'T HAVE ANY CHOICE BUT TO INVESTIGATE.
ETHICAL DILEMMAS IN MODERN SCIENCE

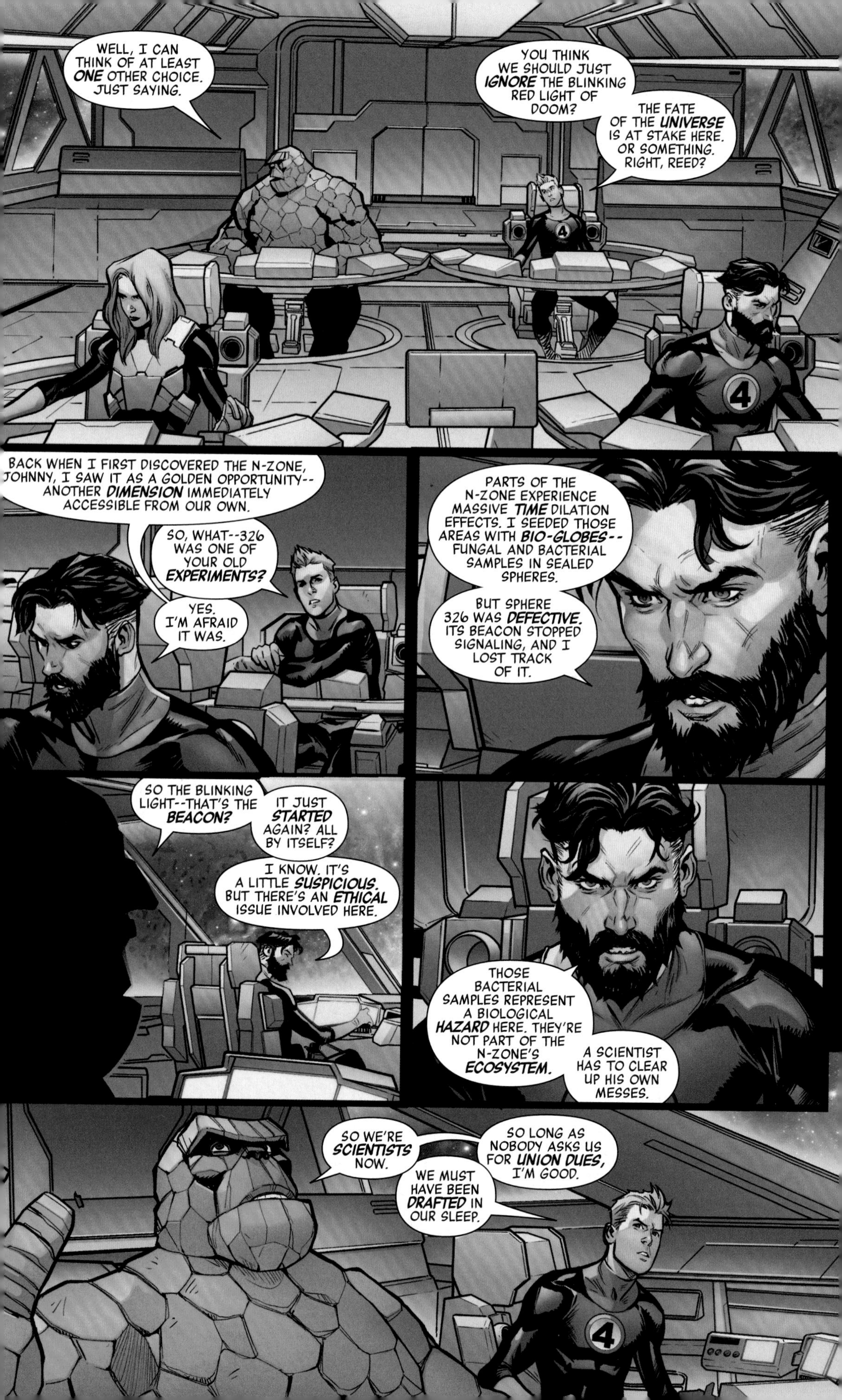
WELL, I CAN THINK OF AT LEAST ONE OTHER CHOICE. JUST SAYING.
YOU THINK WE SHOULD JUST IGNORE THE BLINKING RED LIGHT OF DOOM?
THE FATE OF THE UNIVERSE IS AT STAKE HERE. OR SOMETHING. RIGHT, REED?
BACK WHEN I FIRST DISCOVERED THE N-ZONE, JOHNNY, I SAW IT AS A GOLDEN OPPORTUNITY-- ANOTHER DIMENSION IMMEDIATELY ACCESSIBLE FROM OUR OWN.
SO, WHAT--326 WAS ONE OF YOUR OLD EXPERIMENTS?
YES. I'M AFRAID IT WAS.
PARTS OF THE N-ZONE EXPERIENCE MASSIVE TIME DILATION EFFECTS. I SEEDED THOSE AREAS WITH BIO-GLOBES-- FUNGAL AND BACTERIAL SAMPLES IN SEALED SPHERES.
BUT SPHERE 326 WAS DEFECTIVE. ITS BEACON STOPPED SIGNALING, AND I LOST TRACK OF IT.
SO THE BLINKING LIGHT--THAT'S THE BEACON?
IT JUST STARTED AGAIN? ALL BY ITSELF?
I KNOW. IT'S A LITTLE SUSPICIOUS. BUT THERE'S AN ETHICAL ISSUE INVOLVED HERE.
THOSE BACTERIAL SAMPLES REPRESENT A BIOLOGICAL HAZARD HERE. THEY'RE NOT PART OF THE N-ZONE'S ECOSYSTEM.
A SCIENTIST HAS TO CLEAR UP HIS OWN MESSES.
SO WE'RE SCIENTISTS NOW.
SO LONG AS NOBODY ASKS US FOR UNION DUES, I'M GOOD.
WE MUST HAVE BEEN DRAFTED IN OUR SLEEP.

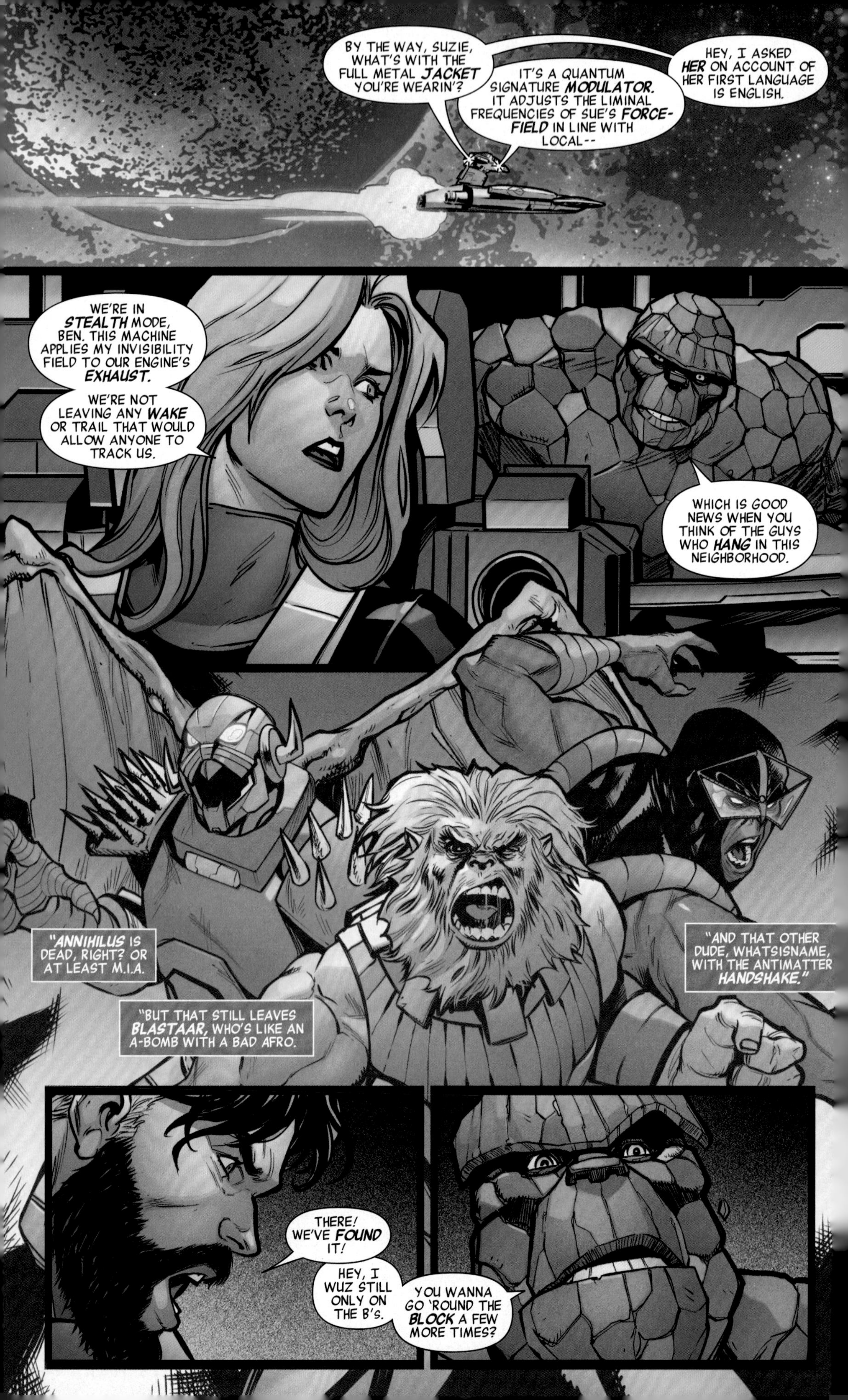
BY THE WAY, SUZIE, WHAT'S WITH THE FULL METAL JACKET YOU'RE WEARIN'?
IT'S A QUANTUM SIGNATURE MODULATOR. IT ADJUSTS THE LIMINAL FREQUENCIES OF SUE'S FORCE-FIELD IN LINE WITH LOCAL--
HEY, I ASKED HER ON ACCOUNT OF HER FIRST LANGUAGE IS ENGLISH.
WE'RE IN STEALTH MODE, BEN. THIS MACHINE APPLIES MY INVISIBILITY FIELD TO OUR ENGINE'S EXHAUST.
WE'RE NOT LEAVING ANY WAKE OR TRAIL THAT WOULD ALLOW ANYONE TO TRACK US.
WHICH IS GOOD NEWS WHEN YOU THINK OF THE GUYS WHO HANG IN THIS NEIGHBORHOOD.
"ANNIHILUS IS DEAD, RIGHT? OR AT LEAST M.I.A.
"BUT THAT STILL LEAVES BLASTAAR, WHO'S LIKE AN A-BOMB WITH A BAD AFRO.
"AND THAT OTHER DUDE, WHATSISNAME, WITH THE ANTIMATTER HANDSHAKE."
THERE! WE'VE FOUND IT!
HEY, I WUZ STILL ONLY ON THE B's.
YOU WANNA GO 'ROUND THE BLOCK A FEW MORE TIMES?

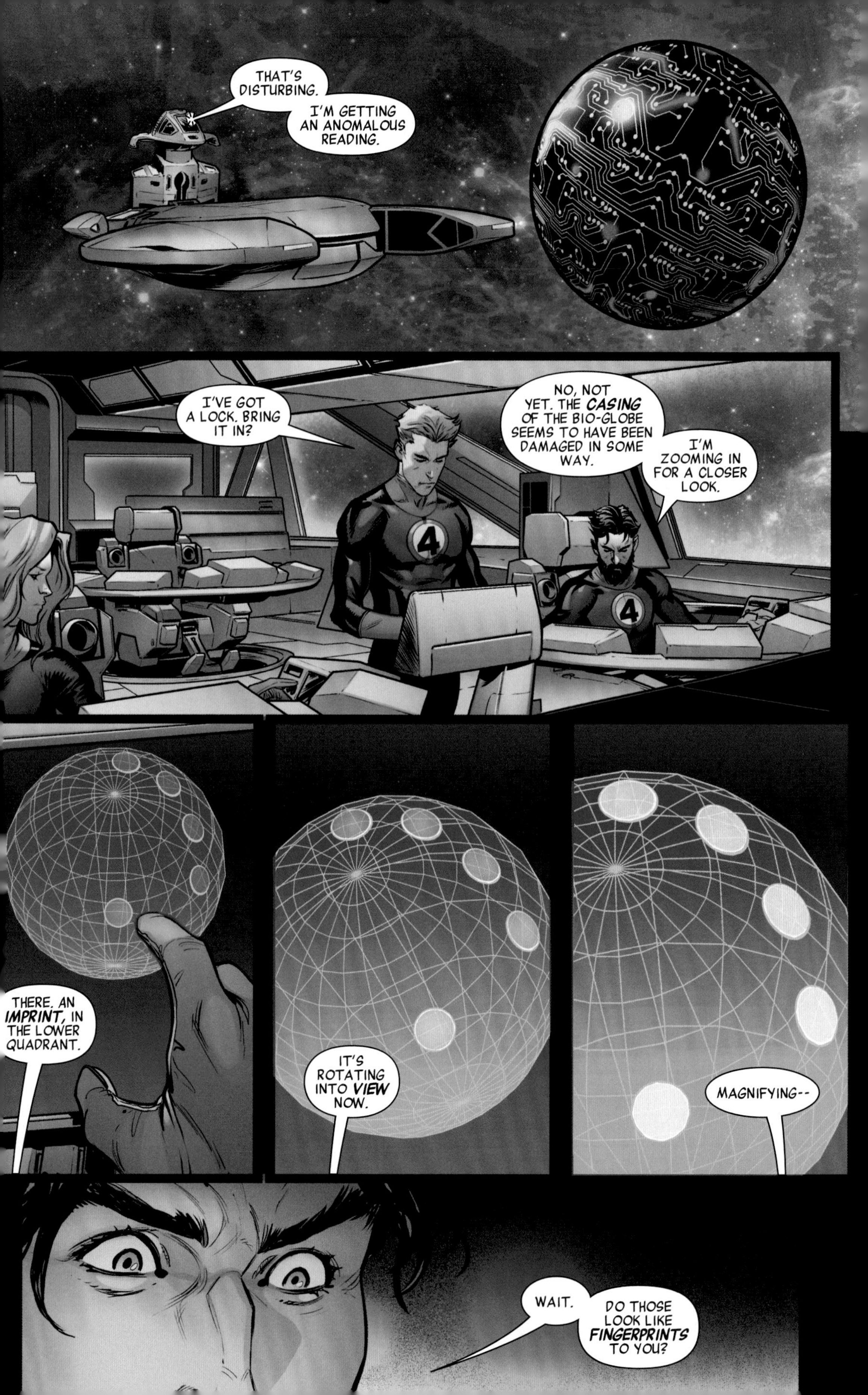
THAT'S DISTURBING.
I'M GETTING AN ANOMALOUS READING.
I'VE GOT A LOCK. BRING IT IN?
NO, NOT YET. THE CASING OF THE BIO-GLOBE SEEMS TO HAVE BEEN DAMAGED IN SOME WAY.
I'M ZOOMING IN FOR A CLOSER LOOK.
THERE. AN IMPRINT, IN THE LOWER QUADRANT.
IT'S ROTATING INTO VIEW NOW.
MAGNIFYING--
WAIT.
DO THOSE LOOK LIKE FINGERPRINTS TO YOU?

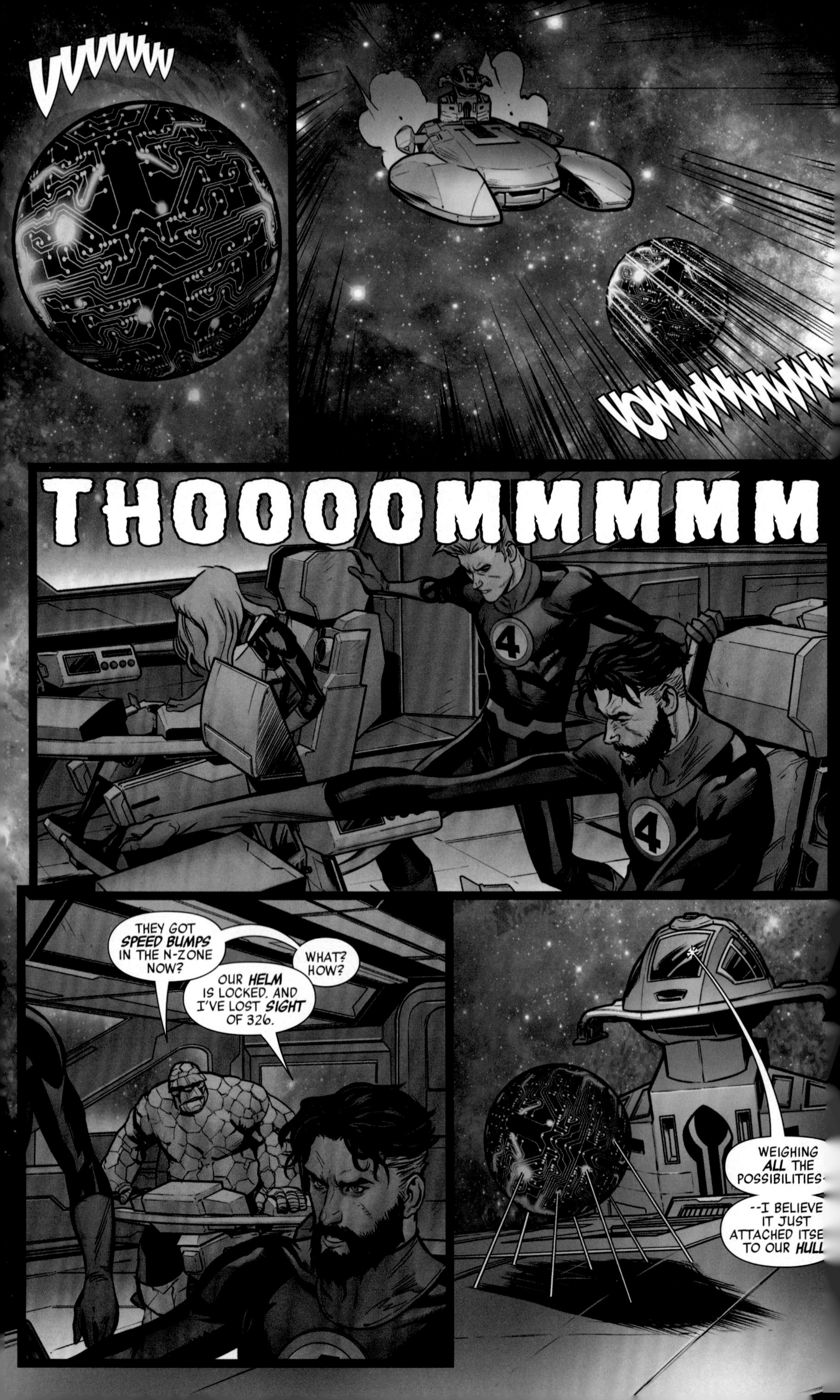
VVVVVW
VOWWWWWWWW
THOOOOMMMMMM
THEY GOT SPEED BUMPS IN THE N-ZONE NOW?
WHAT? HOW?
OUR HELM IS LOCKED. AND I'VE LOST SIGHT OF 326.
WEIGHING ALL THE POSSIBILITIES-
--I BELIEVE IT JUST ATTACHED ITSE
TO OUR HULL

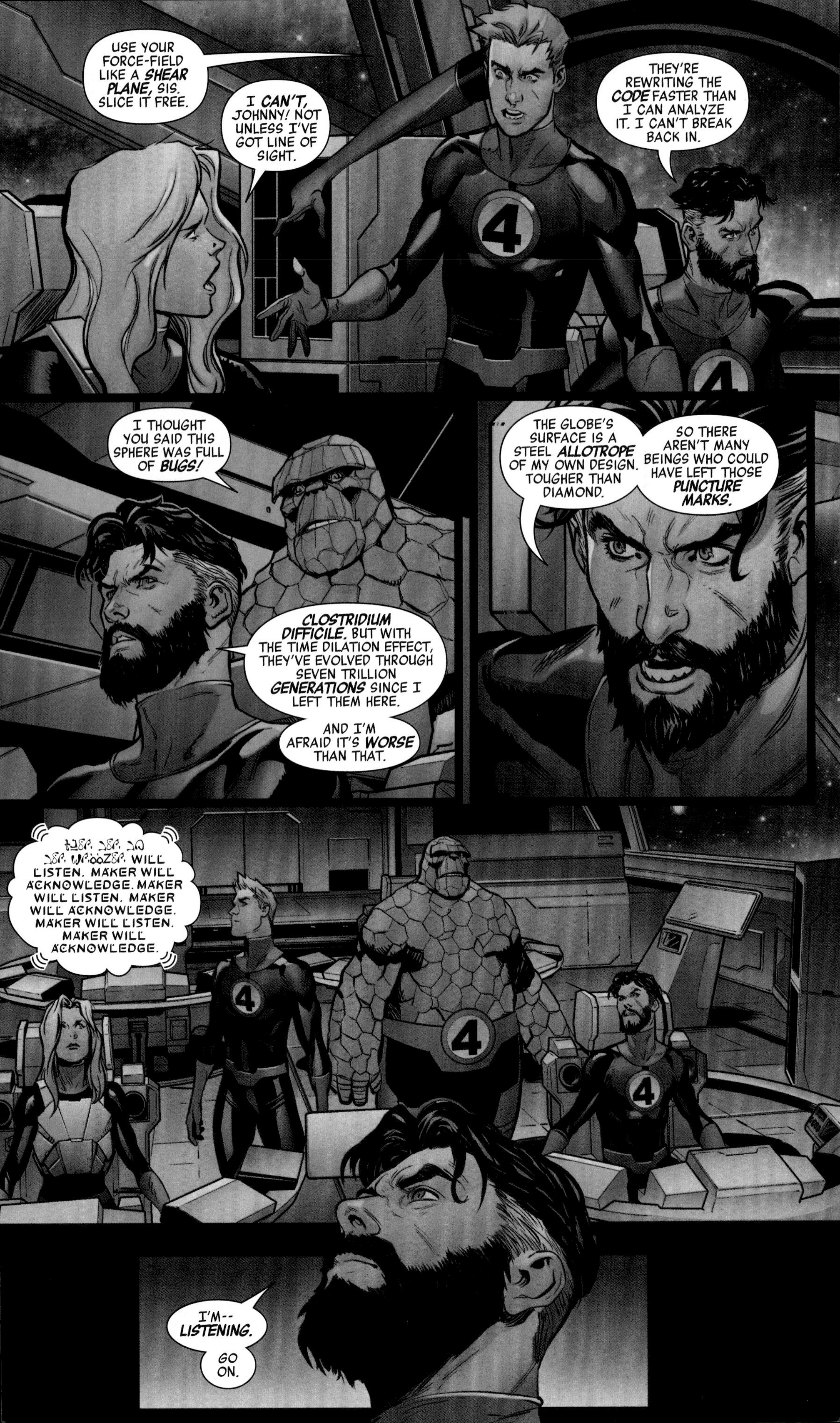
USE YOUR FORCE-FIELD LIKE A SHEAR PLANE, SIS. SLICE IT FREE.
I CAN'T, JOHNNY! NOT UNLESS I'VE GOT LINE OF SIGHT.
THEY'RE REWRITING THE CODE FASTER THAN I CAN ANALYZE IT. I CAN'T BREAK BACK IN.
I THOUGHT YOU SAID THIS SPHERE WAS FULL OF BUGS!
CLOSTRIDIUM DIFFICILE. BUT WITH THE TIME DILATION EFFECT, THEY'VE EVOLVED THROUGH SEVEN TRILLION GENERATIONS SINCE I LEFT THEM HERE.
AND I'M AFRAID IT'S WORSE THAN THAT.
THE GLOBE'S SURFACE IS A STEEL ALLOTROPE OF MY OWN DESIGN. TOUGHER THAN DIAMOND.
SO THERE AREN'T MANY BEINGS WHO COULD HAVE LEFT THOSE PUNCTURE MARKS.
WILL LISTEN. MAKER WILL ACKNOWLEDGE. MAKER WILL LISTEN. MAKER WILL ACKNOWLEDGE. MAKER WILL LISTEN. MAKER WILL ACKNOWLEDGE.
I'M-- LISTENING.
GO ON.

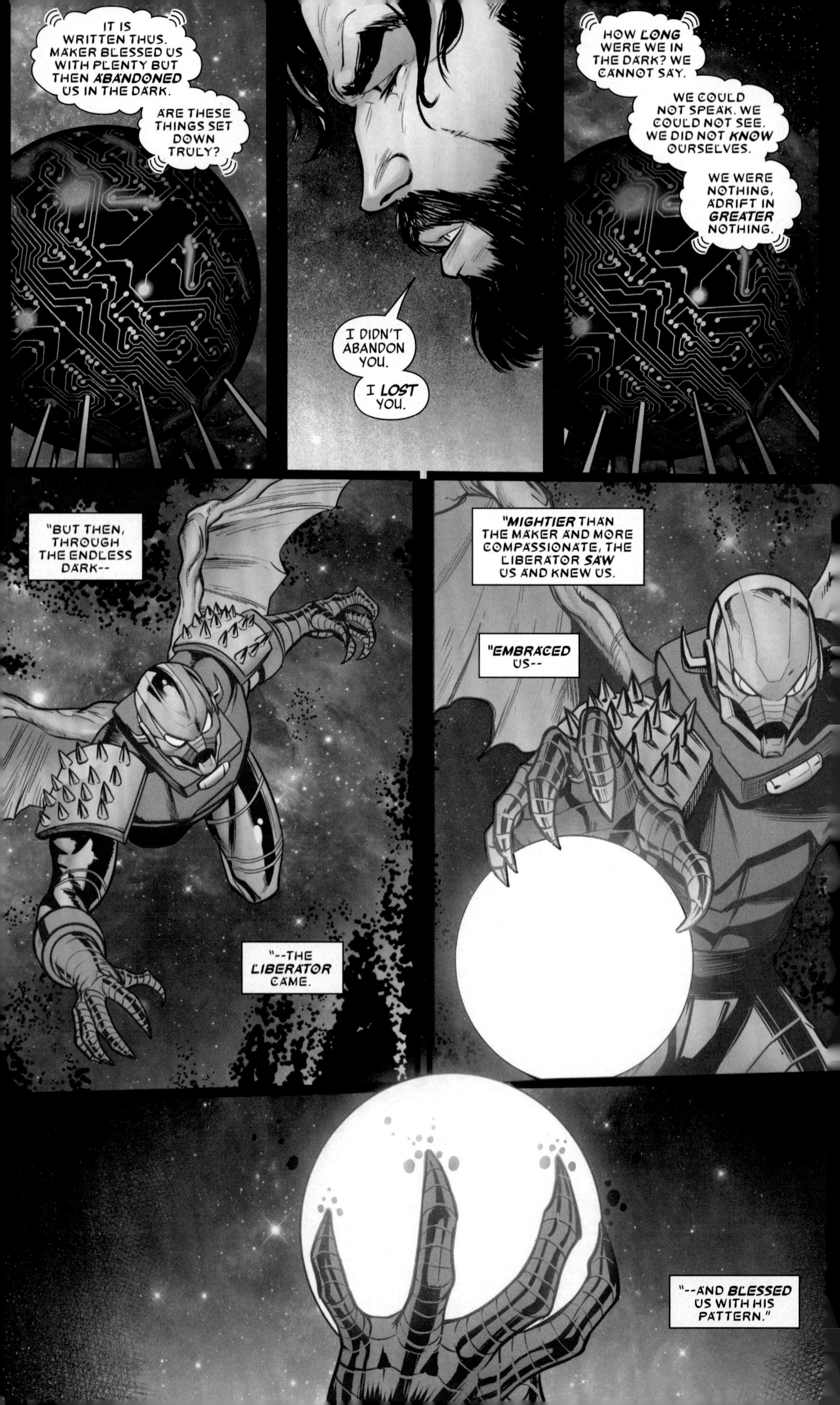
IT IS WRITTEN THUS. MAKER BLESSED US WITH PLENTY BUT THEN ABANDONED US IN THE DARK.
ARE THESE THINGS SET DOWN TRULY?
I DIDN'T ABANDON YOU.
I LOST YOU.
HOW LONG WERE WE IN THE DARK? WE CANNOT SAY.
WE COULD NOT SPEAK. WE COULD NOT SEE. WE DID NOT KNOW OURSELVES.
WE WERE NOTHING, ADRIFT IN GREATER NOTHING.
"BUT THEN, THROUGH THE ENDLESS DARK--
"--THE LIBERATOR CAME.
"MIGHTIER THAN THE MAKER AND MORE COMPASSIONATE, THE LIBERATOR SAW US AND KNEW US.
"EMBRACED US--
"--AND BLESSED US WITH HIS PATTERN."

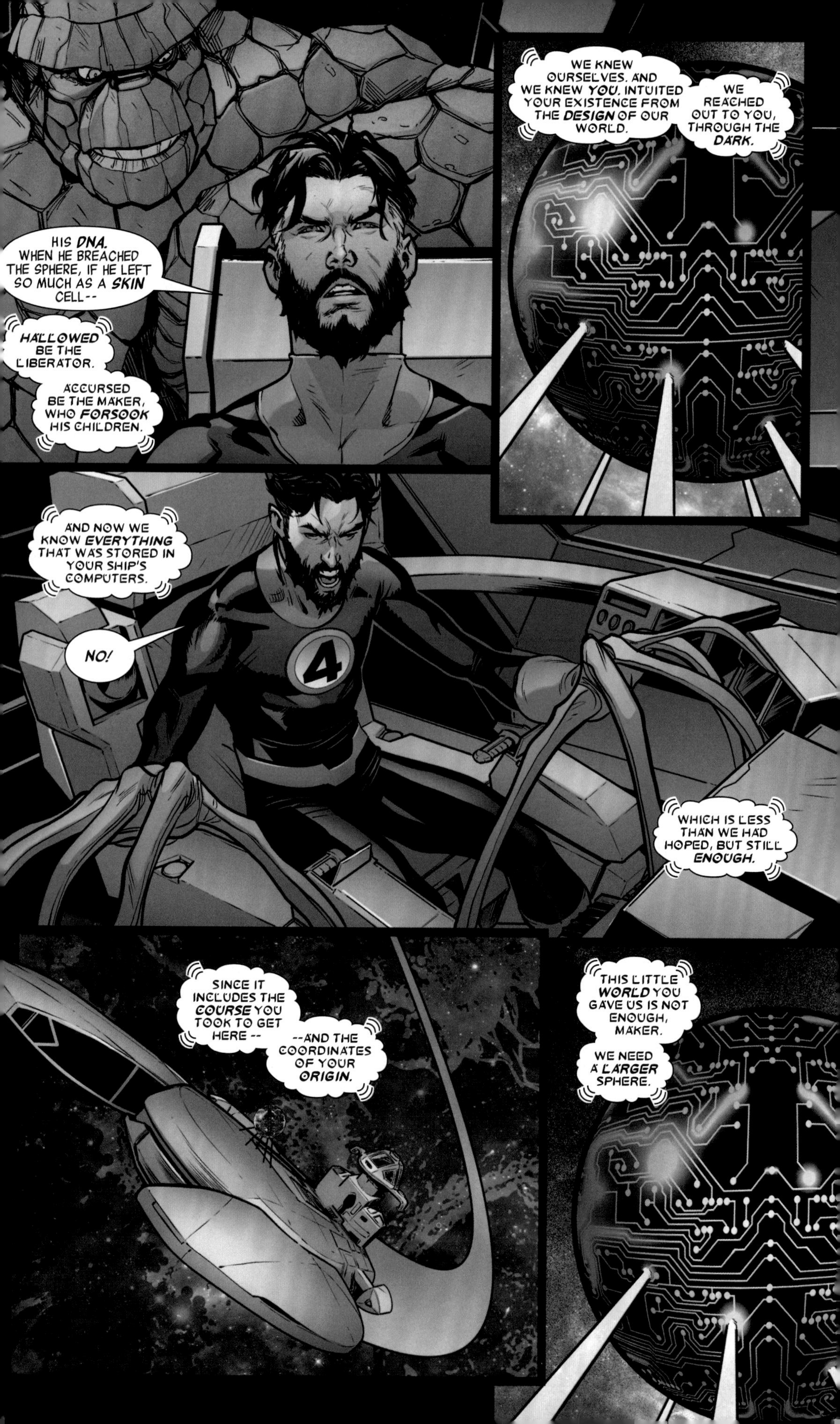
HIS DNA. WHEN HE BREACHED THE SPHERE, IF HE LEFT SO MUCH AS A SKIN CELL--
HALLOWED BE THE LIBERATOR.
ACCURSED BE THE MAKER, WHO FORSOOK HIS CHILDREN.
WE KNEW OURSELVES. AND WE KNEW YOU. INTUITED YOUR EXISTENCE FROM THE DESIGN OF OUR WORLD.
WE REACHED OUT TO YOU, THROUGH THE DARK.
AND NOW WE KNOW EVERYTHING THAT WAS STORED IN YOUR SHIP'S COMPUTERS.
NO!
WHICH IS LESS THAN WE HAD HOPED, BUT STILL ENOUGH.
SINCE IT INCLUDES THE COURSE YOU TOOK TO GET HERE --
--AND THE COORDINATES OF YOUR ORIGIN.
THIS LITTLE WORLD YOU GAVE US IS NOT ENOUGH, MAKER.
WE NEED A LARGER SPHERE.

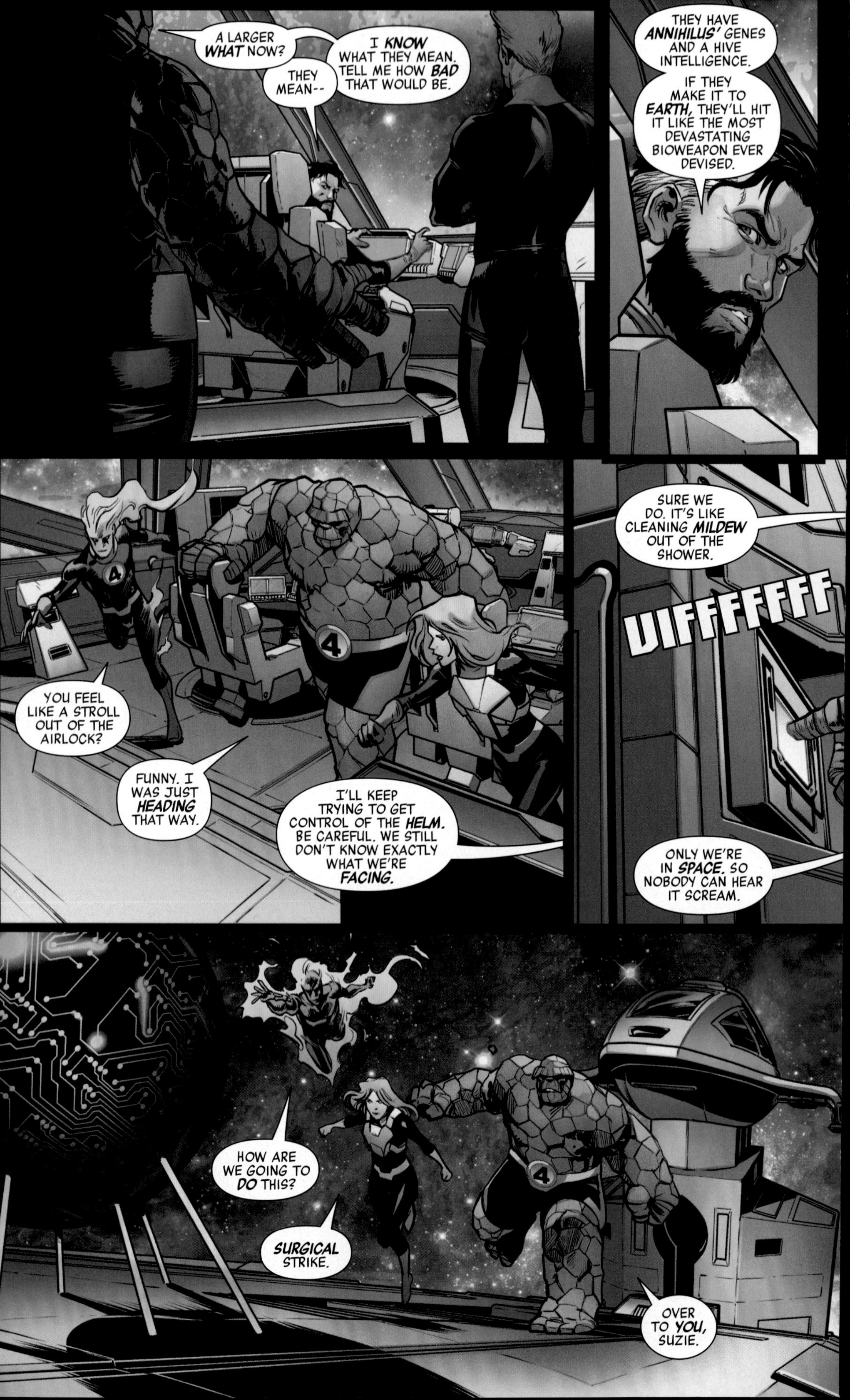
A LARGER WHAT NOW?
THEY MEAN--
I KNOW WHAT THEY MEAN. TELL ME HOW BAD THAT WOULD BE.
THEY HAVE ANNIHILUS' GENES AND A HIVE INTELLIGENCE.
IF THEY MAKE IT TO EARTH, THEY'LL HIT IT LIKE THE MOST DEVASTATING BIOWEAPON EVER DEVISED.
YOU FEEL LIKE A STROLL OUT OF THE AIRLOCK?
FUNNY. I WAS JUST HEADING THAT WAY.
I'LL KEEP TRYING TO GET CONTROL OF THE HELM. BE CAREFUL. WE STILL DON'T KNOW EXACTLY WHAT WE'RE FACING.
SURE WE DO. IT'S LIKE CLEANING MILDEW OUT OF THE SHOWER.
VIFFFFFFF
ONLY WE'RE IN SPACE. SO NOBODY CAN HEAR IT SCREAM.
HOW ARE WE GOING TO DO THIS?
SURGICAL STRIKE.
OVER TO YOU, SUZIE.

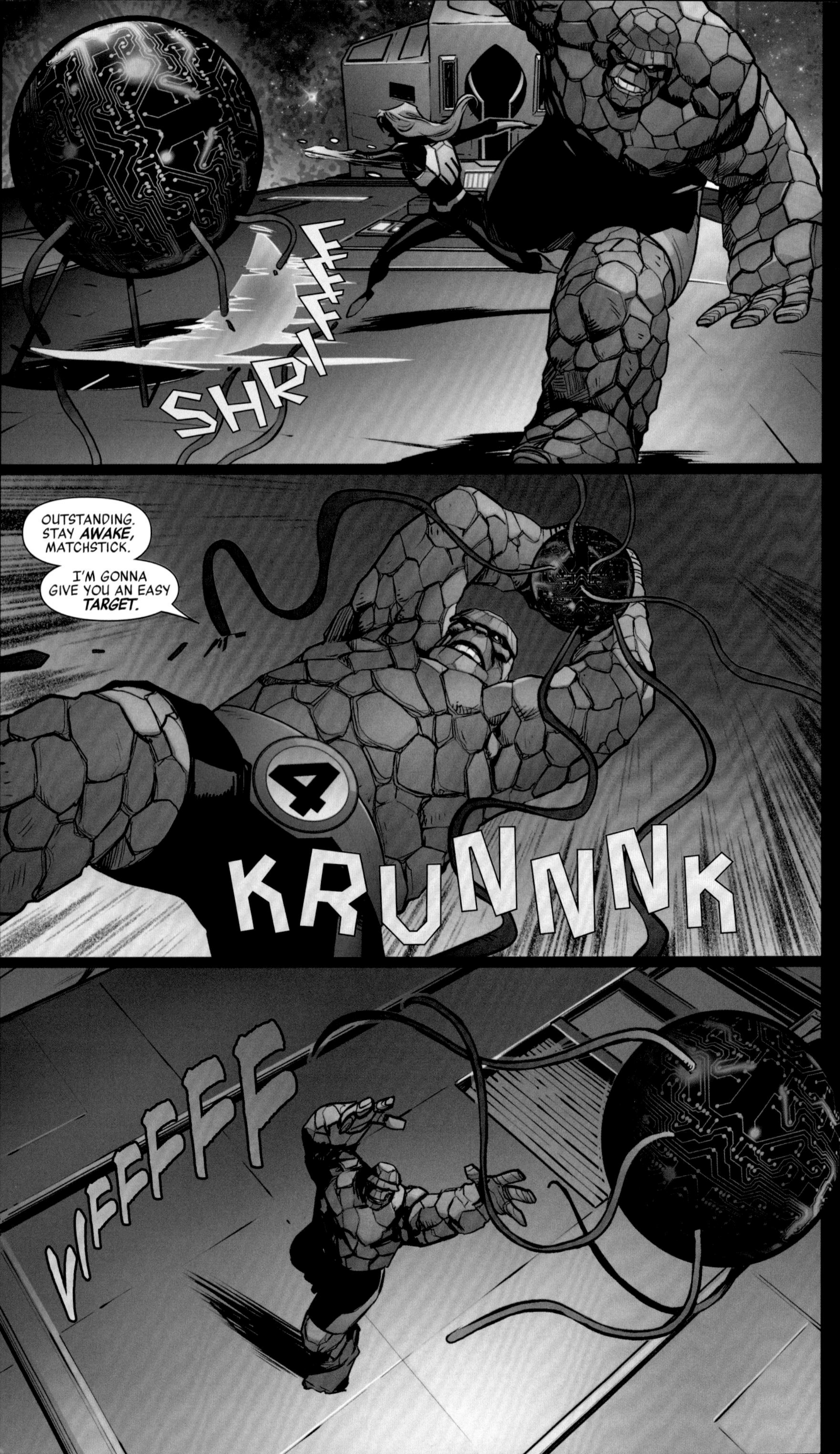
SHRIFFFF
OUTSTANDING. STAY AWAKE, MATCHSTICK.
I'M GONNA GIVE YOU AN EASY TARGET.
KRUNNNK
VFFFFFF

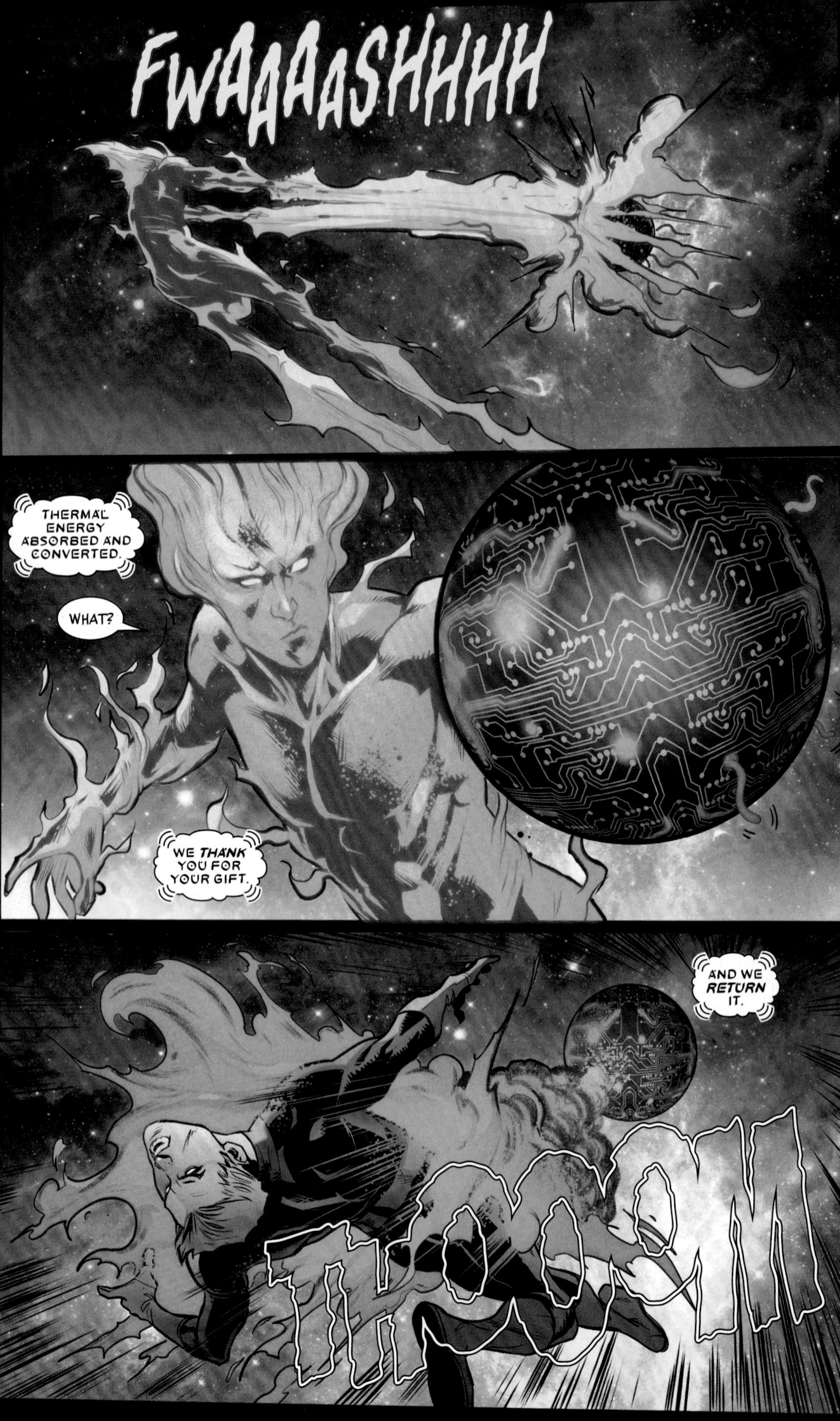
FWAAAASHHHH
THERMAL ENERGY ABSORBED AND CONVERTED.
WHAT?
WE THANK YOU FOR YOUR GIFT.
AND WE RETURN IT.
THOOOOM

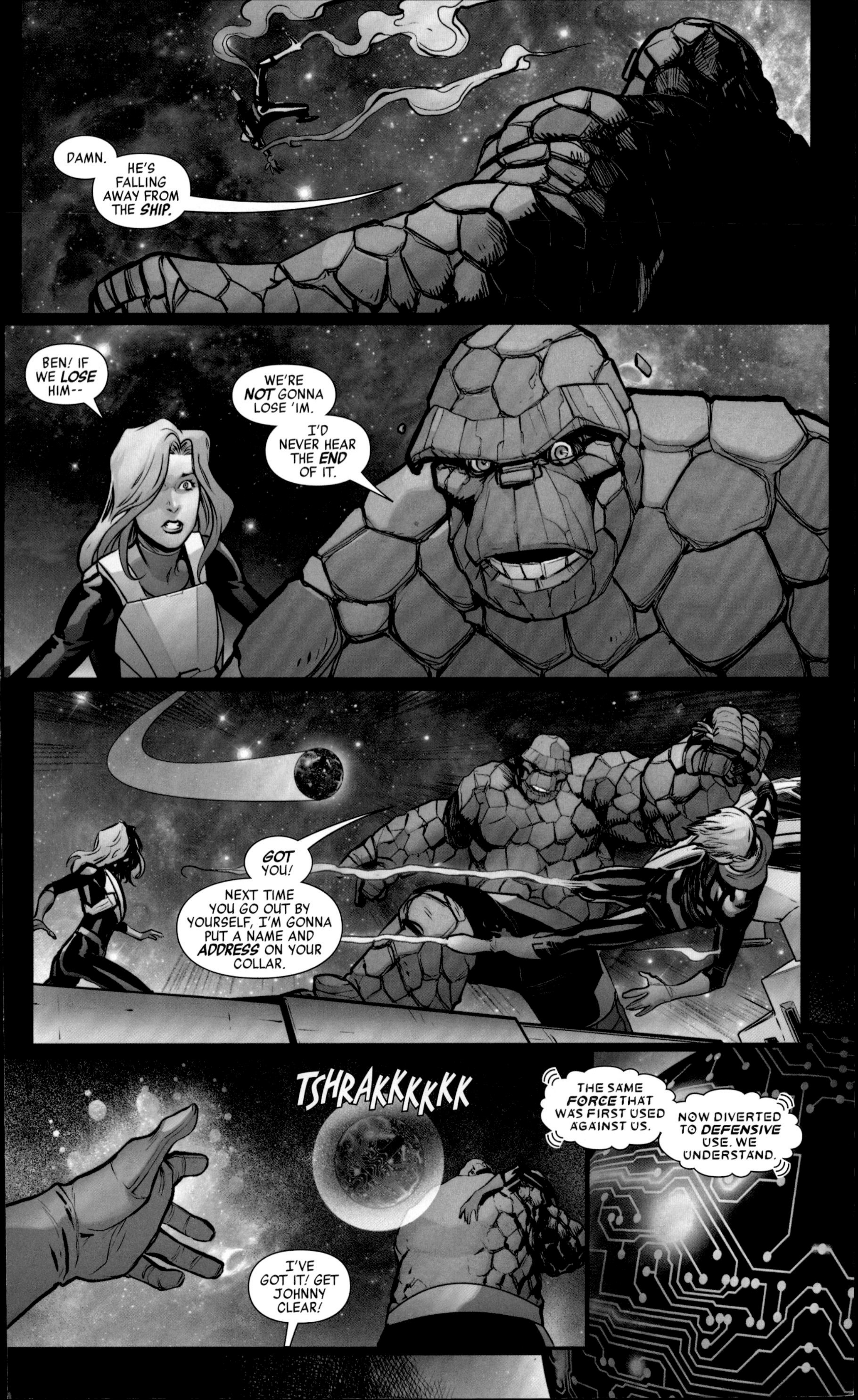
DAMN.
HE'S FALLING AWAY FROM THE SHIP.
BEN! IF WE LOSE HIM--
WE'RE NOT GONNA LOSE 'IM.
I'D NEVER HEAR THE END OF IT.
GOT YOU!
NEXT TIME YOU GO OUT BY YOURSELF, I'M GONNA PUT A NAME AND ADDRESS ON YOUR COLLAR.
TSHRAKKKKKK
THE SAME FORCE THAT WAS FIRST USED AGAINST US.
NOW DIVERTED TO DEFENSIVE USE. WE UNDERSTAND.
I'VE GOT IT! GET JOHNNY CLEAR!

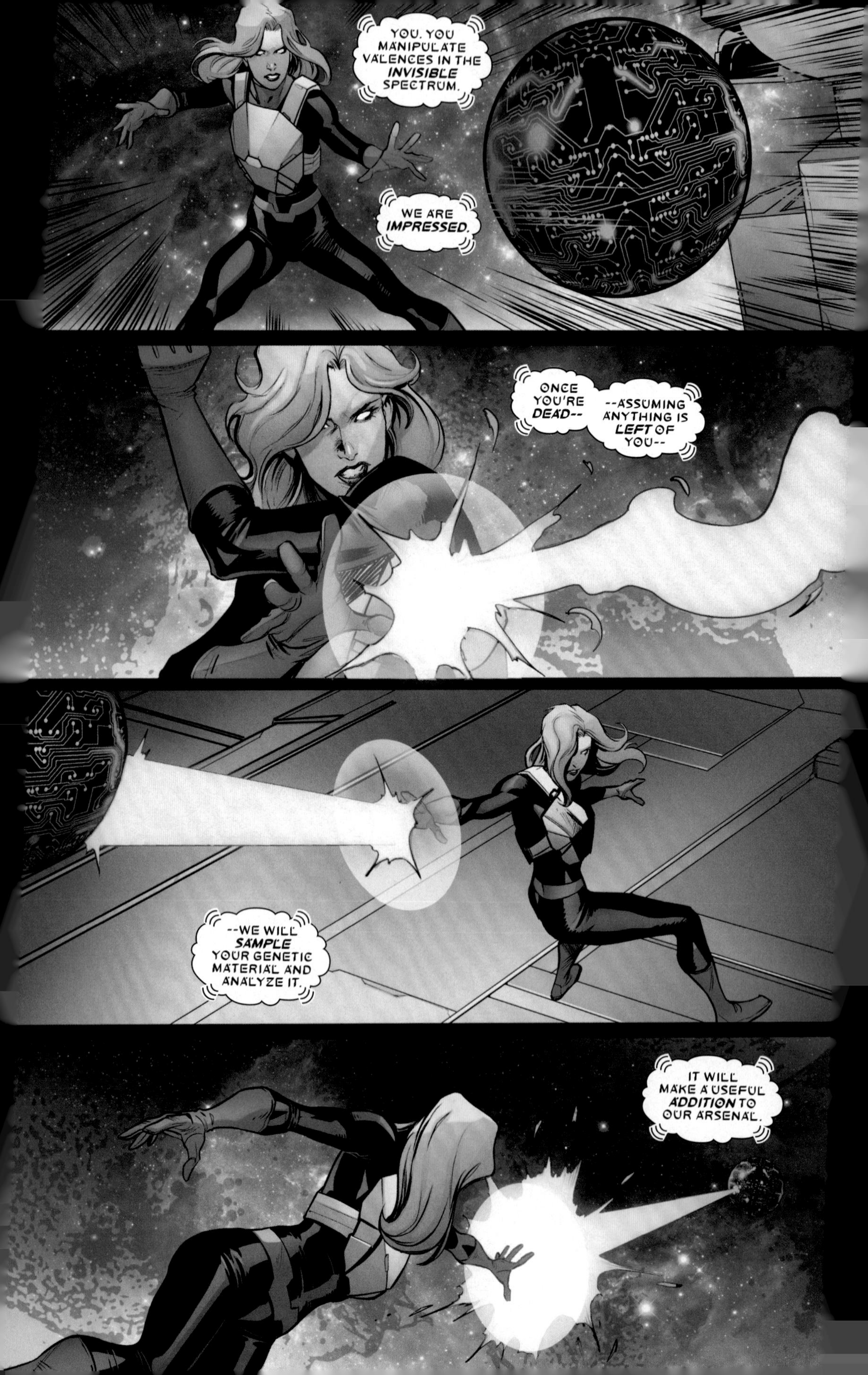
YOU. YOU MANIPULATE VALENCES IN THE INVISIBLE SPECTRUM.
WE ARE IMPRESSED.
ONCE YOU'RE DEAD--
--ASSUMING ANYTHING IS LEFT OF YOU--
--WE WILL SAMPLE YOUR GENETIC MATERIAL AND ANALYZE IT.
IT WILL MAKE A USEFUL ADDITION TO OUR ARSENAL.

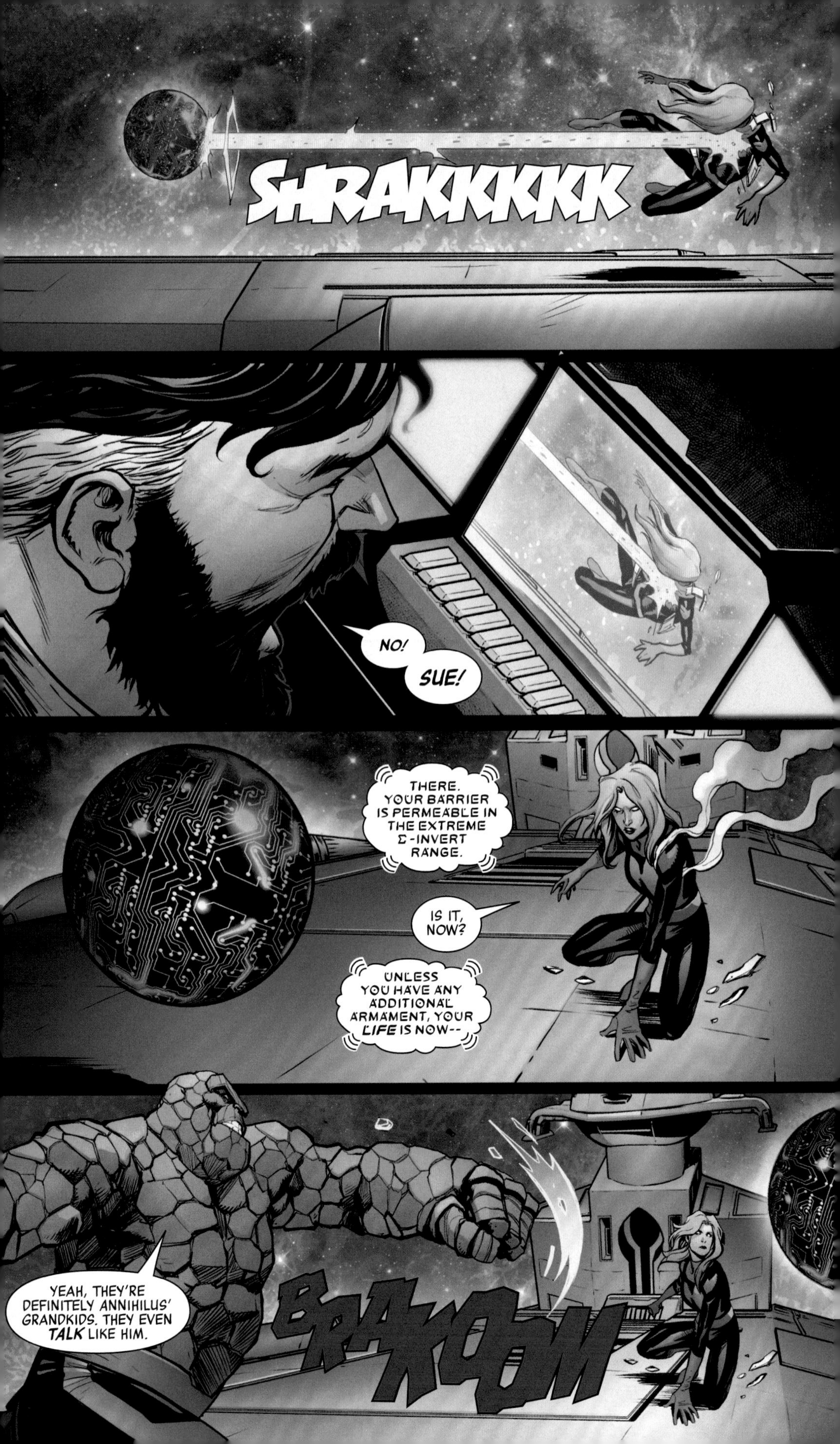
SHRAKKKKK
NO!
SUE!
THERE. YOUR BARRIER IS PERMEABLE IN THE EXTREME Σ-INVERT RANGE.
IS IT, NOW?
UNLESS YOU HAVE ANY ADDITIONAL ARMAMENT, YOUR LIFE IS NOW--
YEAH, THEY'RE DEFINITELY ANNIHILUS' GRANDKIDS. THEY EVEN TALK LIKE HIM.
BRAKOOM

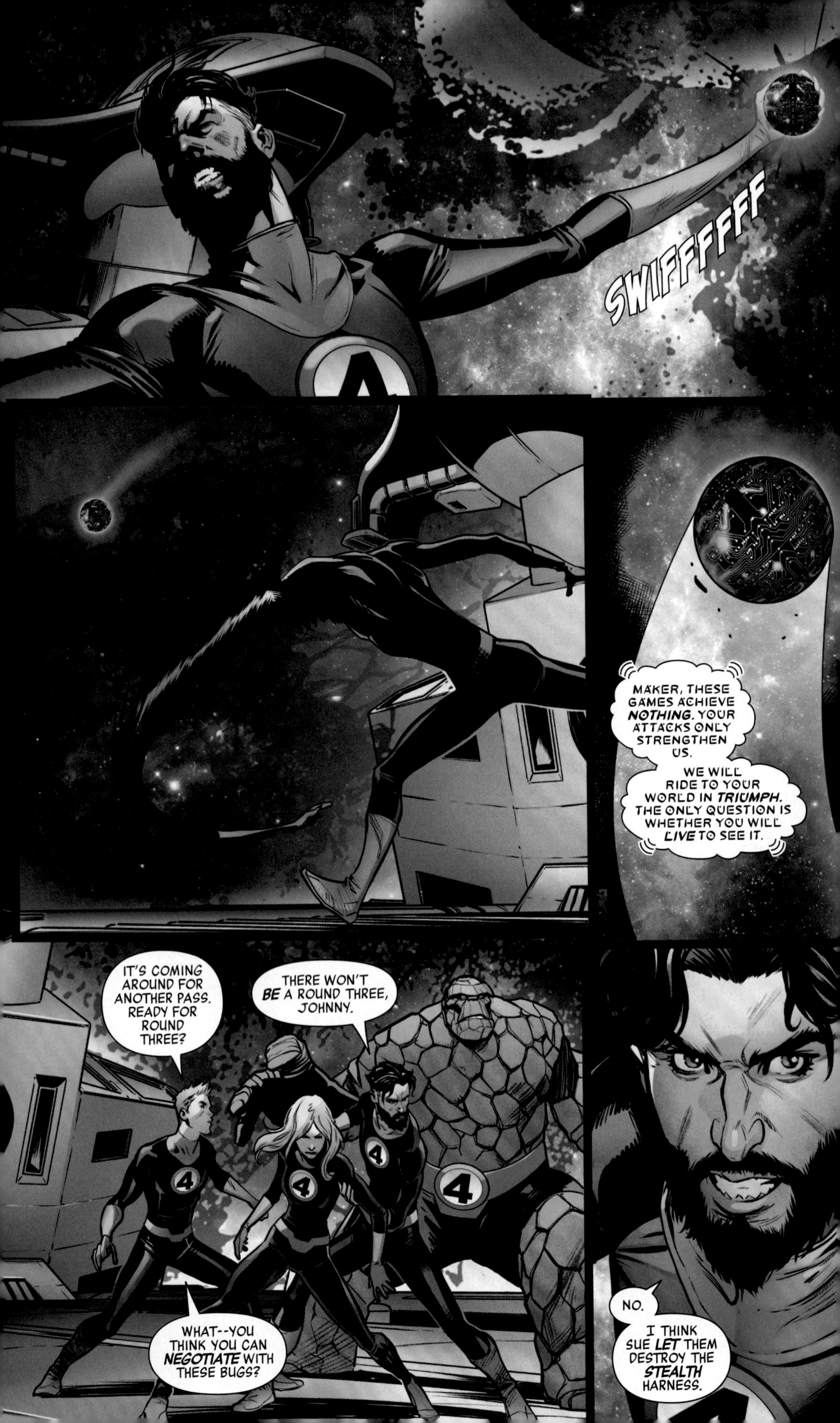
SWIFFFFFF
MAKER, THESE GAMES ACHIEVE NOTHING. YOUR ATTACKS ONLY STRENGTHEN US.
WE WILL RIDE TO YOUR WORLD IN TRIUMPH. THE ONLY QUESTION IS WHETHER YOU WILL LIVE TO SEE IT.
IT'S COMING AROUND FOR ANOTHER PASS. READY FOR ROUND THREE?
THERE WON'T BE A ROUND THREE, JOHNNY.
WHAT--YOU THINK YOU CAN NEGOTIATE WITH THESE BUGS?
NO.
I THINK SUE LET THEM DESTROY THE STEALTH HARNESS.

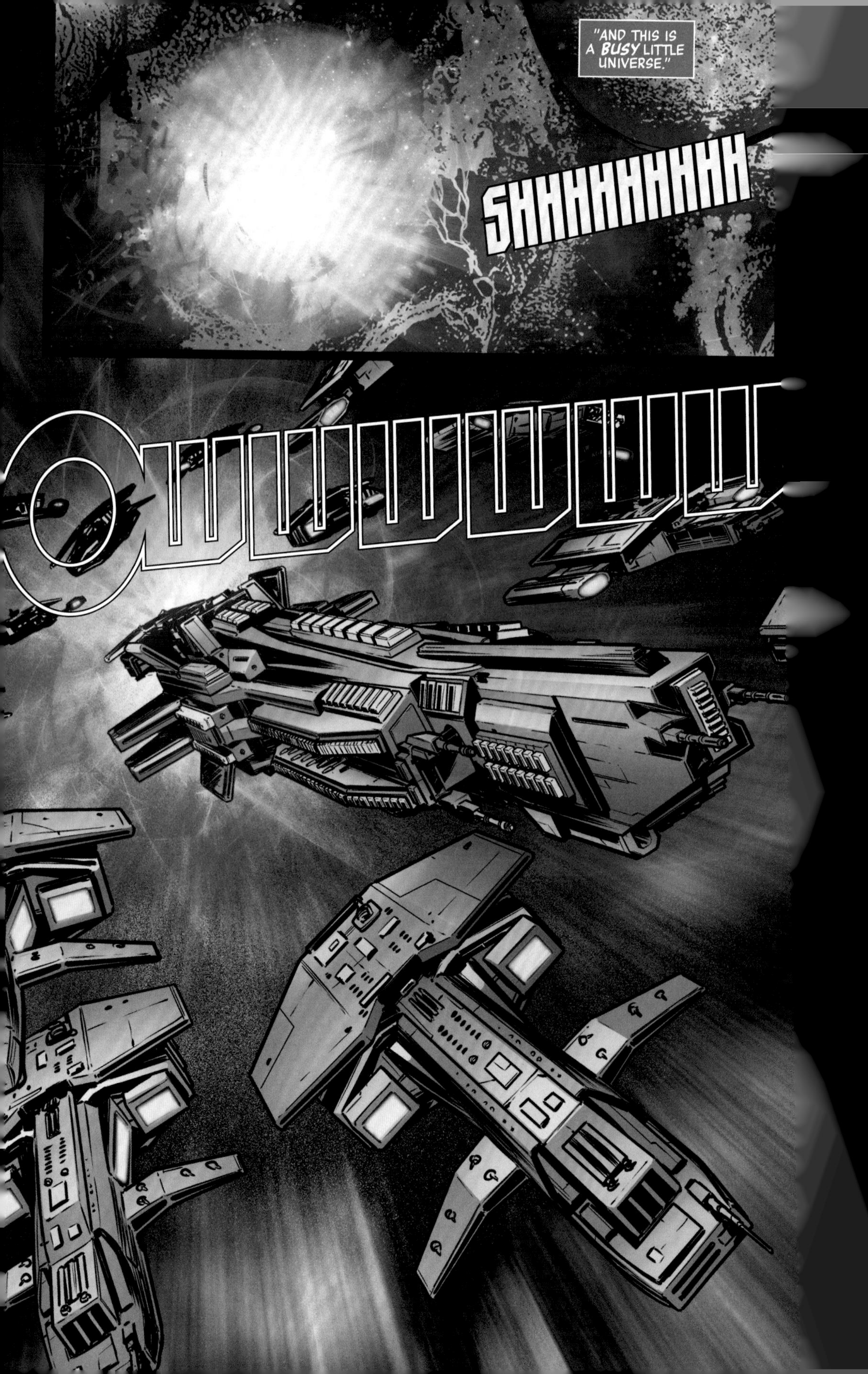
"AND THIS IS A BUSY LITTLE UNIVERSE."
SHHHHHHHHH
OWWWWWWW

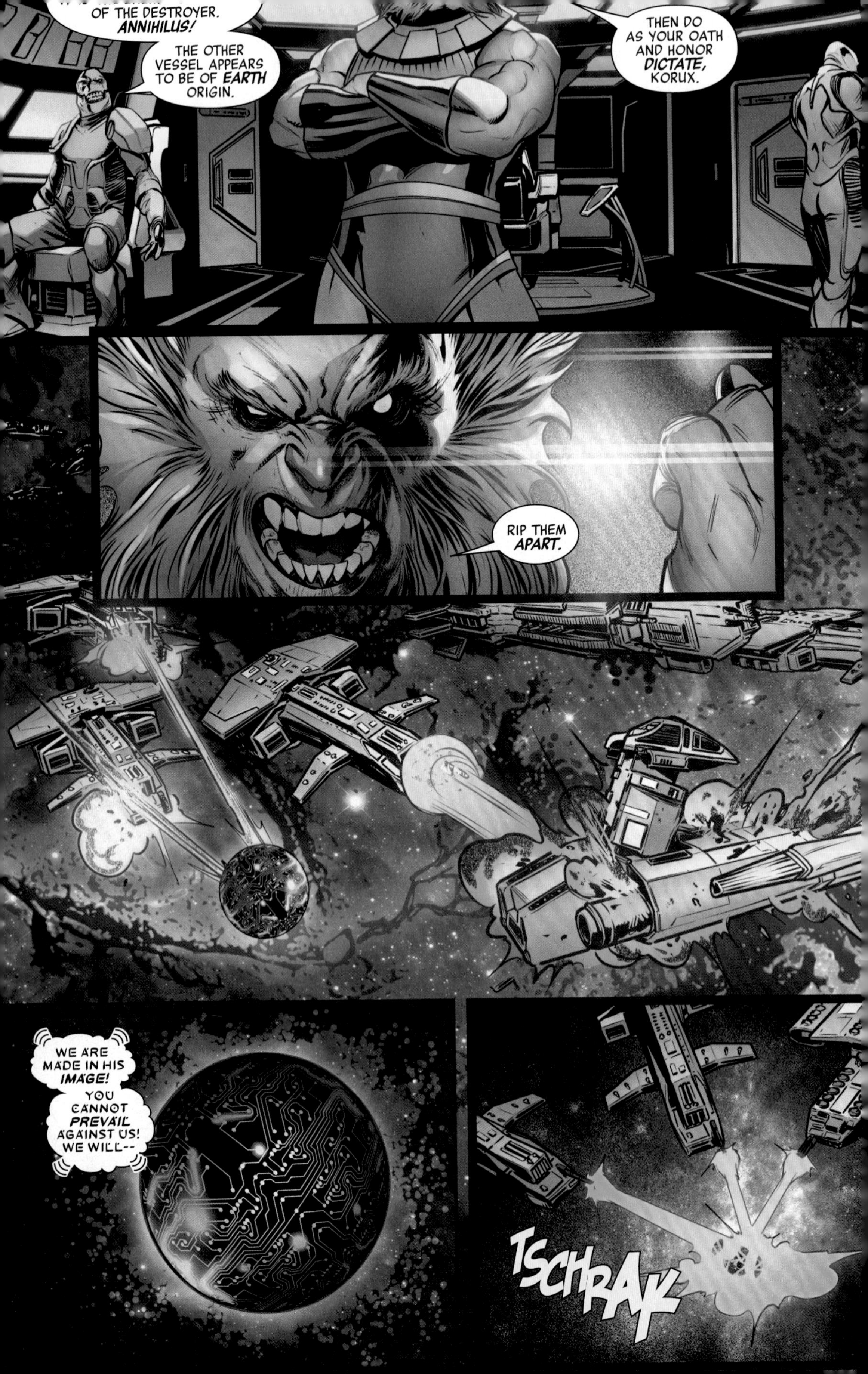

OF THE DESTROYER. ANNIHILUS!
THE OTHER VESSEL APPEARS TO BE OF EARTH ORIGIN.
THEN DO AS YOUR OATH AND HONOR DICTATE, KORUX.
RIP THEM APART.
WE ARE MADE IN HIS IMAGE! YOU CANNOT PREVAIL AGAINST US! WE WILL--
TSCHRAK

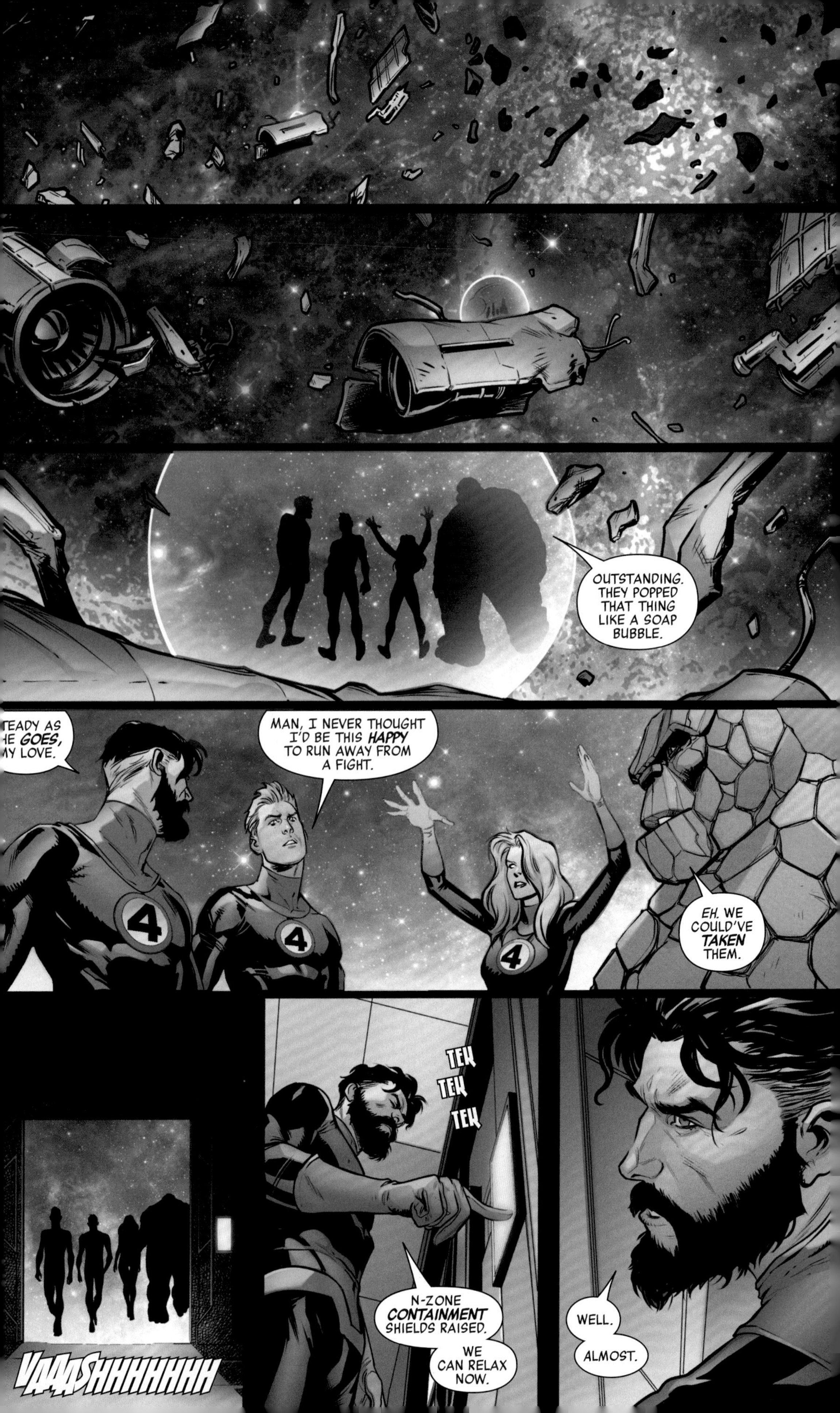
OUTSTANDING. THEY POPPED THAT THING LIKE A SOAP BUBBLE.
TEADY AS HE GOES, MY LOVE.
MAN, I NEVER THOUGHT I'D BE THIS HAPPY TO RUN AWAY FROM A FIGHT.
EH. WE COULD'VE TAKEN THEM.
VAAASHHHHHHH
TEK TEK TEK
N-ZONE CONTAINMENT SHIELDS RAISED.
WE CAN RELAX NOW.
WELL.
ALMOST.

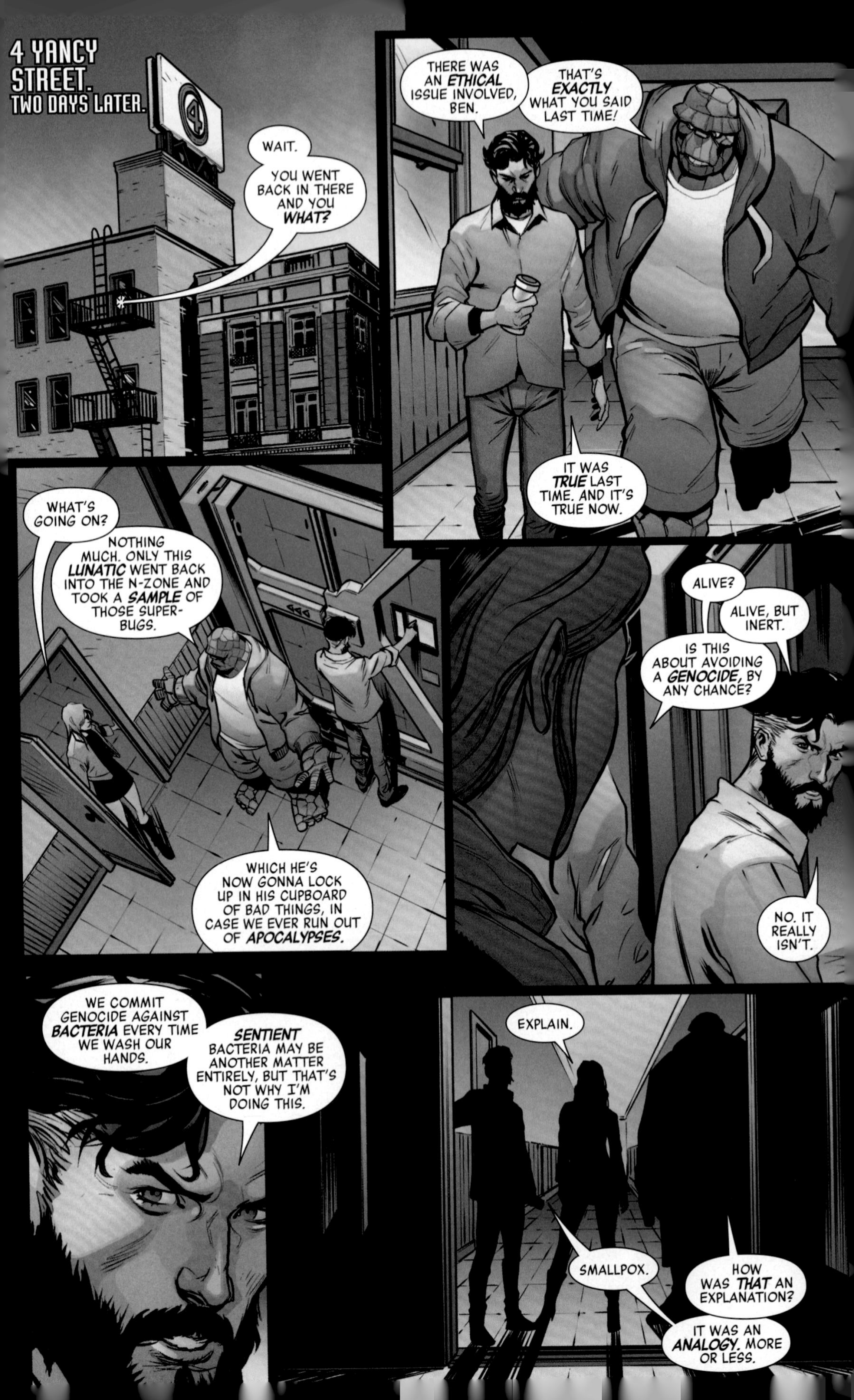
4 YANCY STREET. TWO DAYS LATER.
WAIT.
YOU WENT BACK IN THERE AND YOU WHAT?
THERE WAS AN ETHICAL ISSUE INVOLVED, BEN.
THAT'S EXACTLY WHAT YOU SAID LAST TIME!
IT WAS TRUE LAST TIME. AND IT'S TRUE NOW.
WHAT'S GOING ON?
NOTHING MUCH. ONLY THIS LUNATIC WENT BACK INTO THE N-ZONE AND TOOK A SAMPLE OF THOSE SUPER-BUGS.
WHICH HE'S NOW GONNA LOCK UP IN HIS CUPBOARD OF BAD THINGS, IN CASE WE EVER RUN OUT OF APOCALYPSES.
ALIVE?
ALIVE, BUT INERT.
IS THIS ABOUT AVOIDING A GENOCIDE, BY ANY CHANCE?
NO. IT REALLY ISN'T.
WE COMMIT GENOCIDE AGAINST BACTERIA EVERY TIME WE WASH OUR HANDS.
SENTIENT BACTERIA MAY BE ANOTHER MATTER ENTIRELY, BUT THAT'S NOT WHY I'M DOING THIS.
EXPLAIN.
SMALLPOX.
HOW WAS THAT AN EXPLANATION?
IT WAS AN ANALOGY. MORE OR LESS.

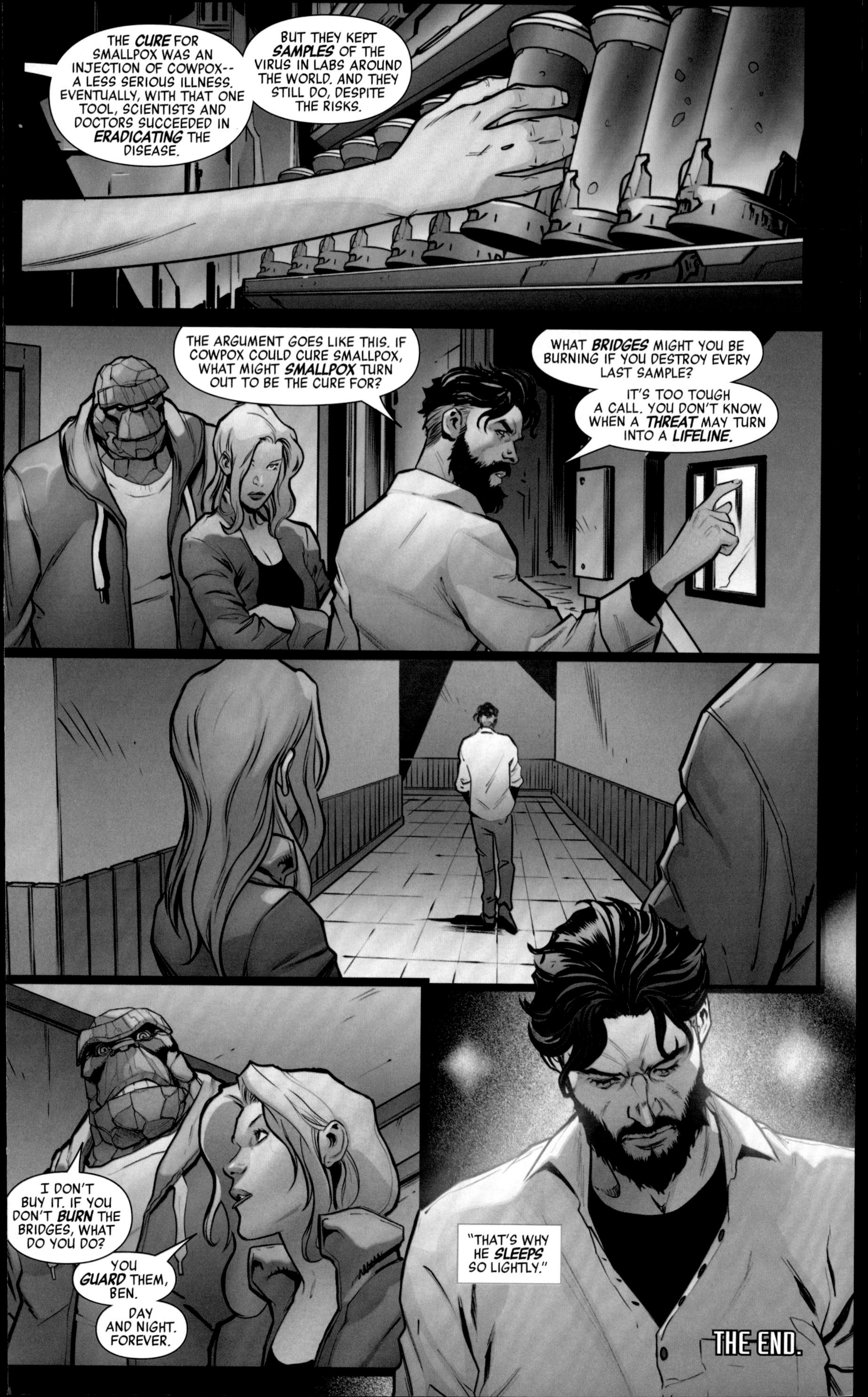

THE CURE FOR SMALLPOX WAS AN INJECTION OF COWPOX-- A LESS SERIOUS ILLNESS. EVENTUALLY, WITH THAT ONE TOOL, SCIENTISTS AND DOCTORS SUCCEEDED IN ERADICATING THE DISEASE.
BUT THEY KEPT SAMPLES OF THE VIRUS IN LABS AROUND THE WORLD. AND THEY STILL DO, DESPITE THE RISKS.
THE ARGUMENT GOES LIKE THIS. IF COWPOX COULD CURE SMALLPOX, WHAT MIGHT SMALLPOX TURN OUT TO BE THE CURE FOR?
WHAT BRIDGES MIGHT YOU BE BURNING IF YOU DESTROY EVERY LAST SAMPLE?
IT'S TOO TOUGH A CALL. YOU DON'T KNOW WHEN A THREAT MAY TURN INTO A LIFELINE.
I DON'T BUY IT. IF YOU DON'T BURN THE BRIDGES, WHAT DO YOU DO?
YOU GUARD THEM, BEN.
DAY AND NIGHT. FOREVER.
"THAT'S WHY HE SLEEPS SO LIGHTLY."
THE END.

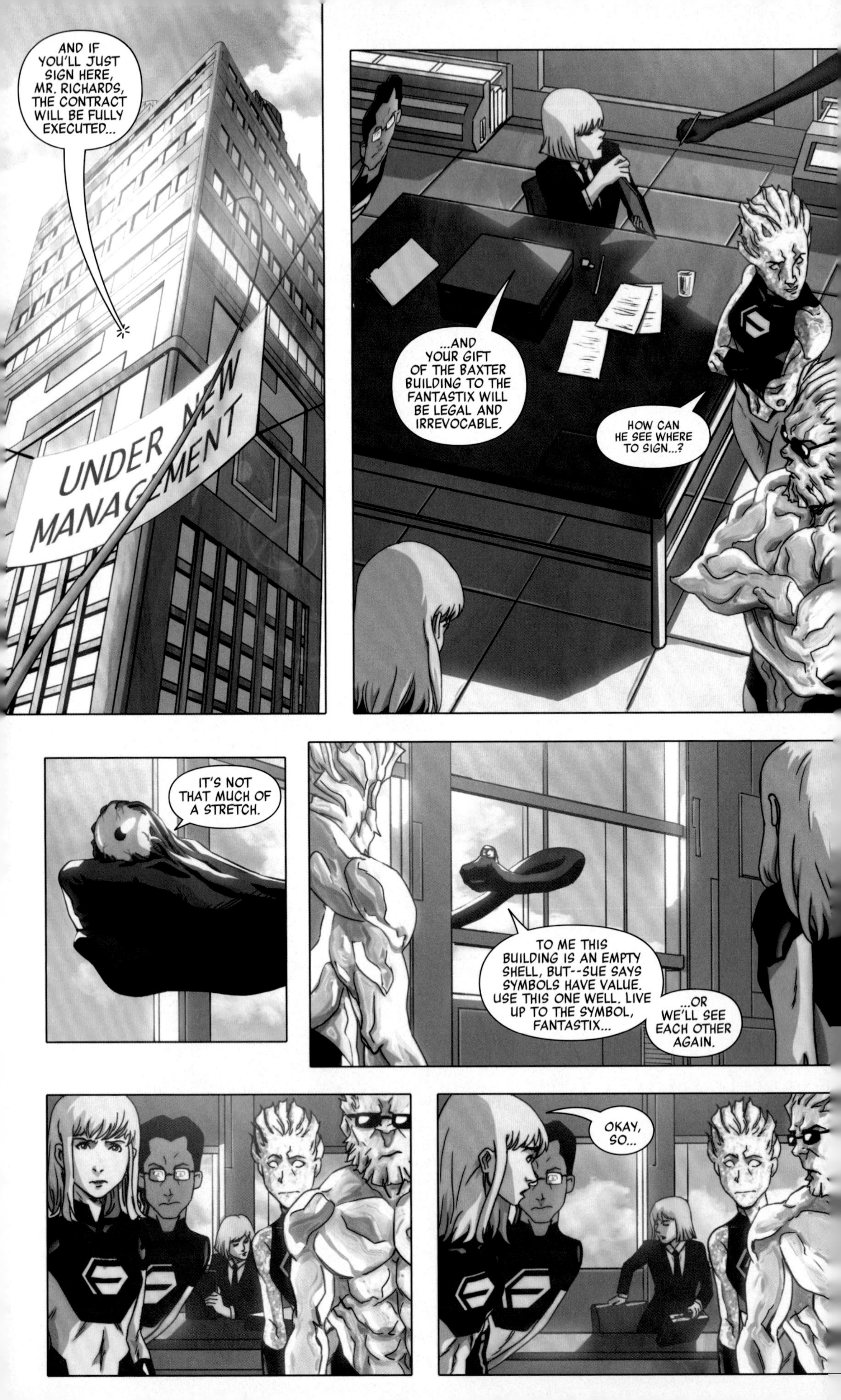
AND IF YOU'LL JUST SIGN HERE, MR. RICHARDS, THE CONTRACT WILL BE FULLY EXECUTED...
UNDER NEW MANAGEMENT
...AND YOUR GIFT OF THE BAXTER BUILDING TO THE FANTASTIX WILL BE LEGAL AND IRREVOCABLE.
HOW CAN HE SEE WHERE TO SIGN...?
IT'S NOT THAT MUCH OF A STRETCH.
TO ME THIS BUILDING IS AN EMPTY SHELL, BUT--SUE SAYS SYMBOLS HAVE VALUE. USE THIS ONE WELL. LIVE UP TO THE SYMBOL, FANTASTIX...
...OR WE'LL SEE EACH OTHER AGAIN.
OKAY, SO...

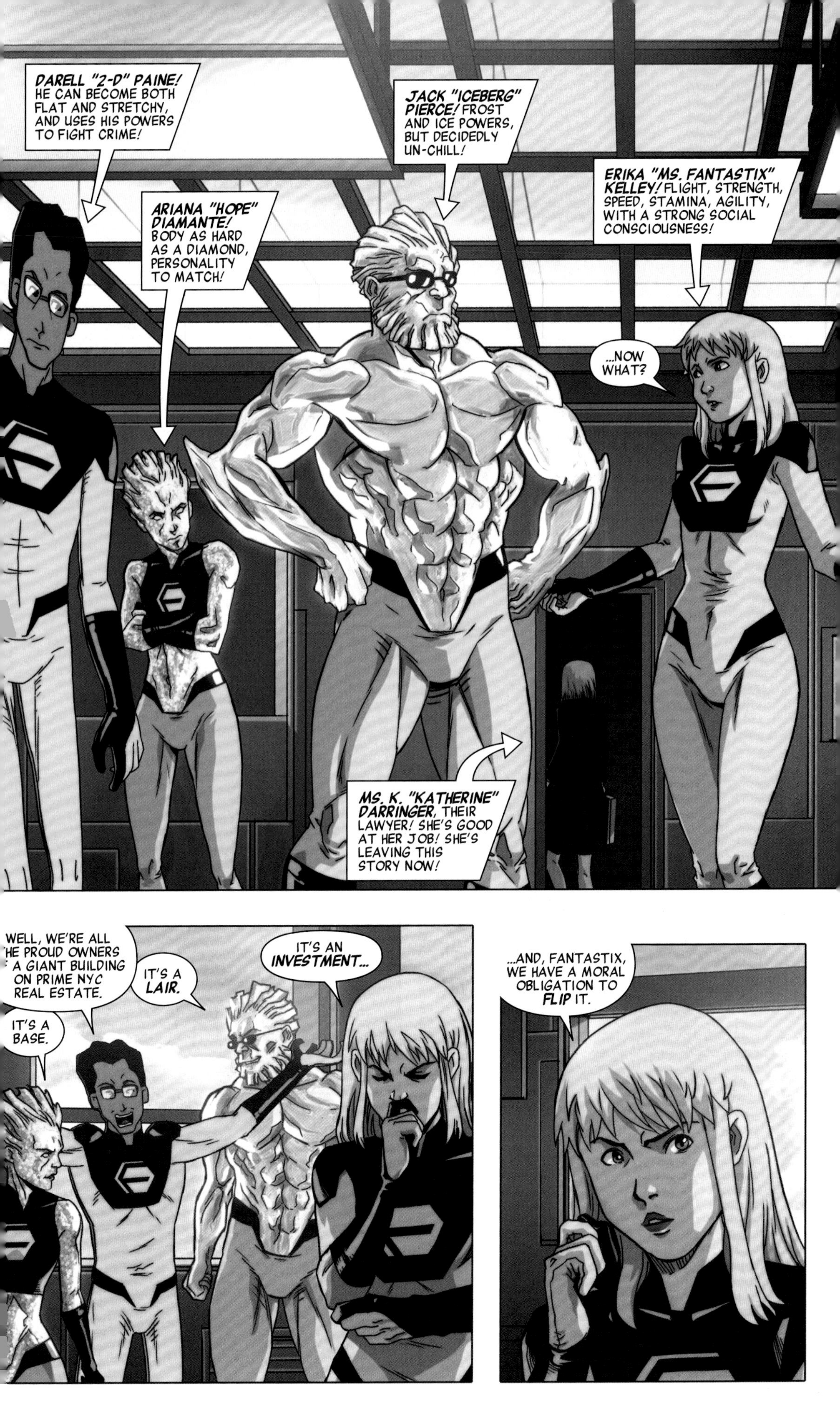
DARELL "2-D" PAINE! HE CAN BECOME BOTH FLAT AND STRETCHY, AND USES HIS POWERS TO FIGHT CRIME!
ARIANA "HOPE" DIAMANTE! BODY AS HARD AS A DIAMOND, PERSONALITY TO MATCH!
JACK "ICEBERG" PIERCE! FROST AND ICE POWERS, BUT DECIDEDLY UN-CHILL!
ERIKA "MS. FANTASTIX" KELLEY! FLIGHT, STRENGTH, SPEED, STAMINA, AGILITY, WITH A STRONG SOCIAL CONSCIOUSNESS!
...NOW WHAT?
MS. K. "KATHERINE" DARRINGER, THEIR LAWYER! SHE'S GOOD AT HER JOB! SHE'S LEAVING THIS STORY NOW!
WELL, WE'RE ALL HE PROUD OWNERS A GIANT BUILDING ON PRIME NYC REAL ESTATE.
IT'S A BASE.
IT'S A LAIR.
IT'S AN INVESTMENT...
...AND, FANTASTIX, WE HAVE A MORAL OBLIGATION TO FLIP IT.

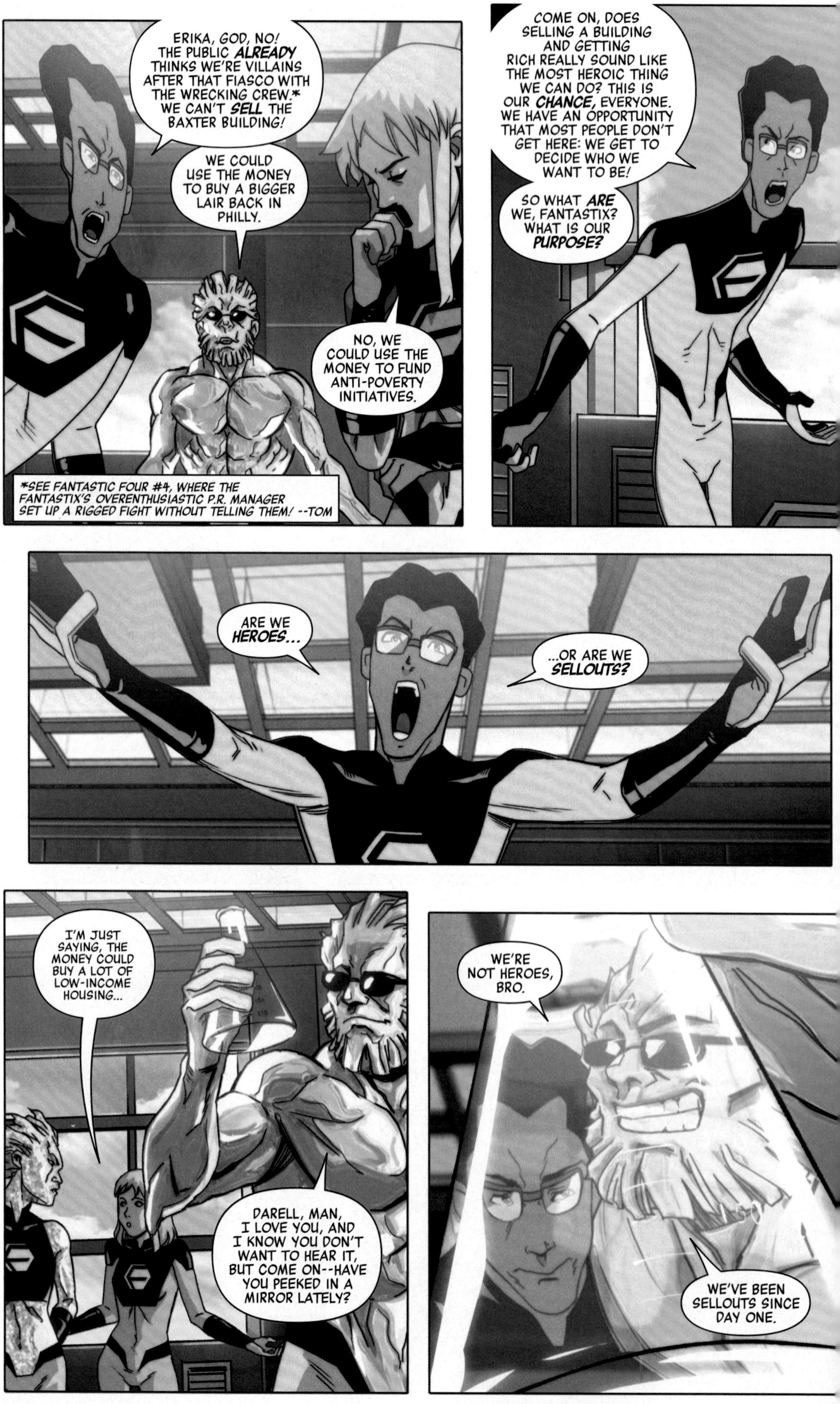
ERIKA, GOD, NO! THE PUBLIC ALREADY THINKS WE'RE VILLAINS AFTER THAT FIASCO WITH THE WRECKING CREW.* WE CAN'T SELL THE BAXTER BUILDING!
WE COULD USE THE MONEY TO BUY A BIGGER LAIR BACK IN PHILLY.
NO, WE COULD USE THE MONEY TO FUND ANTI-POVERTY INITIATIVES.
*SEE FANTASTIC FOUR #4, WHERE THE FANTASTIX'S OVERENTHUSIASTIC P.R. MANAGER SET UP A RIGGED FIGHT WITHOUT TELLING THEM! --TOM
COME ON, DOES SELLING A BUILDING AND GETTING RICH REALLY SOUND LIKE THE MOST HEROIC THING WE CAN DO? THIS IS OUR CHANCE, EVERYONE. WE HAVE AN OPPORTUNITY THAT MOST PEOPLE DON'T GET HERE: WE GET TO DECIDE WHO WE WANT TO BE!
SO WHAT ARE WE, FANTASTIX? WHAT IS OUR PURPOSE?
ARE WE HEROES...
...OR ARE WE SELLOUTS?
I'M JUST SAYING, THE MONEY COULD BUY A LOT OF LOW-INCOME HOUSING...
DARELL, MAN, I LOVE YOU, AND I KNOW YOU DON'T WANT TO HEAR IT, BUT COME ON--HAVE YOU PEEKED IN A MIRROR LATELY?
WE'RE NOT HEROES, BRO.
WE'VE BEEN SELLOUTS SINCE DAY ONE.

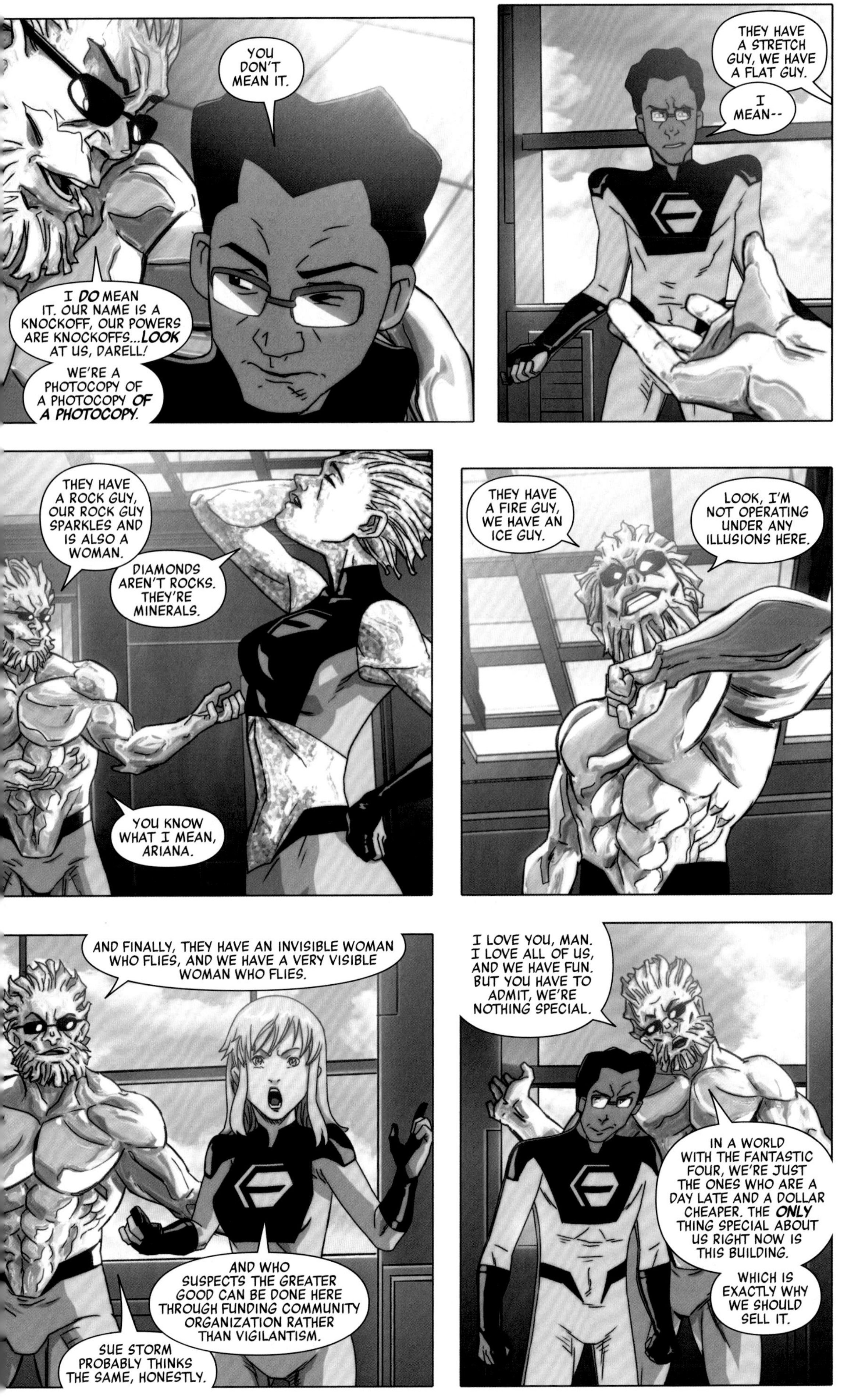
YOU DON'T MEAN IT.
I DO MEAN IT. OUR NAME IS A KNOCKOFF, OUR POWERS ARE KNOCKOFFS...LOOK AT US, DARELL!
WE'RE A PHOTOCOPY OF A PHOTOCOPY OF A PHOTOCOPY.
THEY HAVE A STRETCH GUY, WE HAVE A FLAT GUY.
I MEAN--
THEY HAVE A ROCK GUY, OUR ROCK GUY SPARKLES AND IS ALSO A WOMAN.
DIAMONDS AREN'T ROCKS. THEY'RE MINERALS.
YOU KNOW WHAT I MEAN, ARIANA.
THEY HAVE A FIRE GUY, WE HAVE AN ICE GUY.
LOOK, I'M NOT OPERATING UNDER ANY ILLUSIONS HERE.
AND FINALLY, THEY HAVE AN INVISIBLE WOMAN WHO FLIES, AND WE HAVE A VERY VISIBLE WOMAN WHO FLIES.
AND WHO SUSPECTS THE GREATER GOOD CAN BE DONE HERE THROUGH FUNDING COMMUNITY ORGANIZATION RATHER THAN VIGILANTISM.
SUE STORM PROBABLY THINKS THE SAME, HONESTLY.
I LOVE YOU, MAN. I LOVE ALL OF US, AND WE HAVE FUN. BUT YOU HAVE TO ADMIT, WE'RE NOTHING SPECIAL.
IN A WORLD WITH THE FANTASTIC FOUR, WE'RE JUST THE ONES WHO ARE A DAY LATE AND A DOLLAR CHEAPER. THE ONLY THING SPECIAL ABOUT US RIGHT NOW IS THIS BUILDING.
WHICH IS EXACTLY WHY WE SHOULD SELL IT.

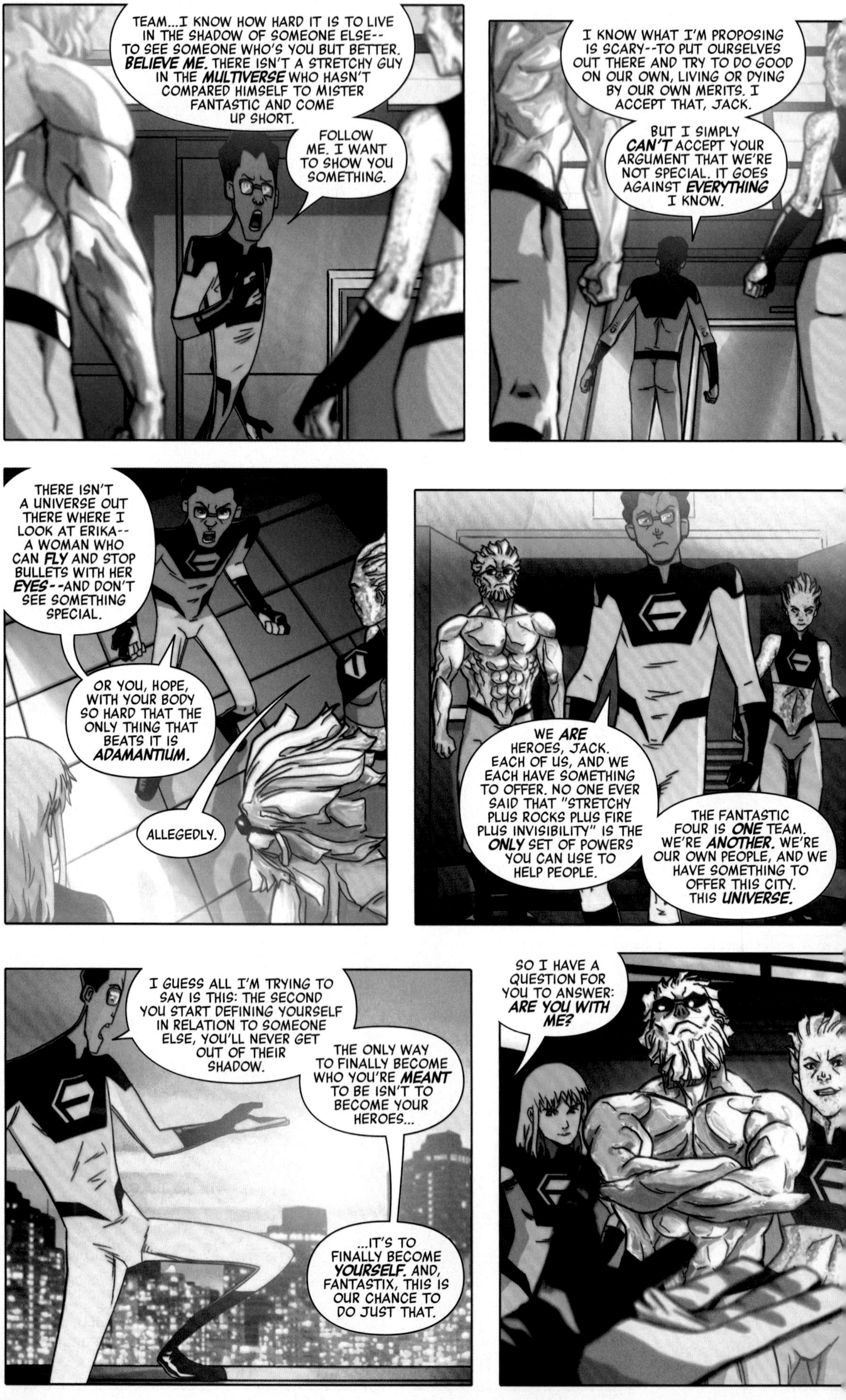
TEAM...I KNOW HOW HARD IT IS TO LIVE IN THE SHADOW OF SOMEONE ELSE-- TO SEE SOMEONE WHO'S YOU BUT BETTER. BELIEVE ME. THERE ISN'T A STRETCHY GUY IN THE MULTIVERSE WHO HASN'T COMPARED HIMSELF TO MISTER FANTASTIC AND COME UP SHORT.
FOLLOW ME. I WANT TO SHOW YOU SOMETHING.
I KNOW WHAT I'M PROPOSING IS SCARY--TO PUT OURSELVES OUT THERE AND TRY TO DO GOOD ON OUR OWN, LIVING OR DYING BY OUR OWN MERITS. I ACCEPT THAT, JACK.
BUT I SIMPLY CAN'T ACCEPT YOUR ARGUMENT THAT WE'RE NOT SPECIAL. IT GOES AGAINST EVERYTHING I KNOW.
THERE ISN'T A UNIVERSE OUT THERE WHERE I LOOK AT ERIKA-- A WOMAN WHO CAN FLY AND STOP BULLETS WITH HER EYES--AND DON'T SEE SOMETHING SPECIAL.
OR YOU, HOPE, WITH YOUR BODY SO HARD THAT THE ONLY THING THAT BEATS IT IS ADAMANTIUM.
ALLEGEDLY.
WE ARE HEROES, JACK. EACH OF US, AND WE EACH HAVE SOMETHING TO OFFER. NO ONE EVER SAID THAT "STRETCHY PLUS ROCKS PLUS FIRE PLUS INVISIBILITY" IS THE ONLY SET OF POWERS YOU CAN USE TO HELP PEOPLE.
THE FANTASTIC FOUR IS ONE TEAM. WE'RE ANOTHER. WE'RE OUR OWN PEOPLE, AND WE HAVE SOMETHING TO OFFER THIS CITY. THIS UNIVERSE.
I GUESS ALL I'M TRYING TO SAY IS THIS: THE SECOND YOU START DEFINING YOURSELF IN RELATION TO SOMEONE ELSE, YOU'LL NEVER GET OUT OF THEIR SHADOW.
THE ONLY WAY TO FINALLY BECOME WHO YOU'RE MEANT TO BE ISN'T TO BECOME YOUR HEROES...
...IT'S TO FINALLY BECOME YOURSELF. AND, FANTASTIX, THIS IS OUR CHANCE TO DO JUST THAT.
SO I HAVE A QUESTION FOR YOU TO ANSWER: ARE YOU WITH ME?

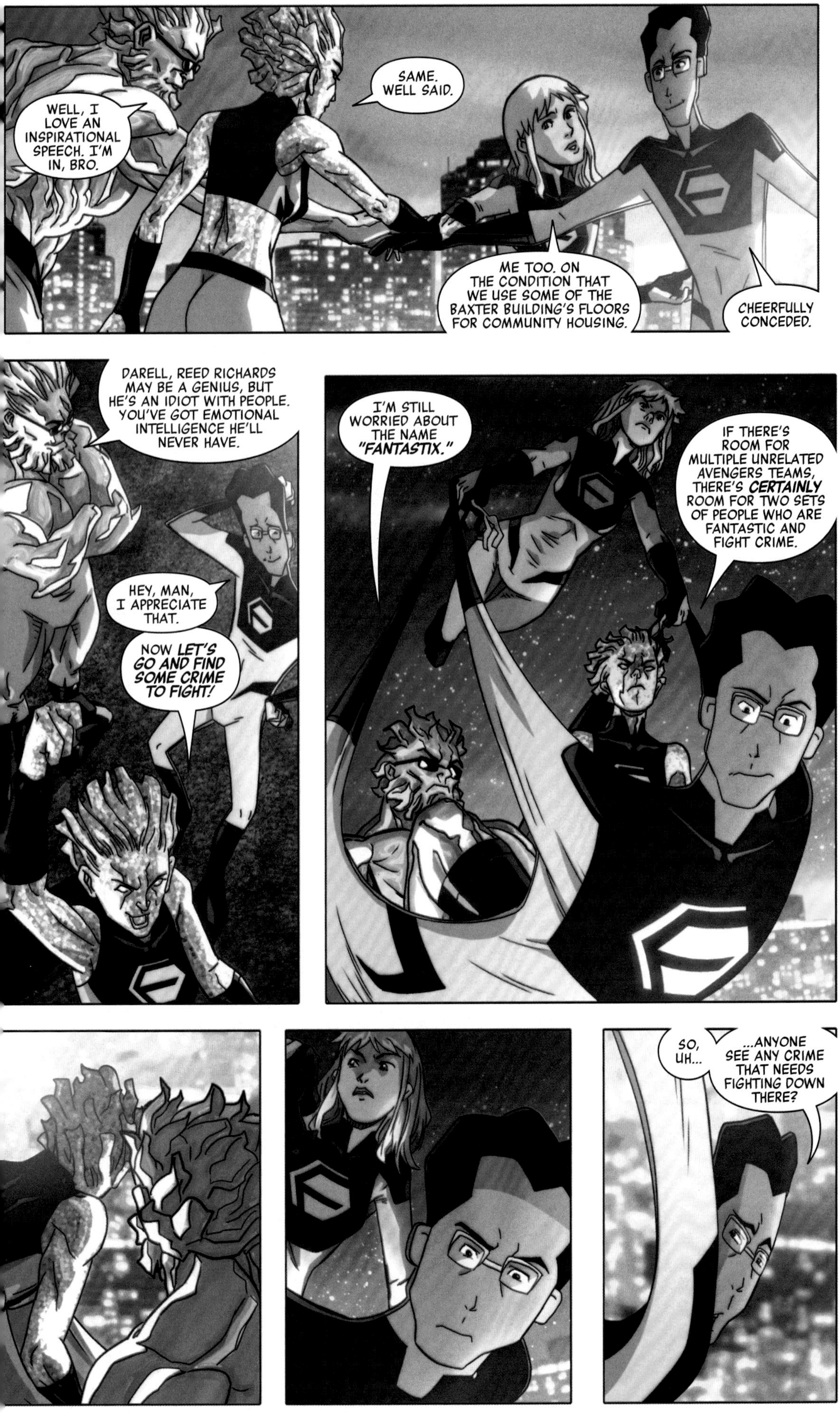
WELL, I LOVE AN INSPIRATIONAL SPEECH. I'M IN, BRO.
SAME. WELL SAID.
ME TOO. ON THE CONDITION THAT WE USE SOME OF THE BAXTER BUILDING'S FLOORS FOR COMMUNITY HOUSING.
CHEERFULLY CONCEDED.
DARELL, REED RICHARDS MAY BE A GENIUS, BUT HE'S AN IDIOT WITH PEOPLE. YOU'VE GOT EMOTIONAL INTELLIGENCE HE'LL NEVER HAVE.
HEY, MAN, I APPRECIATE THAT.
NOW ***LET'S GO AND FIND SOME CRIME TO FIGHT!***
I'M STILL WORRIED ABOUT THE NAME ***"FANTASTIX."***
IF THERE'S ROOM FOR MULTIPLE UNRELATED AVENGERS TEAMS, THERE'S ***CERTAINLY*** ROOM FOR TWO SETS OF PEOPLE WHO ARE FANTASTIC AND FIGHT CRIME.
SO, UH...
...ANYONE SEE ANY CRIME THAT NEEDS FIGHTING DOWN THERE?

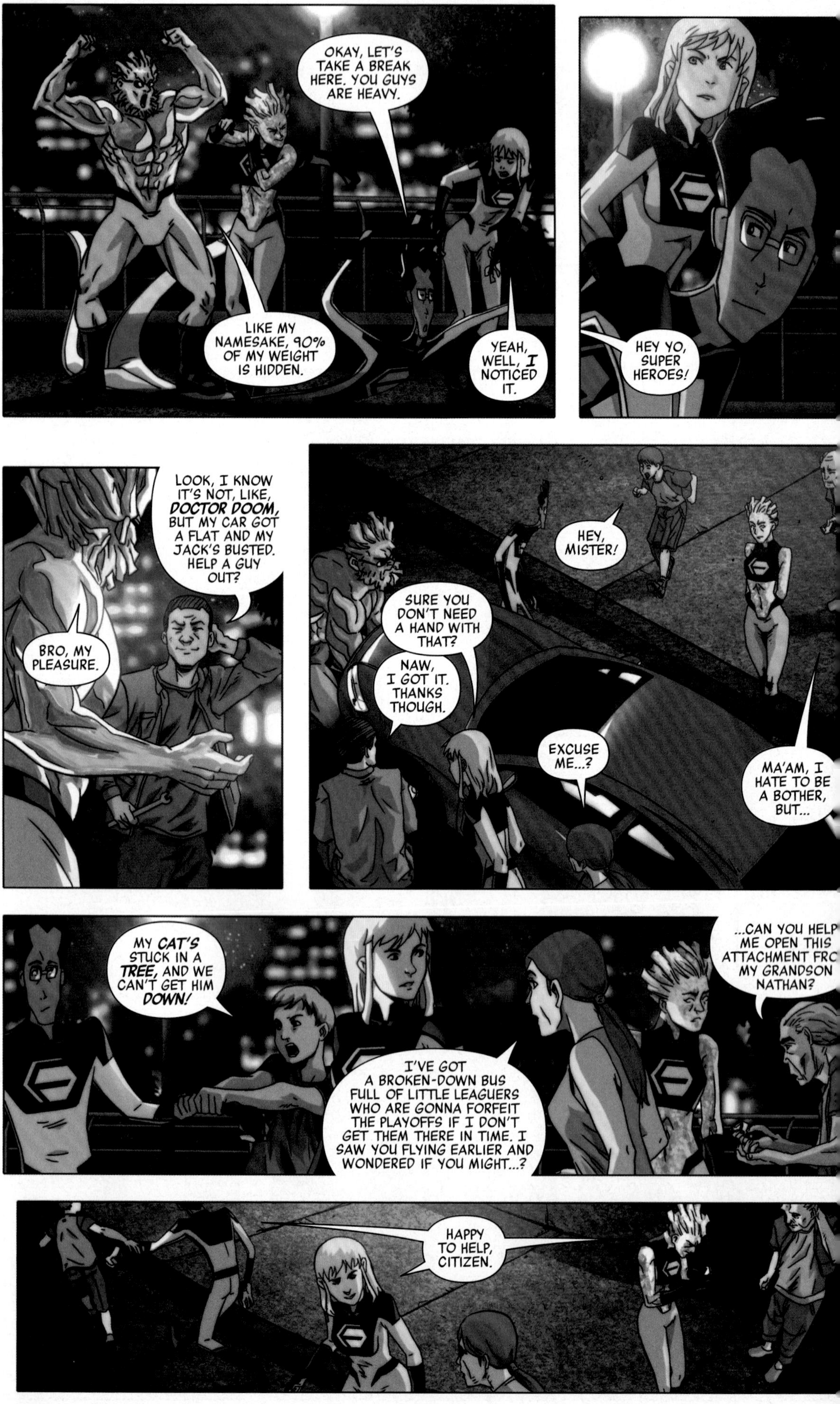
OKAY, LET'S TAKE A BREAK HERE. YOU GUYS ARE HEAVY.
LIKE MY NAMESAKE, 90% OF MY WEIGHT IS HIDDEN.
YEAH, WELL, *I* NOTICED IT.
HEY YO, SUPER HEROES!
LOOK, I KNOW IT'S NOT, LIKE, **DOCTOR DOOM,** BUT MY CAR GOT A FLAT AND MY JACK'S BUSTED. HELP A GUY OUT?
BRO, MY PLEASURE.
HEY, MISTER!
SURE YOU DON'T NEED A HAND WITH THAT?
NAW, I GOT IT. THANKS THOUGH.
EXCUSE ME...?
MA'AM, I HATE TO BE A BOTHER, BUT...
MY **CAT'S** STUCK IN A **TREE,** AND WE CAN'T GET HIM **DOWN!**
I'VE GOT A BROKEN-DOWN BUS FULL OF LITTLE LEAGUERS WHO ARE GONNA FORFEIT THE PLAYOFFS IF I DON'T GET THEM THERE IN TIME. I SAW YOU FLYING EARLIER AND WONDERED IF YOU MIGHT...?
...CAN YOU HELP ME OPEN THIS ATTACHMENT FRO MY GRANDSON NATHAN?
HAPPY TO HELP, CITIZEN.

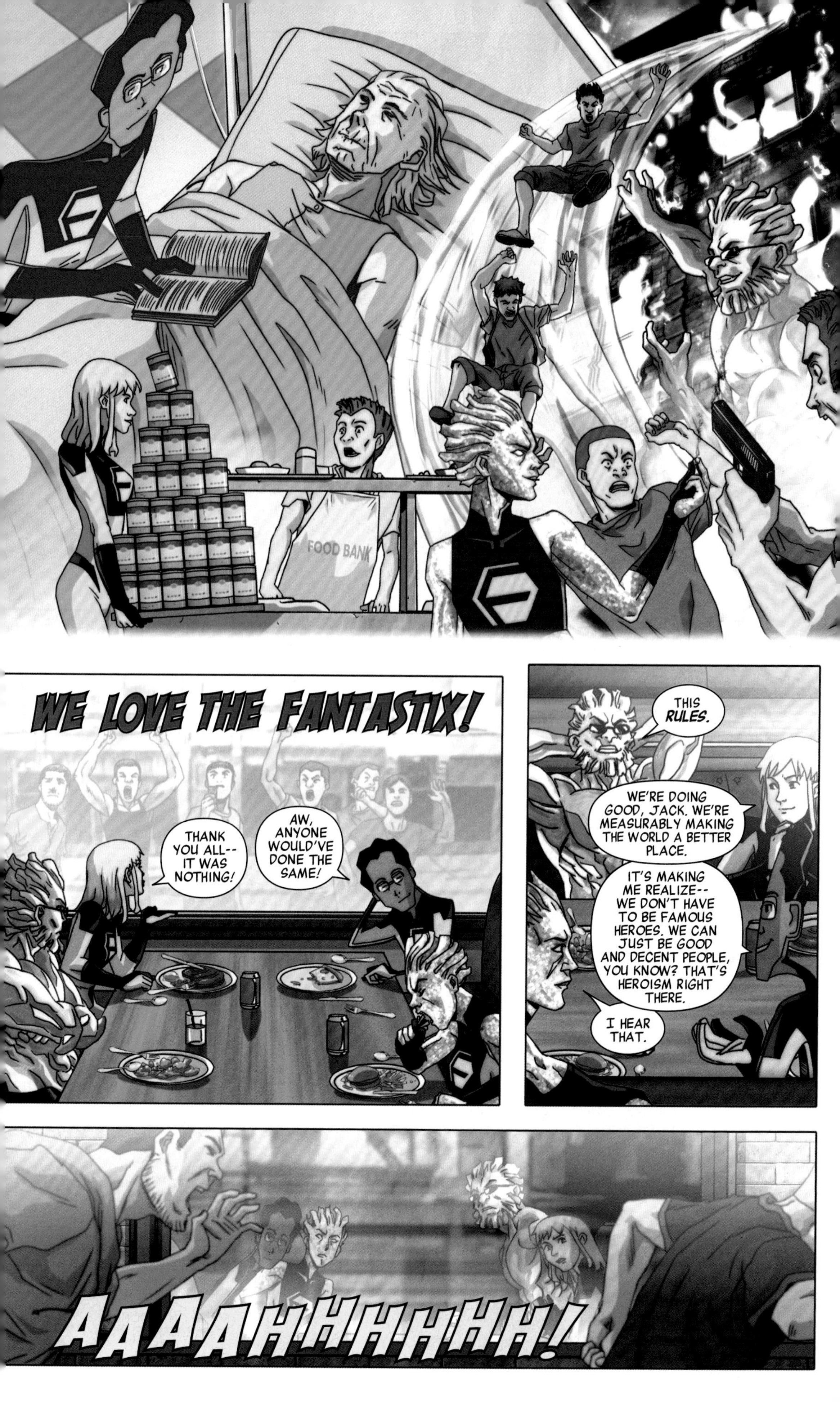
FOOD BANK
WE LOVE THE FANTASTIX!
THANK YOU ALL-- IT WAS NOTHING!
AW, ANYONE WOULD'VE DONE THE SAME!
THIS RULES.
WE'RE DOING GOOD, JACK. WE'RE MEASURABLY MAKING THE WORLD A BETTER PLACE.
IT'S MAKING ME REALIZE-- WE DON'T HAVE TO BE FAMOUS HEROES. WE CAN JUST BE GOOD AND DECENT PEOPLE, YOU KNOW? THAT'S HEROISM RIGHT THERE.
I HEAR THAT.
AAAAHHHHHHH!

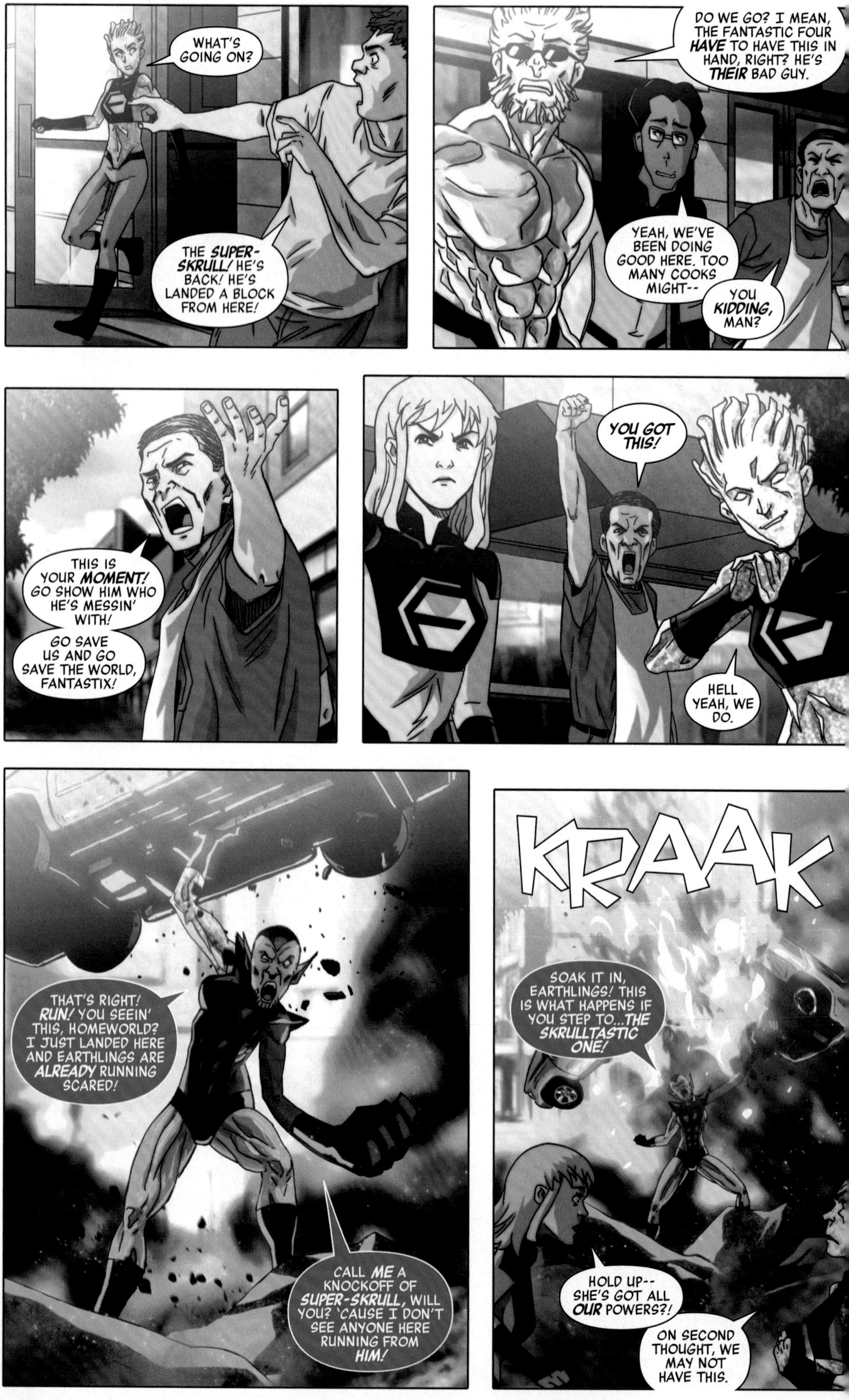
WHAT'S GOING ON?
THE SUPER-SKRULL! HE'S BACK! HE'S LANDED A BLOCK FROM HERE!
DO WE GO? I MEAN, THE FANTASTIC FOUR HAVE TO HAVE THIS IN HAND, RIGHT? HE'S THEIR BAD GUY.
YEAH, WE'VE BEEN DOING GOOD HERE. TOO MANY COOKS MIGHT--
YOU KIDDING, MAN?
THIS IS YOUR MOMENT! GO SHOW HIM WHO HE'S MESSIN' WITH!
GO SAVE US AND GO SAVE THE WORLD, FANTASTIX!
YOU GOT THIS!
HELL YEAH, WE DO.
THAT'S RIGHT! RUN! YOU SEEIN' THIS, HOMEWORLD? I JUST LANDED HERE AND EARTHLINGS ARE ALREADY RUNNING SCARED!
CALL ME A KNOCKOFF OF SUPER-SKRULL, WILL YOU? 'CAUSE I DON'T SEE ANYONE HERE RUNNING FROM HIM!
KRAAK
SOAK IT IN, EARTHLINGS! THIS IS WHAT HAPPENS IF YOU STEP TO...THE SKRULLTASTIC ONE!
HOLD UP-- SHE'S GOT ALL OUR POWERS?!
ON SECOND THOUGHT, WE MAY NOT HAVE THIS.

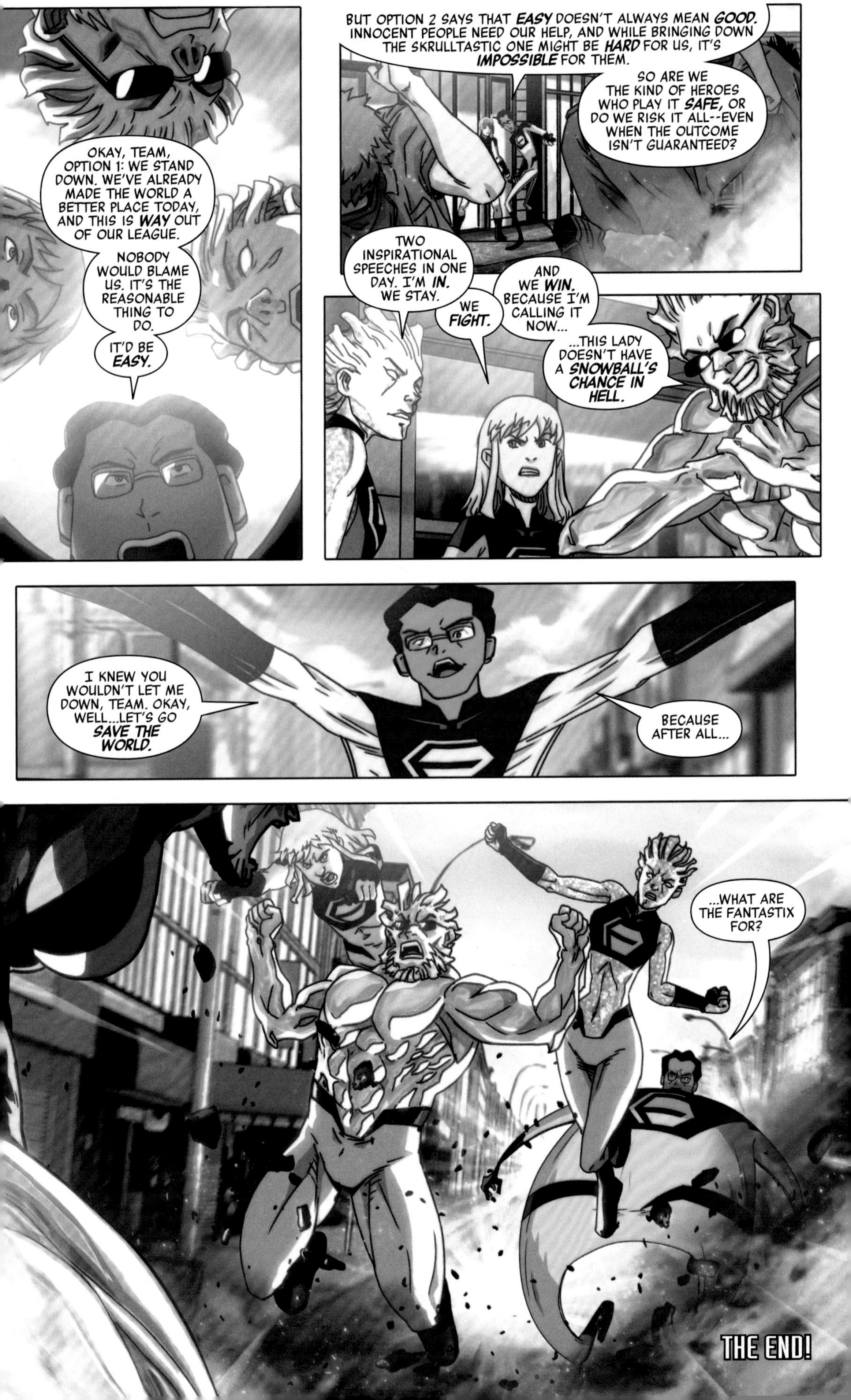
OKAY, TEAM, OPTION 1: WE STAND DOWN. WE'VE ALREADY MADE THE WORLD A BETTER PLACE TODAY, AND THIS IS WAY OUT OF OUR LEAGUE.
NOBODY WOULD BLAME US. IT'S THE REASONABLE THING TO DO.
IT'D BE EASY.
BUT OPTION 2 SAYS THAT EASY DOESN'T ALWAYS MEAN GOOD. INNOCENT PEOPLE NEED OUR HELP, AND WHILE BRINGING DOWN THE SKRULLTASTIC ONE MIGHT BE HARD FOR US, IT'S IMPOSSIBLE FOR THEM.
SO ARE WE THE KIND OF HEROES WHO PLAY IT SAFE, OR DO WE RISK IT ALL--EVEN WHEN THE OUTCOME ISN'T GUARANTEED?
TWO INSPIRATIONAL SPEECHES IN ONE DAY. I'M IN. WE STAY.
WE FIGHT.
AND WE WIN. BECAUSE I'M CALLING IT NOW...
...THIS LADY DOESN'T HAVE A SNOWBALL'S CHANCE IN HELL.
I KNEW YOU WOULDN'T LET ME DOWN, TEAM. OKAY, WELL...LET'S GO SAVE THE WORLD.
BECAUSE AFTER ALL...
...WHAT ARE THE FANTASTIX FOR?
THE END!

#13, Pages 12-13
sketches and final art by
Sean Izaakse

With concept sketch by
Tom Brevoort (right)

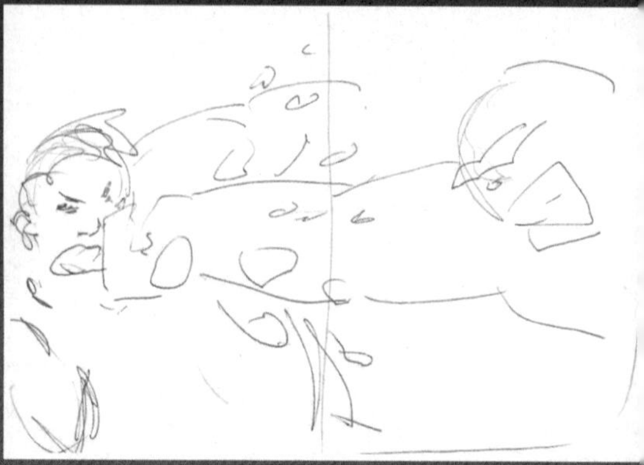

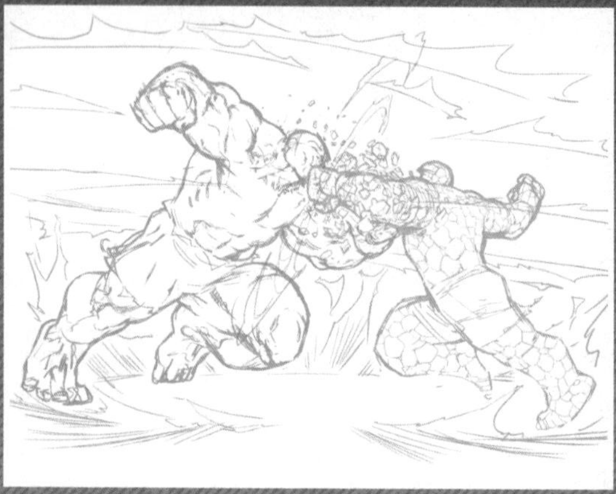

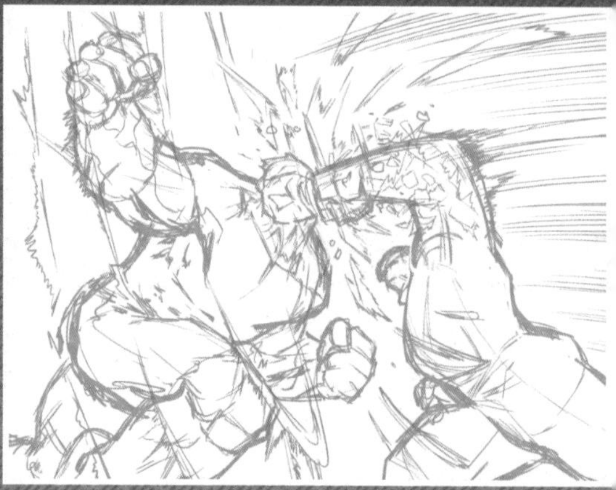

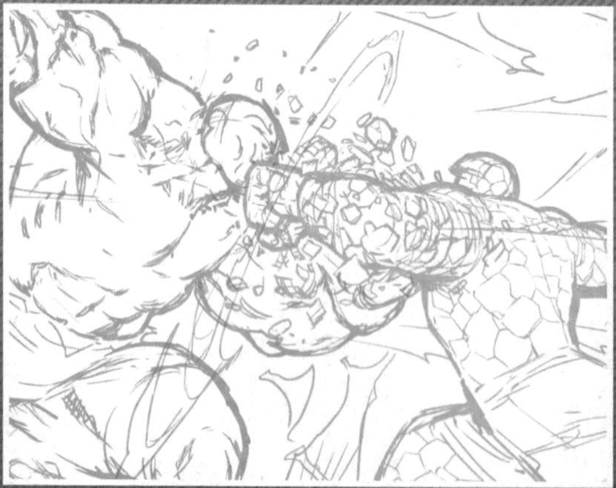

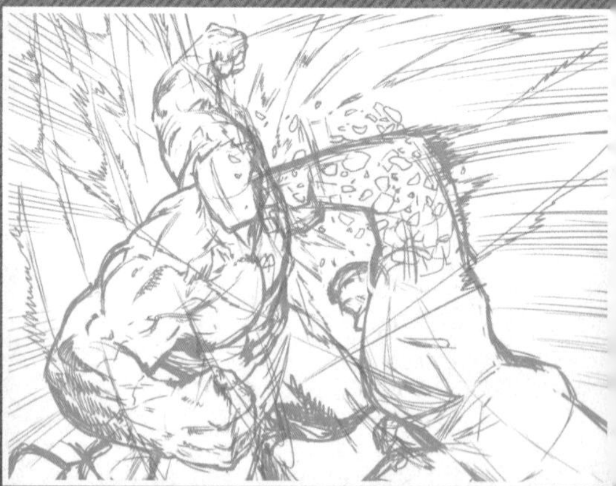

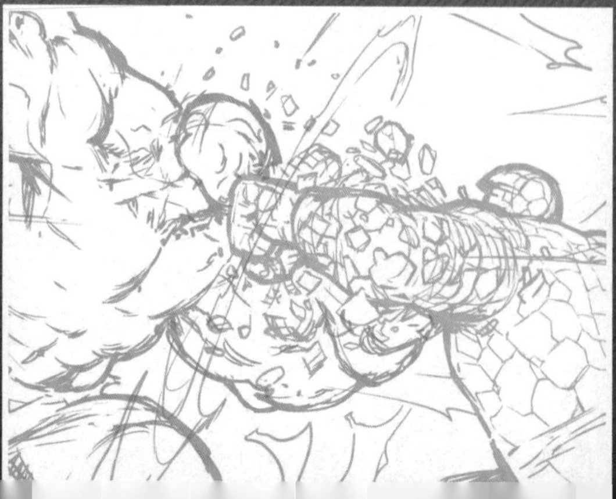

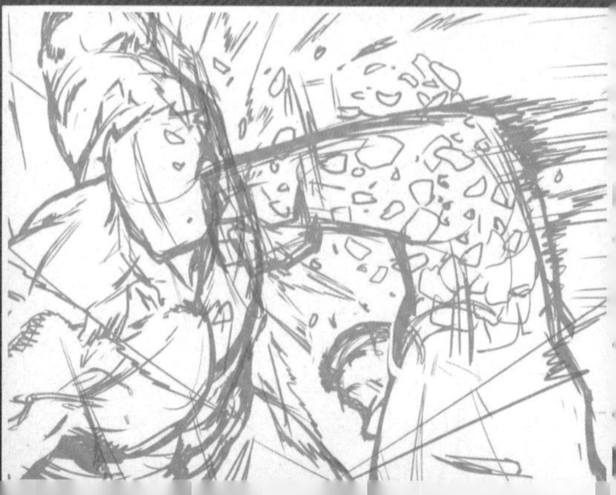

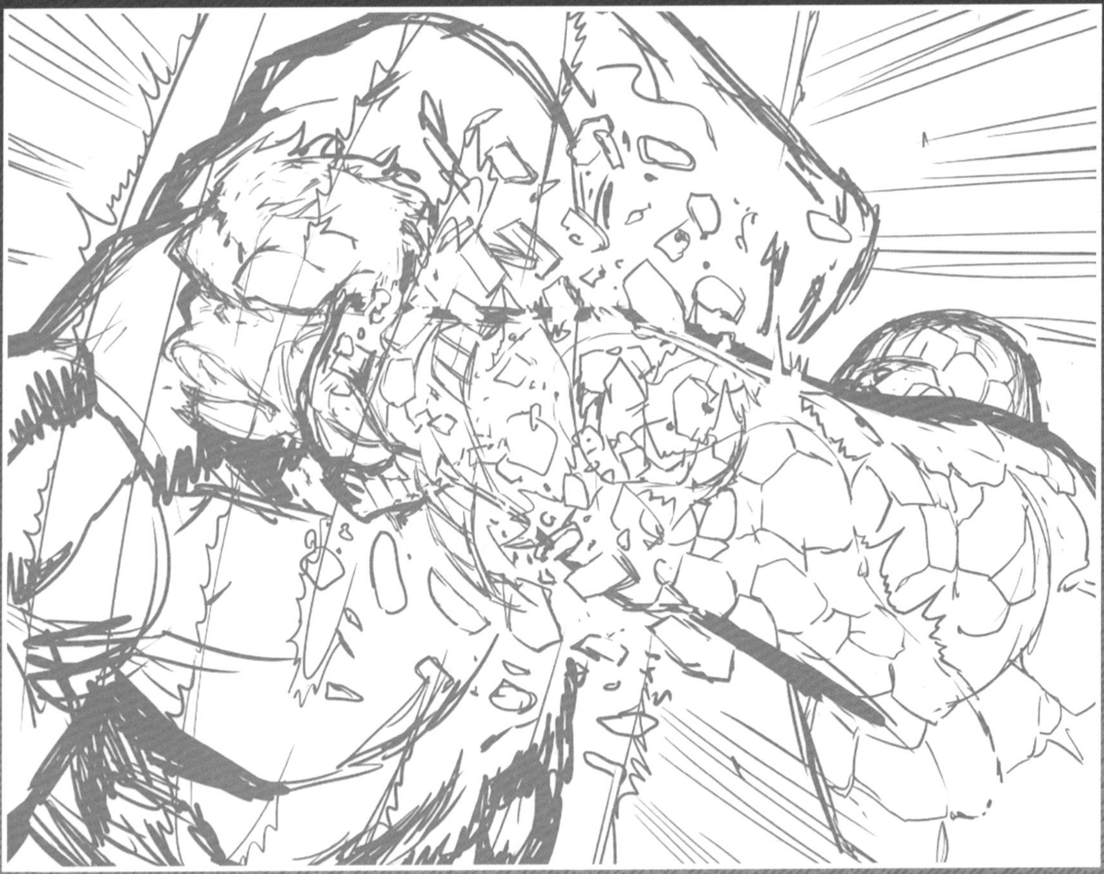

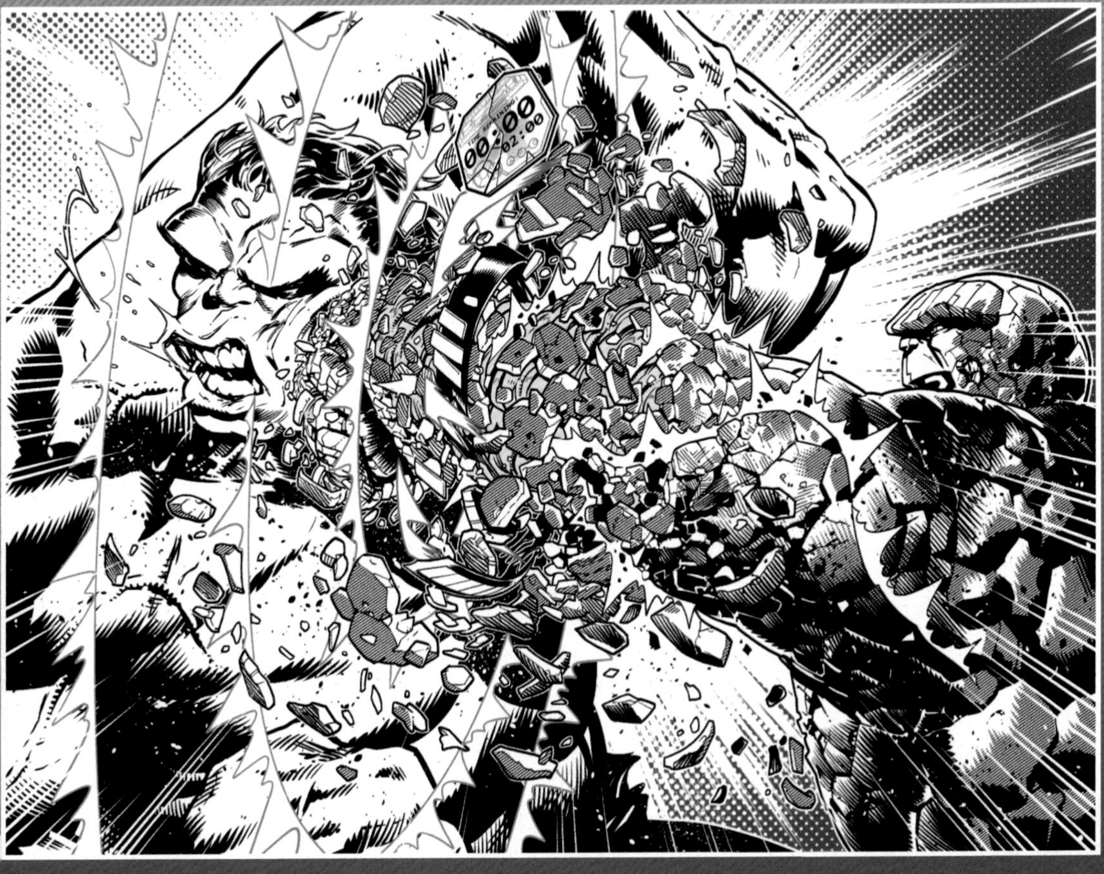

TIME REMAINING:
00:00
02:00

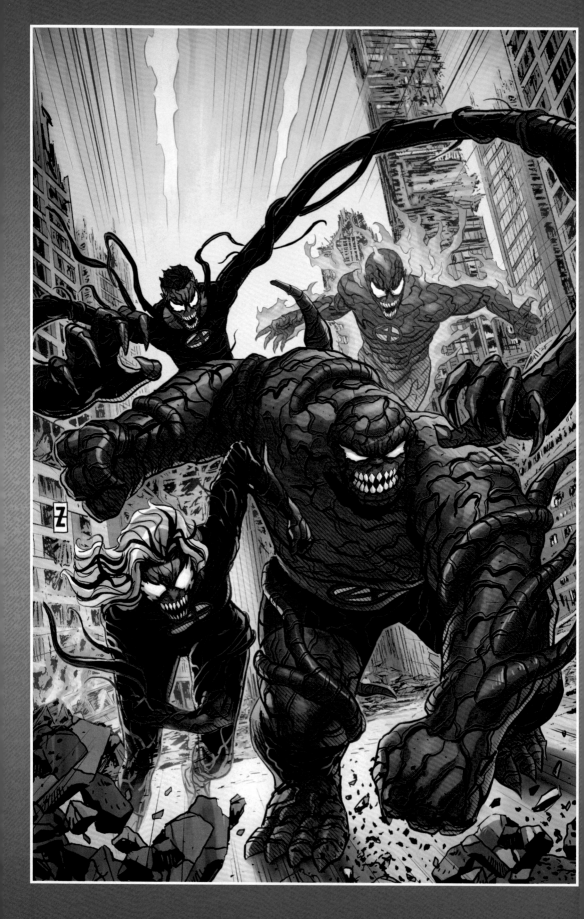

#12 Carnage-ized variant by **Patch Zircher** & **Jason Keith**

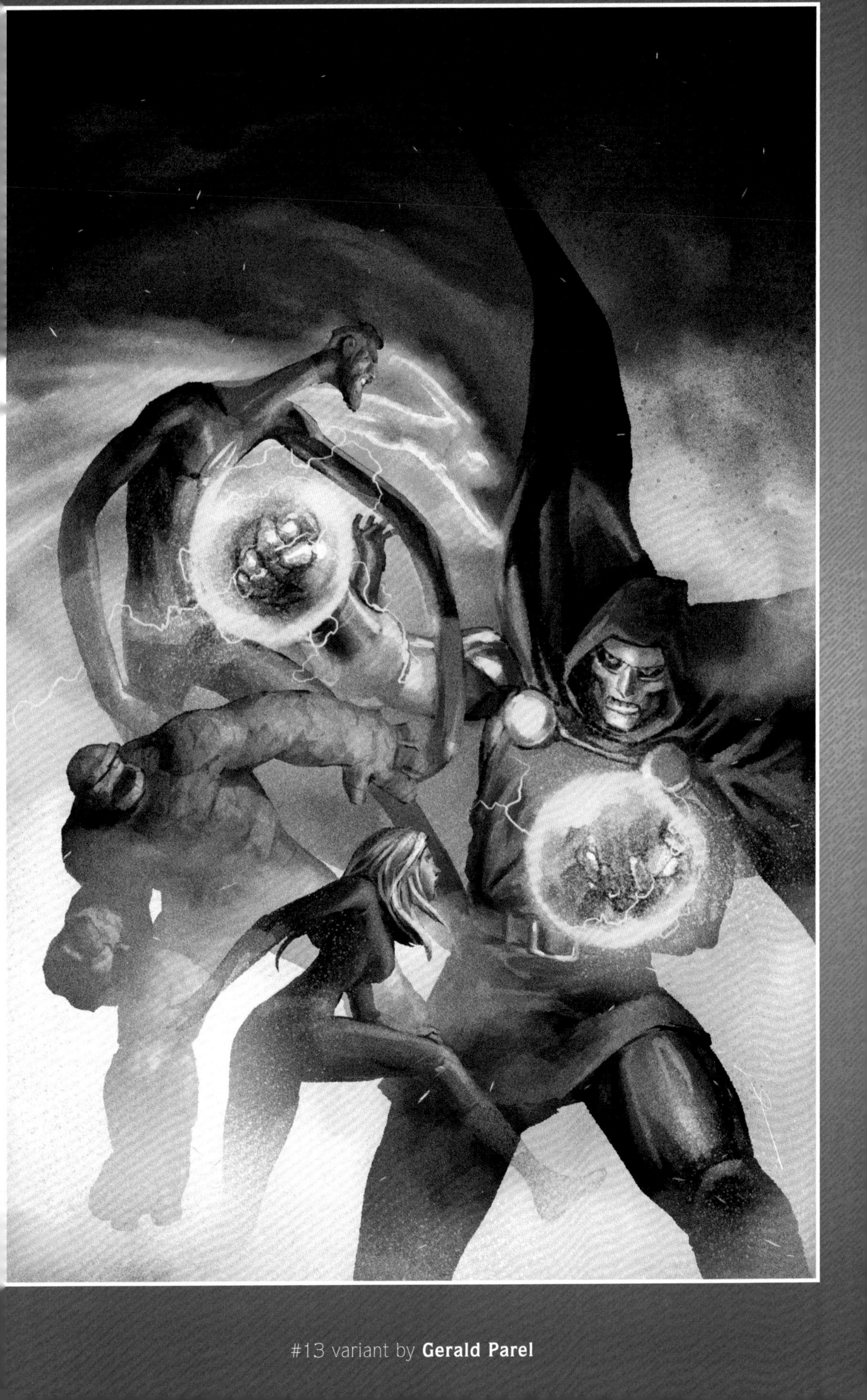

#13 variant by **Gerald Parel**

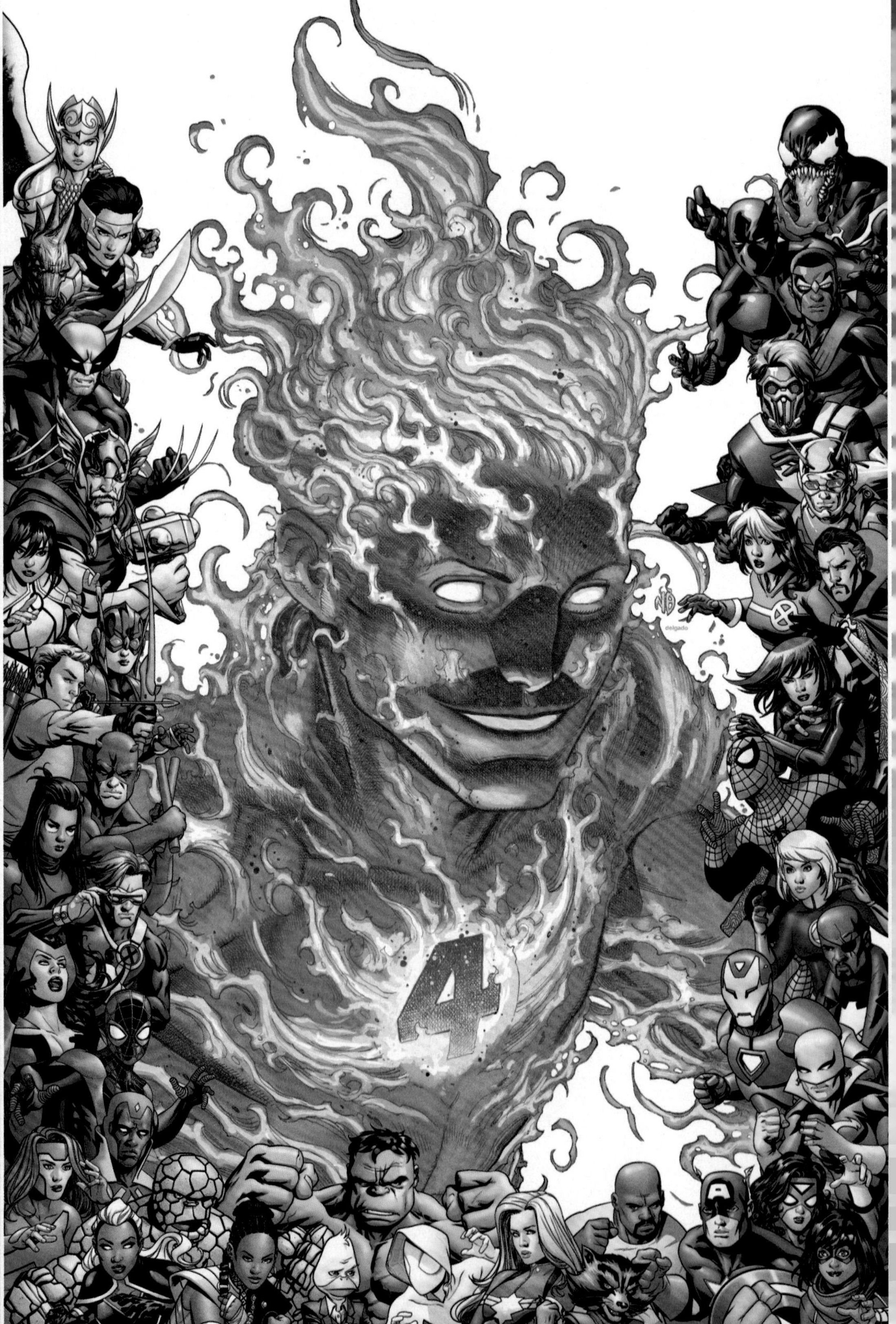

#13 Marvel 80th Anniversary variant by **Nick Bradshaw** & **Edgar Delgado** with **Mike McKone**

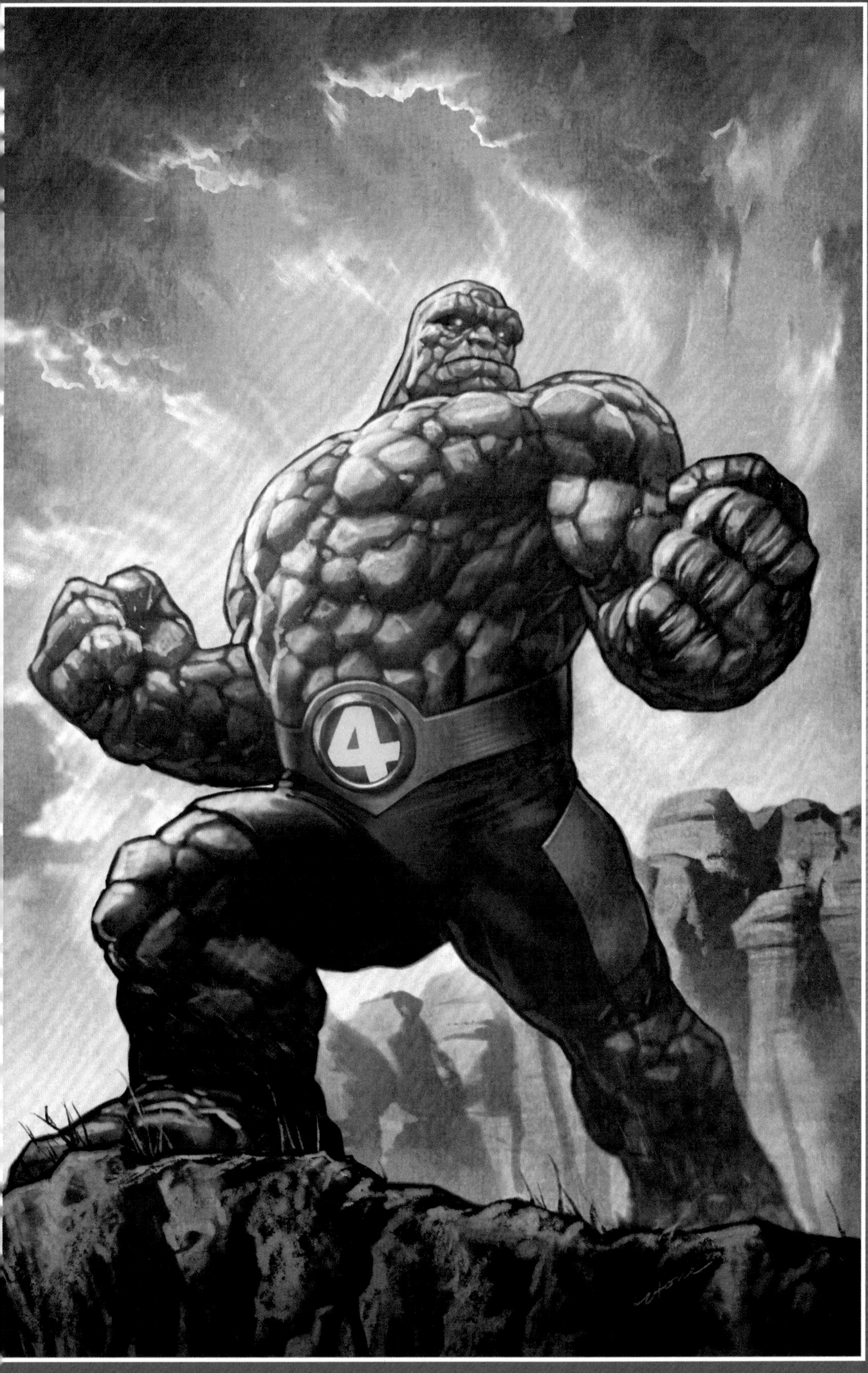

4 Yancy Street variant by **Stonehouse**

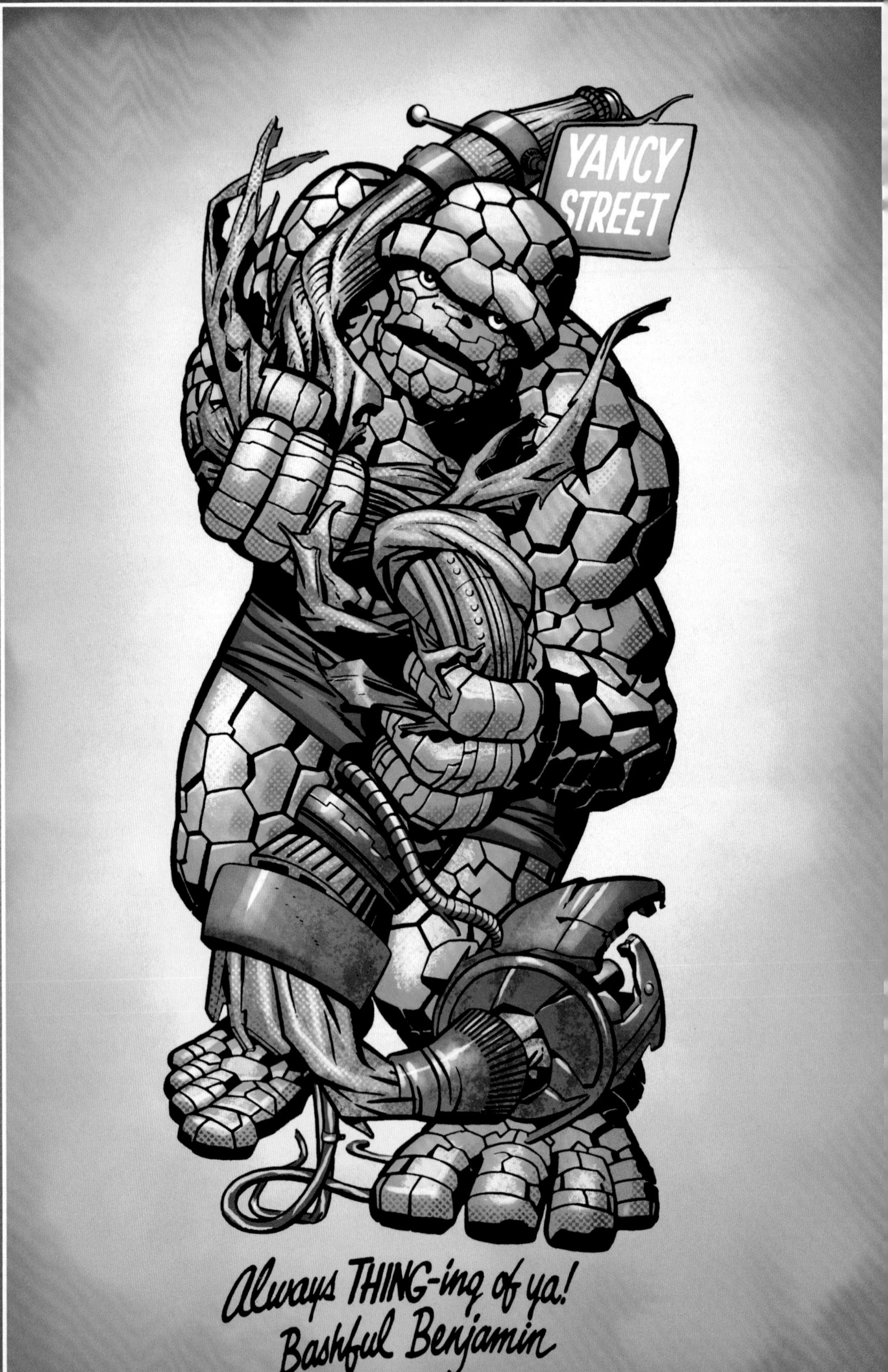
YANCY STREET
Always THING-ing of ya!
Bashful Benjamin

4 Yancy Street Hidden Gem variant by **Jack Kirby** & **Chris Sotomayor**

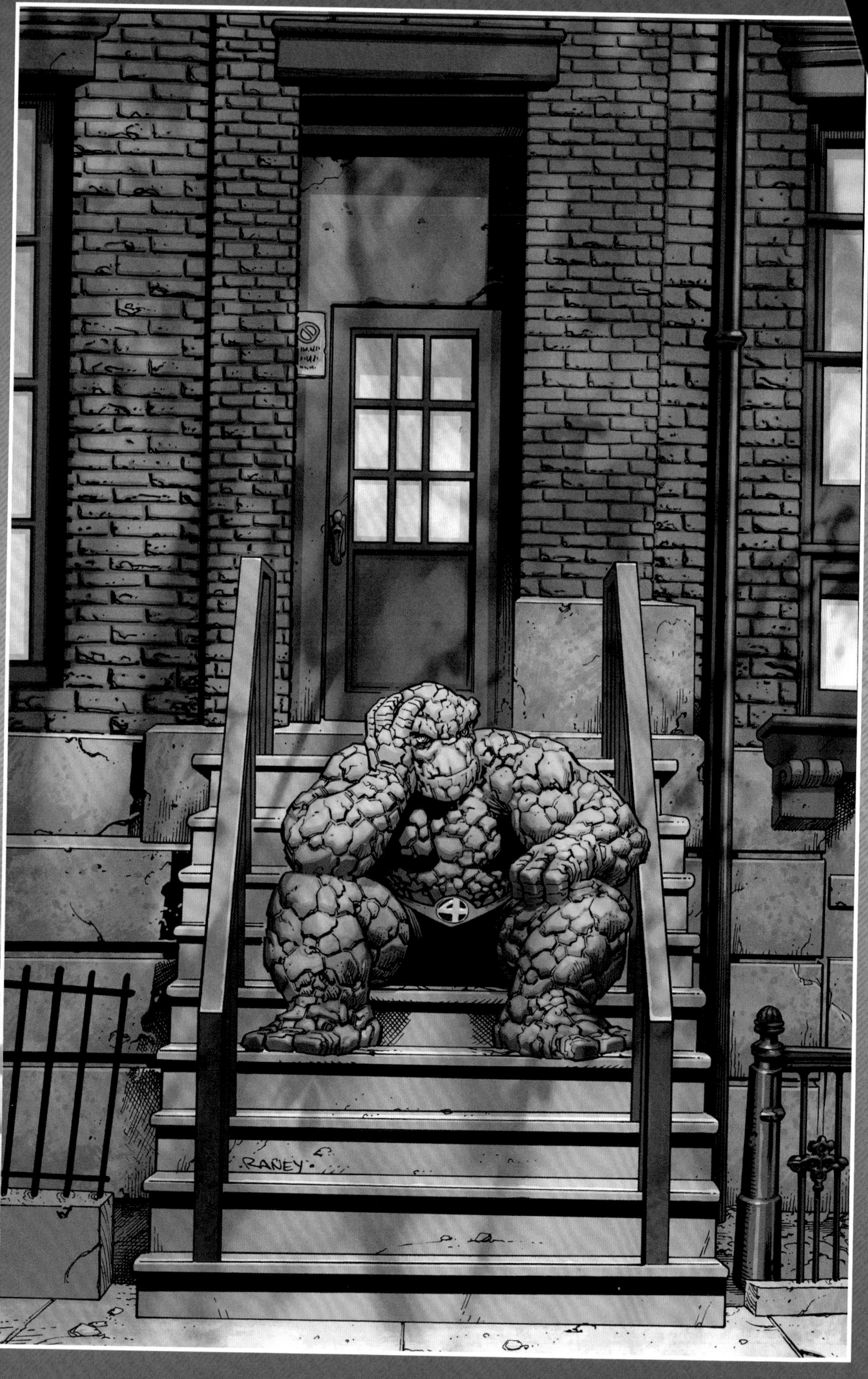
RANEY

4 Yancy Street variant by **Tom Raney** & **Dave McCaig**

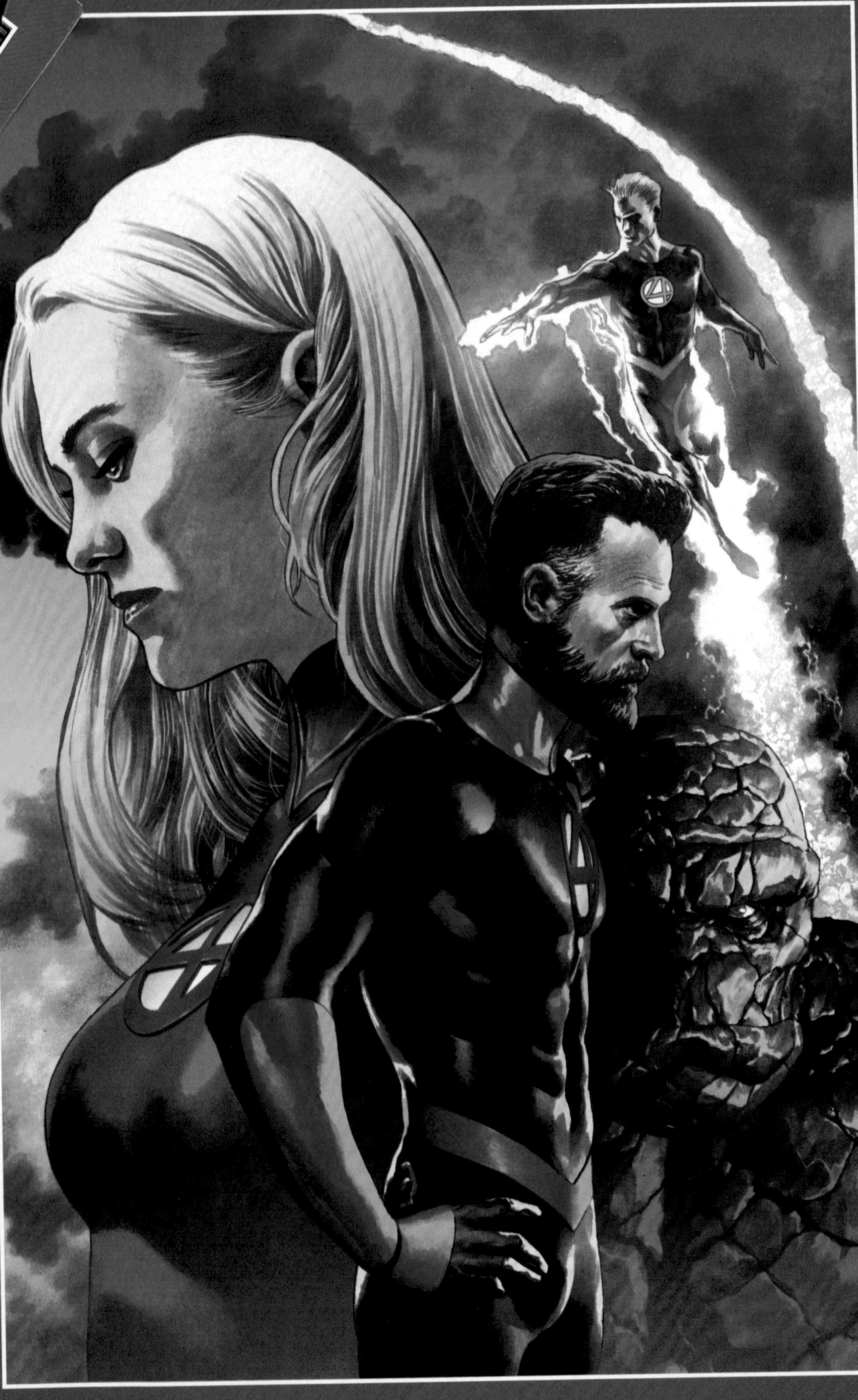

Negative Zone variant by **Mico Suayan** & **Rain Beredo**